Li Bennich-Björkman, Sergiy Kurbatov (Eds.)

WHEN THE FUTURE CAME

The Collapse of the Soviet Union and the Emergence of National Memory in Post-Soviet History Textbooks

Bibliografische Information der Deutschen Nationalbibliothek
Die Deutsche Nationalbibliothek verzeichnet diese Publikation in der Deutschen Nationalbibliografie; detaillierte bibliografische Daten sind im Internet über http://dnb.d-nb.de abrufbar.

Bibliographic information published by the Deutsche Nationalbibliothek
Die Deutsche Nationalbibliothek lists this publication in the Deutsche Nationalbibliografie; detailed bibliographic data are available in the Internet at http://dnb.d-nb.de.

Cover picture: Illustration "Perestroika" showing late soviet people with banners in their hands. On the top left there is a stylized portrait of Gorbatchev, on the top right corner the stylized image of the "Snickers" chocolate bar, with the McDonald's logo in the top center. © Copyright 2019 by Gregory Avoyan.

ISBN-13: 978-3-8382-1335-4

© *ibidem*-Verlag, Stuttgart 2019

Alle Rechte vorbehalten

Das Werk einschließlich aller seiner Teile ist urheberrechtlich geschützt. Jede Verwertung außerhalb der engen Grenzen des Urheberrechtsgesetzes ist ohne Zustimmung des Verlages unzulässig und strafbar. Dies gilt insbesondere für Vervielfältigungen, Übersetzungen, Mikroverfilmungen und elektronische Speicherformen sowie die Einspeicherung und Verarbeitung in elektronischen Systemen.

All rights reserved. No part of this publication may be reproduced, stored in or introduced into a retrieval system, or transmitted, in any form, or by any means (electronic, mechanical, photocopying, recording or otherwise) without the prior written permission of the publisher. Any person who does any unauthorized act in relation to this publication may be liable to criminal prosecution and civil claims for damages.

Printed in the EU

Soviet and Post-Soviet Politics and Society (SPPS)   Vol. 211
ISSN 1614-3515

General Editor: Andreas Umland,   Commissioning Editor: Max Jakob Horstmann,
Institute for Euro-Atlantic Cooperation, Kyiv, umland@stanfordalumni.org   London, mjh@ibidem.eu

EDITORIAL COMMITTEE*

DOMESTIC & COMPARATIVE POLITICS
Prof. **Ellen Bos**, *Andrássy University of Budapest*
Dr. **Gergana Dimova**, *University of Winchester*
Dr. **Andrey Kazantsev**, *MGIMO (U) MID RF, Moscow*
Prof. **Heiko Pleines**, *University of Bremen*
Prof. **Richard Sakwa**, *University of Kent at Canterbury*
Dr. **Sarah Whitmore**, *Oxford Brookes University*
Dr. **Harald Wydra**, *University of Cambridge*

SOCIETY, CLASS & ETHNICITY
Col. **David Glantz**, *"Journal of Slavic Military Studies"*
Dr. **Marlène Laruelle**, *George Washington University*
Dr. **Stephen Shulman**, *Southern Illinois University*
Prof. **Stefan Troebst**, *University of Leipzig*

POLITICAL ECONOMY & PUBLIC POLICY
Dr. **Andreas Goldthau**, *Central European University*
Dr. **Robert Kravchuk**, *University of North Carolina*
Dr. **David Lane**, *University of Cambridge*
Dr. **Carol Leonard**, *Higher School of Economics, Moscow*
Dr. **Maria Popova**, *McGill University, Montreal*

FOREIGN POLICY & INTERNATIONAL AFFAIRS
Dr. **Peter Duncan**, *University College London*
Prof. **Andreas Heinemann-Grüder**, *University of Bonn*
Prof. **Gerhard Mangott**, *University of Innsbruck*
Dr. **Diana Schmidt-Pfister**, *University of Konstanz*
Dr. **Lisbeth Tarlow**, *Harvard University, Cambridge*
Dr. **Christian Wipperfürth**, *N-Ost Network, Berlin*
Dr. **William Zimmerman**, *University of Michigan*

HISTORY, CULTURE & THOUGHT
Dr. **Catherine Andreyev**, *University of Oxford*
Prof. **Mark Bassin**, *Södertörn University*
Prof. **Karsten Brüggemann**, *Tallinn University*
Dr. **Alexander Etkind**, *University of Cambridge*
Dr. **Gasan Gusejnov**, *Moscow State University*
Prof. **Leonid Luks**, *Catholic University of Eichstaett*
Dr. **Olga Malinova**, *Russian Academy of Sciences*
Dr. **Richard Mole**, *University College London*
Prof. **Andrei Rogatchevski**, *University of Tromsø*
Dr. **Mark Tauger**, *West Virginia University*

ADVISORY BOARD*

Prof. **Dominique Arel**, *University of Ottawa*
Prof. **Jörg Baberowski**, *Humboldt University of Berlin*
Prof. **Margarita Balmaceda**, *Seton Hall University*
Dr. **John Barber**, *University of Cambridge*
Prof. **Timm Beichelt**, *European University Viadrina*
Dr. **Katrin Boeckh**, *University of Munich*
Prof. em. **Archie Brown**, *University of Oxford*
Dr. **Vyacheslav Bryukhovetsky**, *Kyiv-Mohyla Academy*
Prof. **Timothy Colton**, *Harvard University, Cambridge*
Prof. **Paul D'Anieri**, *University of Florida*
Dr. **Heike Dörrenbächer**, *Friedrich Naumann Foundation*
Dr. **John Dunlop**, *Hoover Institution, Stanford, California*
Dr. **Sabine Fischer**, *SWP, Berlin*
Dr. **Geir Flikke**, *NUPI, Oslo*
Prof. **David Galbreath**, *University of Aberdeen*
Prof. **Alexander Galkin**, *Russian Academy of Sciences*
Prof. **Frank Golczewski**, *University of Hamburg*
Dr. **Nikolas Gvosdev**, *Naval War College, Newport, RI*
Prof. **Mark von Hagen**, *Arizona State University*
Dr. **Guido Hausmann**, *University of Munich*
Prof. **Dale Herspring**, *Kansas State University*
Dr. **Stefani Hoffman**, *Hebrew University of Jerusalem*
Prof. **Mikhail Ilyin**, *MGIMO (U) MID RF, Moscow*
Prof. **Vladimir Kantor**, *Higher School of Economics*
Dr. **Ivan Katchanovski**, *University of Ottawa*
Prof. em. **Andrzej Korbonski**, *University of California*
Dr. **Iris Kempe**, *"Caucasus Analytical Digest"*
Prof. **Herbert Küpper**, *Institut für Ostrecht Regensburg*
Dr. **Rainer Lindner**, *CEEER, Berlin*
Dr. **Vladimir Malakhov**, *Russian Academy of Sciences*

Dr. **Luke March**, *University of Edinburgh*
Prof. **Michael McFaul**, *Stanford University, Palo Alto*
Prof. **Birgit Menzel**, *University of Mainz-Germersheim*
Prof. **Valery Mikhailenko**, *The Urals State University*
Prof. **Emil Pain**, *Higher School of Economics, Moscow*
Dr. **Oleg Podvintsev**, *Russian Academy of Sciences*
Prof. **Olga Popova**, *St. Petersburg State University*
Dr. **Alex Pravda**, *University of Oxford*
Dr. **Erik van Ree**, *University of Amsterdam*
Dr. **Joachim Rogall**, *Robert Bosch Foundation Stuttgart*
Prof. **Peter Rutland**, *Wesleyan University, Middletown*
Prof. **Marat Salikov**, *The Urals State Law Academy*
Dr. **Gwendolyn Sasse**, *University of Oxford*
Prof. **Jutta Scherrer**, *EHESS, Paris*
Prof. **Robert Service**, *University of Oxford*
Mr. **James Sherr**, *RIIA Chatham House London*
Dr. **Oxana Shevel**, *Tufts University, Medford*
Prof. **Eberhard Schneider**, *University of Siegen*
Prof. **Olexander Shnyrkov**, *Shevchenko University, Kyiv*
Prof. **Hans-Henning Schröder**, *SWP, Berlin*
Prof. **Yuri Shapoval**, *Ukrainian Academy of Sciences*
Prof. **Viktor Shnirelman**, *Russian Academy of Sciences*
Dr. **Lisa Sundstrom**, *University of British Columbia*
Dr. **Philip Walters**, *"Religion, State and Society", Oxford*
Prof. **Zenon Wasyliw**, *Ithaca College, New York State*
Dr. **Lucan Way**, *University of Toronto*
Dr. **Markus Wehner**, *"Frankfurter Allgemeine Zeitung"*
Dr. **Andrew Wilson**, *University College London*
Prof. **Jan Zielonka**, *University of Oxford*
Prof. **Andrei Zorin**, *University of Oxford*

* While the Editorial Committee and Advisory Board support the General Editor in the choice and improvement of manuscripts for publication, responsibility for remaining errors and misinterpretations in the series' volumes lies with the books' authors.

Soviet and Post-Soviet Politics and Society (SPPS)
ISSN 1614-3515

Founded in 2004 and refereed since 2007, SPPS makes available affordable English-, German-, and Russian-language studies on the history of the countries of the former Soviet bloc from the late Tsarist period to today. It publishes between 5 and 20 volumes per year and focuses on issues in transitions to and from democracy such as economic crisis, identity formation, civil society development, and constitutional reform in CEE and the NIS. SPPS also aims to highlight so far understudied themes in East European studies such as right-wing radicalism, religious life, higher education, or human rights protection. The authors and titles of all previously published volumes are listed at the end of this book. For a full description of the series and reviews of its books, see www.ibidem-verlag.de/red/spps.

Editorial correspondence & manuscripts should be sent to: Dr. Andreas Umland, Institute for Euro-Atlantic Cooperation, vul. Volodymyrska 42, off. 21, UA-01030 Kyiv, Ukraine

Business correspondence & review copy requests should be sent to: *ibidem* Press, Leuschnerstr. 40, 30457 Hannover, Germany; tel.: +49 511 2622200; fax: +49 511 2622201; spps@ibidem.eu.

Authors, reviewers, referees, and editors for (as well as all other persons sympathetic to) SPPS are invited to join its networks at
www.facebook.com/group.php?gid=52638198614
www.linkedin.com/groups?about=&gid=103012
www.xing.com/net/spps-ibidem-verlag/

Recent Volumes

203 Andrei Rogatchevski, Yngvar B. Steinholt, Arve Hansen, David-Emil Wickström
War of Songs
Popular Music and Recent Russia-Ukraine Relations
With a foreword by Artemy Troitsky
ISBN 978-3-8382-1173-2

204 Maria Lipman (ed.)
Russian Voices on Post-Crimea Russia
An Almanac of Counterpoint Essays from 2015–2018
ISBN 978-3-8382-1251-7

205 Ksenia Maksimovtsova
Language Conflicts in Contemporary Estonia, Latvia, and Ukraine
A Comparative Exploration of Discourses in Post-Soviet Russian-Language Digital Media
With a foreword by Ammon Cheskin
ISBN 978-3-8382-1282-1

206 Michal Vít
The EU's Impact on Identity Formation in East Central Europe between 2004 and 2013
Perceptions of the Nation and Europe in Political Parties of the Czech Republic, Poland, and Slovakia
With a foreword by Andrea Pető
ISBN 978-3-8382-1275-3

207 Per A. Rudling
Tarnished Heroes
The Organization of Ukrainian Nationalists in the Memory Politics of Post-Soviet Ukraine
ISBN 978-3-8382-0999-9

208 Kaja Gadowska, Peter Solomon (Eds.)
Legal Change in Post-Communist States
Progress, Reversions, Explanations
ISBN 978-3-8382-1312-5

209 Paweł Kowal, Georges Mink, Iwona Reichardt (Eds.)
Three Revolutions: Mobilization and Change in Contemporary Ukraine I
Theoretical Aspects and Analyses on Religion, Memory, and Identity
ISBN 978-3-8382-1321-7

210 Paweł Kowal, Adam Reichardt, Georges Mink, Iwona Reichardt (Eds.)
Three Revolutions: Mobilization and Change in Contemporary Ukraine II
An Oral History of the Revolution on Granite, Orange Revolution, and Revolution of Dignity
ISBN 978-3-8382-1323-1

Contents

Acknowledgements 7

Li Bennich-Björkman and Sergiy Kurbatov
When the Future Came 9

Natalia Tregubova, Liliya Erushkina, Alexandr Gorylev, and Alexey Rusakov
Russia as the Ambivalent Inheritor of the Soviet Union:
The Case(s) of Russia 29

Alla Marchenko, Yuliya Yurchuk, and Andrey Kashin
Waking Up a "Sleeping Beauty": Rethinking Ukrainian
Perestroika 59

Marharyta Fabrykant and Andrei Dudchik
The Invention of Transition: Perestroika in Belarusian
History Textbooks 91

Diana Bencheci and Valerii Mosneagu
Moldova: Perestroika between Russia, Romania, and
"Moldovan-ness" 137

Li Bennich-Björkman and Sergiy Kurbatov
Which Future Came? Multiple Perestroika(s) as Prisms
of the Soviet and the National 157

Works Cited 175

Index 193

Acknowledgements

Over the years we have been working on this book, several universities have generously hosted our many workshops. In those workshops, the author team gathered to comment, reflect, and discuss, as the individual chapters and the common framework slowly took shape amidst many other pressing duties. We want to express our gratitude to the Institute for Russian and Eurasian Studies (IRES, previously the Uppsala Center for Russian and Eurasian Studies—UCRS), the University of Uppsala, Sweden, and the National Academy of Educational Sciences in Kyiv, Ukraine, for hosting numerous events in the framework of our project and for constantly supporting our activities. It was a great pleasure for us to hold workshops at the State University of Moldova in Chisenau, Moldova and the Lobachevsky State University of Nizhny Novgorod in Nizhny Novgorod, Russia. Special thanks are extended to the leaders of IRES and the National Academy of Educational Sciences, Claes Levinsson and Vasyl Kremen—their contributions are highly appreciated. Numerous colleagues spent time commenting on parts of the manuscript, and we would particularly like to acknowledge the help of Mikhail Suslov, Andrey Rezaev, Leonid Polishchuk, Jörgen Hermansson, and Stanislav Chetoshnykov. Drafts of individual chapters were presented at the 41st World Congress of the International Institute of Sociology (IIS) in Uppsala on 9–10 June 2013 at the regular session "Contemporary Historical Textbooks and the Ways of Representation of the Past in the 21st Century," at which we received valuable feedback.

The possibility of collaboratively developing this book was enabled by a grant from the Swedish Institute, Visby Programme, for which we express our warm gratitude. As editors, we finally wish to express our sincere admiration for all the team members, the authors of the individual chapters: Natalia Tregubova, Liliya Erushkina, Alexander Gorylev, Alexey Rusakov, Alla Marchenko, Yuliya Yurchuk, Andriy Kashyn, Marharyta Fabrykant, Andrei Dudchik, Diana Bencheci, and Valeriu Mosneaga. Their diligence, patience, and hard work, throughout the long process when the book was taking shape, have astonished and gratified us, and without it, no book would ever have materialized.

Uppsala and Kyiv, 5 March, 2019
Li Bennich-Björkman, Sergiy Kurbatov

When the Future Came

Li Bennich-Björkman and Sergiy Kurbatov

Introduction

This is a book about how the changes that brought the Soviet Union to its end, and their aftermath, have gradually formed cultural, collective memories throughout the former Soviet Union. Told through the retrospective lens of official history writing in four post-Soviet countries, the rise of a new order has become embedded in the uniquely national experiences of Russia, Ukraine, Belarus, and Moldova. The book analyzes history textbooks for secondary schools and universities from the 1990s and up to 2012 in these four countries, striving to capture the officially sanctioned national gazes on what constitutes their recent past, gazes that take in the years of perestroika, the collapse of the Soviet Union, and the independent statehood that followed, in partly similar, but mostly divergent narratives between the countries and over time. Focusing on the comparative aspects of how national history textbooks in these countries chose to narrate what to the surrounding world often and incorrectly appeared to be a commonly experienced historical process allows us to understand the various trajectories of sovereignty unfolding since independence in 1991 in these four countries, and beyond them in the former Soviet Union in its entirety. These trajectories range from renouncing the Soviet past and embracing statehood and nation-building in Ukraine, to regretting the loss of Soviet community and deemphasizing independence in Belarus. Not least among these four countries, there is also great diversity in how geopolitical orientations developed after the collapse, which is further explored by getting close to the historiographies of each of them. Today, after the Crimea annexation and the war in Eastern Ukraine, Ukrainians have been looking towards Europe more unanimously than before, whereas Moldova is still vacillating, and is now tending to move in a Russian direction.

Belarus has remained closely tied to Russia, upholding federative or confederative tendencies within the region, while keeping a door open towards the European Union through the Eastern Partnership. Russia, with its long history of empire in the region, has not ceased to strive for dominance over the former republics, although in the 1990s it briefly seemed to be coping with the loss of its former centrality in another, less imperative manner. The predominance of growing national consciousness is likewise diverging between the countries. What was the past, as constructed in the textbooks analyzed in the following pages, contributes to justifying and defending these choices.

The idea behind the book grew out of discussions within a research group bringing together scholars and researchers from Ukraine, Russia, Belarus, Moldova, and Sweden. The dramatic events unfolding in the Soviet Union during the late 1980s and early 1990s, which ultimately led to the collapse of the Union and the rise of fifteen successor states, seemed to be understood and interpreted differently within the group depending on the nationalities of the participants. Whereas some aspects, such as the attention paid to the last president of the Soviet Union, Mikhail Gorbachev, recurred in many countries, others left markedly different traces. For example, the Chernobyl catastrophe in 1986 played hardly any role in Moldovan memory-making about this time, though it was ascribed a major role in Ukraine. Even more striking, the perceived significance of perestroika and the collapse as such differed between countries. Did they mark a radical shift, or simply discontinuity that reverted to continuity?

While in the Western literature on Eastern Europe and this era, perestroika, the collapse of the Soviet Union, and the emergence of the new post-Soviet states form a compelling narrative of major historical breakpoints, something less dramaturgically and analytically coherent can be glimpsed in the former Soviet Union's own historiographies. Were there indeed such wide discrepancies in what happened when the Soviet Union collapsed and new countries came to life that there would be reason to speak not of one but several perestroikas, with particular national flavors and specific approaches to the past and future?

Not only did initial discussions within the group reveal divergences when it came to descriptions of what happened, but it became clear that normative assessments of the collapse and its consequences varied just as much, perhaps mirroring, we believed, dominant discourses in the countries of origin. Was the collapse of the Soviet Union an opening for progress and new freedom, or was it, on the contrary, to be grieved as a lost opportunity for future generations of post-Soviet inhabitants who were forced to struggle alone to find a way in a neoliberal world, without the soothing community of the Soviet family? Assessments differed profoundly. Where, we started to ask ourselves, did these assessments come from and how were they formed? Why were they so divergent? After all, these countries all shared a reasonably common Soviet past when it came to formal and informal institutions, and had all endured what on the surface seemed to be reasonably similar processes of radical change. Remembering these historic processes that ended the 20th century and marked the beginning of the 21st takes place in many layers and corners of the societies involved, but to see how the "we," the state, chooses to interpret and memorialize these transformations into new existences, and bring it forward to new generations, textbooks are a natural source, one form of officially approved guidelines to the past.

How are national memories formed in relation to the collapse of the Soviet Union in these country contexts? What do these processes of memorialization point to in terms of historical determinism, room for agency, and relations within and among society, the public, and the elites?

These are the core questions that our discussions pointed to, and that structure the inquiries of the individual country chapters that form the empirical core of this book. These chapters focus on the national contexts of and textbook contents in Russia, Belarus, Moldova, and Ukraine, whereas the comparison—which the country analyses make possible—dominates the last chapter. In that chapter, insights are brought together into an attempt to expose overall patterns of similarities and differences, particularly in addressing the Soviet past, the national consequences of the collapse, and the overall themes of historical determinism, structuralism, and agency — and, significantly, whose agency.

A Four-Country Study

The four former Soviet republics studied here were all previously part of Tsarist Russia, with some modifications. Bessarabia, present-day Moldova, became part of Tsarist Russia in 1812, but between the two world wars it was a Romanian territory and as such was claimed by the Soviets in 1940. The Transnistrian region was then added to Bessarabia, to form the Soviet Republic of Moldova. The Western Ukrainian regions of Galicia, Volhynia, and Bukovina and Transcarpathia used to be part of the Habsburg Empire until the end of World War I, and then during the interwar period of Poland, Romania, and Czechoslovakia, respectively. Ukraine is thus marked by historical legacies of different empires and states: the main territory of Ukraine was integrated into the Soviet Union in 1922 as a result of tensions and Civil War between the parties involved, while Western Ukraine — as mentioned — was made into Soviet territory much later, at the beginning of World War II as a result of the Molotov-Ribbentrop Pact and its secret division of territories between Nazi Germany and the Soviet Union. Ukraine offers an interesting complexity, with its present western territories being latecomers, and its Eastern, Southern, and Central parts originally in the Union. The Soviet-enforced collectivization was brutal in Eastern Ukraine, where millions of people did not survive the Great Famine, the Holodomor, of 1932–1933 (Conquest; Applebaum, *Red Famine*). Moreover, tens of thousands of Ukrainians were later deported in the great Ukrainian purges of 1937–1938 (Applebaum, *Gulag*). The Autonomous Crimean Republic had belonged to the Russian Soviet Federative Socialistic Republic, but in 1954 it was transferred to the Ukrainian Soviet Socialistic Republic pursuant to the Decree of the Presidium of Supreme Soviet of the USSR of 19 February. Regional differences in the processes of integration into the Soviet Union came to influence the forms of Sovietization in Ukraine, and subsequently shaped the attitudes of the population towards Soviet rule. The legacy of these "different" Sovietizations compounds the ambivalence in the national identity of Ukrainians, including in attitudes towards perestroika, the collapse of the Soviet Union, and the independence of Ukraine.

The choice of the studied countries is not random. Whereas Russia, most of present-day Ukraine, and Belarus belong to the original group of territories in the Soviet Union as established in 1922, Moldova represents the group of Soviet latecomers (together with the three Baltic States and western parts of Ukraine and Belarus), though sharing with the three others the characteristic of having been strongly formed over time by Russian influences. Today, they are all states, formerly Soviet republics, where the historical and cultural ties to Russian civilization continue to be deep, and where the Russian language is spoken alongside Belarusian, Ukrainian, and Romanian. In contrast to the Baltic States, where the strong positions of the national languages and cultures distinguished them from Russian influences, the countries studied here—except Western Ukraine—have historically been much more integral to Russian civilization, and therefore could be presumed to historicize the collapse and what followed in a more similar way than would the Baltic States or the countries of the South Caucasus. The Soviet experience, proceeding from the Russian center, was familiar in a sense, and not alien, to the main territories of the four countries chosen. Nevertheless, they have also been formed over centuries by different legacies, mentalities, and territorial preconditions, as is clearly demonstrated in the individual chapters following this one.

Analyzing Post-Soviet Textbooks

Analyzing school and university textbooks, while leaving aside other expressions of official historiography such as statues, monuments, and artwork commissioned by the state, means that the textbook is viewed as the major socialization tool of states: education for the generations coming of age. What is being taught in these books forms part of official socialization intended to create shared values and, not least, shared memories. One of the core assumptions of the influential culturalist theory of how the "soft" resources binding a community together, such as memories, values, and beliefs, are transferred over generations is the importance of early-life socialization (Inglehart and Welzel 94–135, Lockhart 91). Socialization has been understood as the process of transmitting cultural values, either intentionally or unintentionally. Individuals develop their basic orientations and outlooks in a process of cumulative formation in which experiences from different spheres of life are brought together in attempts to form coherent perceptions of the world (Almond and Verba 323–374). The family (Jennings and Niemi; Westholm 137-159), school (Almond and Verba 323–374; Coleman; Eckstein 265–285), the peer group (Coleman), and media and popular culture (Merelman) are all important arenas where individuals interact with one another across generations, and where socialization continuously occurs. The education system has always been a cornerstone of the ideological socialization of society, and schools and universities play important roles in shaping the minds of each generation. Although the individual chapters in this book do not explore how actual teaching practices influence and nuance textbook contents, they do capture—through the textbooks—attempts of socialization in the making. The question of socialization has far-reaching implications for understanding the processes of social continuity and change, since culture, understood as values, convictions, and memories, partly causes action and conditions the speed and depth of social transformation, as sociologist Karl Mannheim had already noted in 1952 (286).

On a personal level, one of the authors of this chapter studied the Soviet version of the history of Ukraine at school and in his initial years of university, though after graduation he instead taught the national version of Ukrainian history. The absence of national history textbooks at the beginning of Ukrainian Independence was acutely felt, and the Ukrainian diaspora and the works of its representatives were the main resources filling this gap. Especially important in this respect was the book by

Orest Subtelny (1941-2016), *Ukraine: A History* (1988), translated into Ukrainian by Yuri Shevchuk and published in 1992. Numerous editions of this book came out during this time.

Methodologically, the individual authors have worked within a common tradition of qualitative research, but using different discursive analytic methods, presented in more detail as necessary in the individual chapters. Otherwise, we have generally striven to make the chapters readable when taken together, although they do differ somewhat in their approaches and emphases. Strikingly, the Belarusian chapter contains an annotated list of school and university textbooks in its annexes, which the others do not. We chose to retain these annexes, since they could contain valuable information for those studying Belarus in particular.

Collective Memory, Memory Politics, and History Textbooks

When a familiar system collapses and the sense of security and safety shatters, the grounds for cultural trauma arise, in what sociologist Piotr Sztompka calls the other face of social change (450). Historians in the analyzed countries address this trauma in various ways: different countries regard the same processes as emotionally traumatic, but also the opposite, as creators of national pride and sentiments of liberation. "All happy families are alike. Every unhappy family is unhappy in its own way" — Leo Tolstoy's famous observation is true not only of families, but metaphorically of countries emerging from the breakup of the Soviet Union as well. Although perestroika was a common stage experienced by all fifteen Soviet republics, each of them lived it in its own way. Independence came to them all, but how statehood was incorporated into national consciousness varied: while some new states rejoiced, others were more placid, even ambivalent. Understanding how the perestroika period was interpreted in the history textbooks of different countries should start from an understanding of specifics at the factual level. By focusing on what happened, who acted, why, and for what purpose, and what the consequences were, the interpretation of the recent past follows a common scheme that makes it possible to identify how parts of history are narrated to respond to perceived needs for continuity or change, drama or business as usual. The following analyses of history textbooks used in secondary schools and universities from the early 1990s and up to 2012 present a kaleidoscope in which the nationally elaborated views of the four countries shift from unaffected in Belarus to euphoric in Ukraine, from frustrated in Moldova to contained in Russia.

History is growing in importance in the post-Soviet area, being the tool both to unite a people and to distinguish a people from those of other post-Soviet countries. Two recent examples from the former Soviet sphere illustrate that. Taras Shevchenko National University of Kyiv included a question in the examinations for the 2013-2014 academic year on the authoritarian regime of Victor Ianukovych. Students were asked to describe this regime's violations of human rights, the Revolution of Dignity, and the Russian occupation of Crimea, and were impicitly to identify with the view of the Ianukovych government as illegitimate. Also, on 9 April 2015, four "decommunization" laws were adopted by the Ukrainian parliament: 1) On Access to Archives of Repressive Agencies of Totalitarian Communist Regime of 1917-1991; 2) On the Condemnation of the Communist and National Socialist (Nazi) Regimes, and Prohibition of Propaganda of Their Symbols; 3) On the Legal Status and Honoring the Memory of Fighters for Ukraine's Independence in the Twentieth Century; and 4) On Perpetuation of the Victory over Nazism in World War II of 1939-1945 (all texts in English are available at the Ukrainian Institute of National Remembrance official website, memory.gov.ua). In Latvia, the national assembly decided to anticipate criminal responsibility for denying that Soviet occupation had occurred, declaring that those who deny this fact can be jailed for up to five years. The Russian Ministry of Foreign Affairs evaluated this action as an immoral attempt to modify/reconstruct history.

Falk Pingel has stated: "Through the teaching of history and geography we create a mesh of reference points in time and space.

Where we come from, where we live, are we allowed or are we entitled to live there? History and geography textbooks attempt to explain our roots, how and why we happen to be living in a certain place and how that place can be described and characterized—in other words, who we really are (7)." It is natural that numerous works are devoted to the problems of textbook research in general (Foster 5–20) and of history textbook research in particular (Repoussi and Tutiaux-Guillon 154–170). Especially interesting is research that tries to analyze the particularities of history textbook narratives in times of active nation-building, when such socialization is "defined and controlled by the ambivalent nexus between ideology and political expectations (that history textbooks contribute to national identity and patriotism), curricula assumptions (that quality history textbooks impact on pedagogical outcomes), and academic rigor and objectivity" (Zajda 185–191). The authors of nation-building narratives usually use history textbooks to promote self-determination (Janmaat and Vickers, 267–275) and, in the case of the post-Soviet states, to portray their nations and national histories as the victims of Russian oppression (Janmaat 307–324).

Closely connected to the use of history is the concept of collective memory. Collective memory comprises tales of the past that come to dominate or prevail within a specific group. This is an original definition of Maurice Halbwachs, usually considered the "founding father" of the concept of collective memory. The literature on collective, cultural, or social memory and history has been growing steadily in recent decades, and these concepts have become fashionable in those parts of the social sciences and humanities concerned with identity and the biographical aspects of human life. However, many of the contributions articulate little that is new, and an implicit vagueness is part of the concept's great attraction. However, Halbwachs' basic insight, confirmed in an influential study by sociologist Robert Bellah et al., that collectives become communities because of a body of shared memories and perceptions of themselves, is crucial and underlines the cognitive aspect of community-building. In their inquiry into middle-class American mentality, Bellah et al. introduced the concept of "community of memory": "In order not to forget that past, a community is involved in retelling its story, its constitutive narrative, and in so doing, it offers examples of the men and women who have embodied and exemplified the meaning of the community" (153).

Collective memories are individually embraced, but they tell about a collective of which individuals feel part, and these memories are a determining element in shaping group identity. Memories are "collective" or "social" as opposed to individual inasmuch as they are shared by individuals identifying themselves as a group and are concerned with essential aspects of that particular group's existence: what constitutes the collective and what are its boundaries, what values it cherishes, and what are its significant points of reference.

Bellah et al. noted that essential elements of the stories constituting the community identify not just virtues and achievements, but also painful shared experiences that point out the fate shared by the community (250–275). Hence, these memories tell "the story of us" and have to be socialized over generations for the group to survive as a collective. The collective could be anything from a family, organization, or particular neighborhood to an ethnic group or state. In the case of the newly independent states founded after the collapse of the Soviet Union, history textbooks created a uniform and didactic "memory space" – "lieu de mémoire" (Nora) – for the official narratives of the past.

In the literature on collective memory, there is a recurrent and often cited divide between the traditionalists, represented by Halbwachs' *Le Mémoire collective*, who reserve the concept for orally transmitted communication, and the revisionists, represented by Jan Assman, who reject this limitation and also consider monuments, written sources, and arts to be transmitters of collective memories. "Cultural memory preserves the store of knowledge from which a group derives an awareness of its unity and pecularity," wrote Assman (130). The major mechanism by which collective memories endure over time is to shape persistent, but in a sense constructed, identities of "who we are," "who we were," and "how we do things in this community."

Multiple voices contribute to shaping historical memory, forming it into a collective resource. Textbooks are far from the only such voices. Family members conversing around the dining table, writers, artists, and songwriters in their novels, paintings, and lyrics, all these are makers of collective memories (Bergman and Jakobsson 61). Museums are important loci for forming, and sometimes changing, cultural memories, telling about the past, interpreting it, articulating views, and making statements. Individual voices and collective expressions intertwine in creating and constructing beliefs and myths about the past, about what happened and why. All these voices can contribute to, and be used in, ongoing memory politics, or politics of memory, whose traces are also found in the struggle over history textbooks.

However, textbooks differ from many other makers of collective memory in that what is stated is an officially sanctioned and recommended understanding—though more so in schools than in universities in the countries studied here. Whereas works of art, novels, or even museums in the end articulate the voices of individual creators or curators who say, "This is the way I view the past—see it through my eyes," history textbooks say to students, "This is the way we should look at our past, and our surrounding world. This is the way we as a community understand and make sense of what happened." A "we" is therefore assumed to be created. What historians do through history textbooks is, metaphorically, to edit the past, forming it into a narrative of the national collective that resonates with the affections and cognitions of the population. This process is connected with constructing collective identities and incorporating the individual "I" into the collective "we." The population, not least of Russia, as this book demonstrates, could comprise several, coexisting populations whose separate memories need to be articulated to make sense of a perceived complexity. The textbooks in Chechnya and Tatarstan analyzed here edit the past differently from those of Russia.

History is the academic subject through which a governing ideology finds a channel to reach the younger generations to form shared mindsets. Textbooks' explicit function is to form a shared understanding, or "gaze," of the national and international past in the minds of young people, inculcated within the authoritative setting of a school or university.

Required for the effective and long-term stability of society, where highly diverse interpretations of national history undermine community, solidarity, and institutions, a common past is a societal resource of crucial importance. George Orwell wrote in *1984*: "Who controls the past controls the future. Who controls the present controls the past" (44). Of the countries studied here, nowhere is Orwell's statement truer than in Moldova, where the power struggle between the Communists, center/right, and liberals has been heated. When the Communists governed the country from 2001 to 2009, the official history shifted as well. The governing political leaders put their mark on what should be the official gaze of the past. In Ukraine, which constitutes the opposite to Moldova in this respect, the national lens is firmly in place over the twenty years covered.

The Ukranian political leaders "controlling" the past, although struggling over political power, were united in their view of how to remember the past, something that even slightly increased after the Orange Revolution in 2004. Any attempts to denationalize the official version of history faced strong resistance, the best-known example of which was the "pro-Russian" policy of Dmytro Tabachnyk, Minister of Education and Sciences of Ukraine from March 2010 to 23 February 2014. Fairly similar, but played out in a state that since 1994 and the election of president Alexander Lukashenko has been increasingly authoritarian, the past in Belarus is narrated in non-nationalist and non-dramatic terms. Political power has not changed since 1994, and the present government encourages stability and continuity.

Recent developments in Russia since 2014, including the annexation of Crimea, military support for the separatist movement in Eastern Ukraine, and increasingly tense relations with the European Union, will probably be reflected in future textbooks in Russia, again shifting the national gaze. However, up to 2012, Russian historiography was open to the complexity embedded in a huge country that must hold together many nationalities, as well as crystallize the specific position of Russia as the successor state of the great Soviet Union. Russia, like Belarus, has been moving in an authoritarian direction since the election of Vladimir Putin in 2000, and no struggle over the past has been evident in history textbooks since then. However, the discussion—pointed out in the Russian chapter—of a common history textbook for the entire Russian Federation indicates a desire on the part of the political leadership to simplify historical remembrance.

Radical Change in Turbulent Times

Whatever futures Mikhail Gorbachev anticipated in 1985, when he officially launched the economic reform policies with the forward-looking name of "restructuring" and the encouragement of further "openness," the final dissolution of the Soviet Union and the rise of fifteen successor states was not among them. After "five years of luxury funerals," as people colloquially referred to the 1980–1985 period, when three General Secretaries and various other high-ranking Soviet officials died (Martirossian 100), the time had finally come for renewal. When the Swedish Embassy in Moscow reported home on 12 January 1990, amidst an unfolding Soviet breakup with uncertain results, the report described a highlystrung and tense Gorbachev visiting the defiant Lithuanian Republic in the process of declaring its independence, trying to prevent the further dissolution of the federation:

> With emphasis he pleads for the necessity of keeping the union together, thinking about all ties—not least the economic ones—that unite the republics. That the defence forces also have to be All-Union based was broadcast in the TV appearance. Gorbachev underlined that he was the Chairman of the Defence Council. He sought to find support for a renewal of the federation through allowing the republics wide-reaching political autonomy. From what he said, he seemed to be particularly worried by the prospect of discrimination against minorities (read "Russians") in individual republics. (Swedish Government; *Foreign Affairs Archives*, 1989-1991, translation by the authors).

Everything indicates that the policies of perestroika were seriously intended to improve the stagnating Soviet economic and political system, improving life for the hundreds of millions living in the territories that stretched from Europe and into Asia. Taking up the competition with the West was a way to increase the legitimacy of the regime. Comparing itself to a West that in the 1980s was glowing with liberal self-confidence, with the United Kingdom, the United States, and West Germany being governed by ideologically committed leaders with liberal and conservative leanings, Moscow had reason to worry. Margaret Thatcher, Ronald Reagan, and Helmut Kohl were united in their vision of challenging the Soviet Union, through military means if necessary, but also relying on the attractions of the Western lifestyle of individual freedom and its associated material affluence.

The last years of Soviet existence circled around power struggles, attempts at more or less failed coups d'état, waves of stronger and lesser aggression towards the republics that with stubborn persistence, and more and more openly, sought to leave the Union. The three Baltic States, with Lithuania as their courageous leader, played a determining role, and violent attacks took place against demonstrations in both Latvia and Lithuania, with people being killed and injured. Independence movements in Georgia, Moldova, and Armenia met with similar brutality.

The breakup process left the Soviet leaders in Moscow trying to manage not only republican leaders with independence aspirations but also the birth of political leadership in the huge and powerful Russian Rederation[1] with its growing demands for sovereignty.

The open conflict between the elected leader of the Russian Federation, Boris Ieltsin, who sided with the independence fighters in the Baltics, and the Soviet leadership in Moscow put further burdens on the already pressed Union leaders.

It is hard to overestimate the significance of the Soviet collapse and its impact on the world in the 21st century. The

---

[1] The existing Russian Federation is composed by a number of territories, where the Russian Republic consists one (and the major one).

political theorist Francis Fukuyama famously contended that with the end of the Soviet Union, we were witnessing not just the end of the Cold War, but the end of history as such in terms of one of the grand ideologies going to the grave (Fukuyama, End of History amd the Last Man). The sociologist Zygmunt Bauman in an interview maintained that "the collapse of communism ushered us into an as-yet-unexplored world: a world without a collective utopia, without a conscious alternative to itself" (25). The disintegration of the Soviet bloc led not only to new geopolitical configurations hardly fathomable before, but also to new conflicts and instances of violence that were scarcely possible without the fall of the Communist system.

The breakup of the Soviet Union was a historical turning point that came as a surprise not only to the rest of the world but also to many who lived in this vast territory. Several political actors recall feelings of surprise and unpreparedness: Independence "fell" upon them without many plans or preparations for the direction in which to move, for how to organize state institutions and a national economy. In Georgia and Moldova, the ethnic tensions that flared amidst severe economic realities escalated into Civil War over questions of territorial integrity (Blakkisrud and Kolstoe 281–298). The conflicts of Transnistria in Moldova and of Abkhazia and South Ossetia in Georgia are today "frozen" but continue to influence international relations and social and political life in these countries. War broke out between Armenia and Azerbaijan over Nagorno-Karabakh, which continues to be a devastating conflict that has halted socioeconomic reforms and increased military spending. Added to this list is the Russian annexation of Crimea in March 2014 and the violent conflict in Ukrainian Donbas, where Russia has allegedly taken an active role by covertly supporting rebellion.

With the exception of the Baltic States, which turned to Europe at an early stage and deliberately tried to shift trading patterns so as to broaden their economic basis, economic and political development has been slow and halting in many of the former republics, leading to a less than positive view of independence. The layers of first Tsarist and then Soviet experience seem to have generated unusually great difficulty adjusting to modern demands on the state in terms of combined democracy and infrastructural (not despotic) state power (Bennich-Björkman 1–18; Gel'man 455–473; Riabov 30–43).

The shift from planned economies to market systems in the 1990s gave birth to a primitive, raw, and often lawless capitalism, since the state structures were reforming at the time and still lacked the instruments, will, and even understanding needed in order to control privatization. *Sale of the Century: Russia's Wild Ride from Communism to Capitalism*, the well-chosen title of Chrystia Freeland's book on Russia's privatization, illustrates what often went on: insider sellouts at suppressed prices that enriched former state managers, nomenklatura, and Komsomol members in just a few years. The second decade of the market economy witnessed some calming of these provocative, sometimes illicit, processes as regulations began to function, but highly significant economic inequalities without the "soothing hand" of a compensating welfare state—which was present to a certain extent during the Soviet era—are among the lasting changes experienced by post-Soviet societies. Many are even worse off economically today than in late 1989, and inequalities have continued to grow, producing a small strata of super-rich ("oligarchs" not least) (Kupatadze 279–299; Lallemand 61–90; Puglisi 99–123; Söderbaum 10–25).

Perestroika — and Beyond

"Gorbachev's proposed reformation is unprecedented in modern history," claimed Cohen and van den Heuvel, who in 1987–1989 interviewed the foremost reformers in Moscow when perestroika was still unfolding (13). Perestroika was intended to reform socialism to become more pluralistic, open minded, and decentralized, opening up property for more private ownership, without giving up socialism as an ideology and while maintaining top-level control and a definite central role for Moscow. In the mythological tradition of returning to "the sacred past," the reformers from the Communist Party of the Soviet Union tried to return to the true, Leninist visions of socialism, including the economic liberalization of the 1920s, the New Economic Policy. Gorbachev never wanted to let go of a more federative structure, believing that the advantages of an integrated Soviet economy demanded close cooperation in the future as well. This was what radical reformers in Moscow saw before them, and what the elites and grassroots in all the republics were to accommodate. In that way, the perestroika reforms were yet another expression of the social engineering that had been the hallmark of the Soviet Union.

Gorbachev's ideas, which entailed not only economic reforms permitting a more market-oriented economy, but also aspirations for civil organization, debate, and even critique, were at the time, and continued to be, controversial. Gorbachev was a reformist, who believed in the potential of positive change and in the will of the many republics and nationalities to keep the Union together. However, his opponents in the Central Committee in Moscow, like the leader of the conservative wing of the party, Yegor Ligachev (b. 1920), developing into outright enemies as the disintegration unfolded, did not share either his liberal credo or his optimism for a unified Soviet future should these large-scale reforms be put into practice.

History proved them right. Gorbachev and his allies had grossly underestimated the forces of social change embedded in the societies of Ukraine, Georgia, Azerbaijan, and the three Baltic States, not least of a nationalist character (Beissinger, 2002, 47–102; Suny 127–163; Szporluk 1–19). The first signs of change revived and gave birth to ideas and actors that in turn pressed for more, and quicker, reforms. Momentum was gathering, activating slumbering identities and resistance (Suny 127–163). Gorbachev, described as a rational and unemotional man, regarded national identity as of no great importance. He accordingly made a number of serious misjudgements and gravely underestimated the lingering longing combined with frustration among the many nationalities squeezed into the Soviet Union's republics, feelings that quickly escaped control. Local elites and populations in the vast territories of the Soviet Union successively demanded first sovereignty and autonomy, and finally full economic and political independence. In most former Soviet republics, the former communist leaders became the leaders of the new states. To some extent, it was a kind of transformation of one particular system of values into its opposite, from the priority of the international to the dominance of the national. The best example of this is the attempt to introduce a mandatory course on "scientific nationalism" in Ukrainian higher educational institutions, severely criticized by some intellectuals (Bystrytsky). This in itself is evidence of the inherent vulnerabilities built into practices of dictatorship and the large-scale centralization required to realize them. The Politbureau in Moscow was too detached from the grassroots sentiments and loyalties in the republics to be able to assess the potential effects of the reforms that had been set in motion.

The termination of the huge Soviet experiment, with its grand industrialization ambitions and its striving to generate a *new Soviet human*, untainted by nationality, historical specificities, and collective memories, was nothing short of a tremendously powerful unintended consequence of ambitious intentions to modernize and reform that changed the path of history. When the summer of 1991 began, the end of which marked the final days of the Soviet Union, the political, economic, and strategic future appeared highly uncertain for the many republics. Just a few months earlier, in the spring, the Swedish Embassy in Moscow, where the developments were followed closely on a daily basis, reported to Stockholm that "the obvious candidates for secession from the union are, aside from the Baltic States, Georgia, Azerbaijan, Moldova, and later maybe Ukraine" (Swedish Government; *Foreign Affairs Archives*, 1989-1991) The Baltic States, Georgia, and Ukraine shared an increasingly strong nationalism, which inspired elite actions and popular mobilization. Those who hoped for and predicted that prospects, including economic ones, would be more promising outside a future federation or confederation also tended to push for secession, whereas those who regarded the alternatives as more limited instead held onto the idea of a federative or at least confederative structure (Darden 3-23; Hale 57-91). Most clearly among the latter were the republics of Central Asia. In the end, the idea of even a loose confederation did not survive a Russia that was pushing for independence and renewed statehood.

Russia as the Ambivalent Inheritor of the Soviet Union: The Case(s) of Russia

Natalia Tregubova, Liliya Erushkina, Alexandr Gorylev, and Alexey Rusakov

Introduction

Russia is a huge country with many regions, oblasts, and autonomous territories that have their own experiences. The Russian understanding of national identity is one of citizenship in a multinational state that is dealing with the challenges of a global world and is in potential confrontation with other states. It is a civil identity, but with ethnic connotations. The relations between terms such as "ethnos," "civil nation," "the unity of one state," and "the state" itself are not particularly clear and allow for various interpretations. Creating a civil identity through history education implies teaching primarily the history of the state or territory, and not that of the ethnic group as such. Because of the constant changes in the borders of the state over time, it is not quite clear what constitutes the basis of the Russian state itself, what constitutes Russian-ness, and whether it is connected with a particular territory, ethnos, religion, or a combination of these. This is reflected in the historiography of the Russian Federation, where the main discourse identifies Russia as the successor state of the Soviet Union *and* a nation like others. Challenged by two nationalistically oriented alternatives, an elite-oriented one in Chechnya and a grassroots-oriented one in Tatarstan, the "domino principle" discourse holds a strong grip on history textbooks in Russia.

There has been a clear tendency towards the reunification of history education in Russia over time, not least since the 2000s, and the central government regulates how much emphasis is to be put on local versus regional history. The recent discussions of a single history textbook provide good evidence for this desire to unify.

Russia's contemporary educational system is built on the reformation of the Soviet system. The 1990s was a time of discussion and of considerable change, from critiques of dehumanized Soviet education, to both the use of non-standardized textbooks and the elaboration of state standards (Dneprov 132-133; Kozlovskaia 4-5). In the 2000s, educational reforms continued, new plans and standards were put into practice, and the modernization of education came to be regarded as a state priority (in 2005, education was proclaimed a "national project"). These transformations gave birth to a system of education that is more flexible and varied than the versions from before 1991 (Smolin 10); at the same time, it retains several features of the old Soviet system, such as centralization and regulation through state standards. However, it does not possess the systematic and uniform Soviet character, and has adapted badly to new market conditions (Kuz'minov 13-14; Tiurina 12-13).

For history education in the 1990s, the reforms resulted in the approval of a concentric structure of historical education instead of a linear one; today the reverse transition is being discussed, from a concentric to a linear structure. A linear structure implies that history is taught in chronological sequence, while a concentric structure suggests that the same historical events and periods are taught several times: at a basic level in secondary school and more deeply in high school. One of the main problems in the reforms has been striking a balance between the new values of liberalism and nationalism that should supposedly be able to coexist (Puzatich 6-10).

These problems and controversies have become apparent in the debate on uniform Russian history textbooks for secondary school that President Vladimir Putin proposed in early 2013. The discussion embraced not only the textbook contents, but also the idea of a single history textbook as such. In 2015-2016, several history textbooks were published, not the proposed single one, and they were designed with regard to the new historical-cultural standard for teaching domestic history. The debate about a univocal history textbook therefore resulted in a compromise of moderate unification.

The Constitution of the Russian Federation protects ideological diversity, expressed in articles 43 and 44 of the Constitution, which proclaim freedom of teaching and support for various forms of education. At the same time, Russia guarantees the right to education, primarily by means of the state federal education standards established by the government and defining the minimum educational content. The whole set of requirements is compulsory for institutions of general education accredited by the state. General education in Russia comprises primary and secondary education, and the Ministry of Education and Science examines and approves school textbooks. As for the institutions of higher education, they generally possess more freedom in creating programs and choosing literature than do secondary schools, and the Ministry does not approve their textbooks; instead, this is done by specially appointed university committees.

At the time of writing, the subject of history consists of parallel courses in world and domestic history—much as in Moldova—with domestic history acquiring more importance over time. As for the textbooks themselves, they are descriptive, yet analytical in comparison with the highly uniform and ideological Soviet textbooks. Nevertheless, looking back at the period around year 2000, there is a clear tendency towards the reunification of education, and recent discussions of a single history textbook provide good evidence for this interpretation.

Traces of the same tendency towards growing uniformity also show themselves in relation to openness to regional diversity. The Russian Federation is a large state with considerable regional differences, not only economic and social, but also concerning ethnic issues at the inter- and intra-regional levels. These regional divisions are viewed in terms of center versus periphery and center versus alternative (i.e., regional) centers, as opposed to Belarus, Moldova (in part), and Ukraine with their prevailing east-west divisions. One of the most important changes came in 2007 with the repeal of a law that allowed the regions (i.e., national republics) in Russia to determine what regional history should be taught and for how long in class. Instead, a flexible state federal standard was introduced that allows 10–15 percent of class time to be spent on regional history. Several republic governments formulated sharp critiques of these changes (for example in Tatarstan and North Ossetia), though it is difficult to say whether or not the role of the regional part of the basic education program has been diminished.

Another tension connected with ethnic issues became manifest in relation to a university textbook from the center. This was the scandal concerning *Russian History 1917–2009*, written by Alexander Vdovin and Alexander Barsenkov, two professors from Moscow State University's history department. The book included controversial statements about Chechen and Jewish people, prompting sharp criticism of the authors as well as intensive reaction in the mass media. As a result, the Academic Council of Moscow State University's history department chose in the end not to accept the textbook. Nevertheless, it has been reprinted three times, is recommended for high school history programs, and remains in circulation.

Unified standards control history education in the Russian Federation. What do these standards imply? For insights into how they are formulated, the document *The Fundamental Core of the Content of General Education* (Kozlov and Kondakov) for primary and secondary education is a good source. The document was formulated by the Russian Academy of Education by request of the Ministry of Science and Education and the Federal Agency of Education in 2009 (here we use the 4th, expanded edition from 2011). The main aim of the document is to define: "1) the system of basic national values; 2) the system of basic concepts; 3) the system of key tasks" (Kozlov and Kondakov 3; translation by the authors). It concerns itself with knowledge and values, which means that textbooks should be consistent, both scientifically and ideologically. Supposedly, the outlined values are basic national values that belong to the peoples, that is, to the many different ethnoses of the Russian Federation.

Teaching history should aim at developing historical thinking, "the basis of a value- oriented person's civil identity"

(Kozlov and Kondakov 24, translation by the authors). The question is whether this teaching includes the values of certain ethnicities. The answer lies in the definition of basic national values, which only include values that "ensure the effective development of the country" (Kozlov and Kondakov 3, translation by the authors). The document exists to help realize "social cohesion and consent in the conditions of growth in the social, ethnic, religious, and cultural diversity of our society through the formation of Russian identity" (Kozlov and Kondakov 4, translation by the authors). It demonstrates that general education in Russia is intended to eliminate separatist tendencies and create citizens with a national identity in which ethnic differences are even accentuated while, it is claimed, the potential for ethnic (as well as social and religious) conflict is lessened.

Furthermore, national identity is understood to be marked by citizenship in a multinational state that must respond to the challenges of a global world and is in potential confrontation with other states. However, there are references to the family as well, implying ethnos in a primordial sense, while simultaneously being connected with the presumably civil "Fatherland." This inconsistency is more distinct in the use of the concept of "the people" in the document to refer to both ethnos ("traditions of the peoples of Russia") and the civil nation ("multinational Russian people") (Kozlov and Kondakov 10, translation by the authors). The inherent tension between civil and ethnic national identities is striking.

Moreover, one characteristic of the document is that it presumes value and belief in the state itself, in the "integrity of the courts and responsibility of authorities" (Kozlov and Kondakov 10, translation by the authors), presenting the state as infallible. Finally, the document claims that these values "unite all Russians" (Kozlov and Kondakov 11, translation by the authors). In this case, all basic values (not only those that directly point to the civil nation) are supposed to create a pan-Russian identity, implying that all identities are necessary but that ethnic identities are subordinate to the national one. Therefore, the relationship between civil and ethnic nationalism is not as transparent as it appears at first glance.

A characteristic aspect of Russian history as a subject is that it includes references to the "history of Russia as an integral part of the world-historical process" (Kozlov and Kondakov 24, translation by the authors) and to "factors of originality in Russian history" (Kozlov and Kondakov 26, translation by the authors). These references imply the specificity of Russian history and its connection with the rest of the world.

Importantly, this means that such a thing as Russian history exists. This includes the history of "ancient peoples and states" in the Russian territory, i.e., of "ancient Russia," "medieval Russia," "Russia in modern times," and "the most recent history of Russia" from the 20th and 21st centuries (Kozlov and Kondakov 26-28, translation by the authors). These headings demonstrate that "Russian history" means the history of the state (or territory when there was no state). In the case of the perestroika period, for example, it is not seen as part of the history of Russia as part of the Soviet Union, but rather as part of the history of the Soviet state (and society), because the purposeful narration of various events and processes characterizes the historical trajectories of the Soviet Union. Therefore, the key point for Russian history connected with perestroika is the "collapse of the world system of socialism" (Kozlov and Kondakov 26, translation by the authors) in terms of the "causes and outcomes of the crisis and the disintegration of the Soviet system" (Kozlov and Kondakov 28, translation by the authors). The focus is on the end of the Soviet world's existence (and not only the Soviet Union itself). The document characterizes the Soviet Union as "a type of state and society" and mentions "the problem of nationality" (in the sense of "ethnicities") (Kozlov and Kondakov 28, translation by the authors). This corresponds to putting the value of civil national identity before that of ethnic identity. However, the question is whether the "nation" is becoming a substitute for the "state," no matter what its borders were or are in specific epochs; another question remains, however: What is particular to this state that makes it Russian?

To sum up, the standards established by the central authorities presuppose the formation of a civil national identity of citizens of this multiethnic state through secondary education (by promoting basic national values). This identity is supposed to coexist with ethnic identity, thereby preventing ethnic conflict. However, a more intensive look at how words are used indicates that the relations between uses of terms such as "ethnos," "civil nation," "the unity of one state," and "the state" itself are not particularly clear and allow for different interpretations. Creating civil identity through history education implies teaching primarily the history of the state or territory, and not that of the ethnic group as such. Because of the constant changes in the borders of the state over time, it is not quite clear what constitutes the basis of the Russian state itself, what is Russian-ness, and whether it is connected with a particular territory, ethnos, religion, or a combination of these. The texts concerning the perestroika period point to the end of Soviet history and the Soviet Union's disintegration, confirming this "statist" perspective.

The Russian Study

Russian history textbooks containing interpretations of perestroika vary greatly in subject, depending on the year and place of publication. To analyze and compare textbooks systematically, constructing a sample that captures their diversity proved necessary, which was done by identifying criteria that are germane in this context. Such a sample is suitable for qualitative research focused on making preliminary generalizations and revealing main tendencies.

The first distinction is whether the textbook is intended for secondary school students or for those at the higher education level. This matters, because the procedures for approving these publications differ, as mentioned above. School textbooks have to adapt to the general educational standards, whereas university textbooks do not need to meet these standards and are much more varied in quantity and content. Edited by the universities themselves, the regional variety is greater in higher education textbooks. With this in mind, we ask whether the interpretation of perestroika in high school textbooks presents a more uniform description of perestroika than do university textbooks. Second, are the high school textbooks *recommended* by the Ministry of Education and Science more coherent and unified in their content than those that are only *allowed* to be published by the Ministry?

A third dimension is the region from which a university textbook originates. To capture the differences, we compare university textbooks from different regions. Our main interest has been in polar cases: Moscow (the center) and the regional centers of autonomous regions with separatist tendencies ("alternative centers") are included, as are regional centers without clear separatist tendencies. The question is whether the textbooks from these last centers are closer to those of Moscow or to those of the alternative centers in their content. Fourth, the textbooks' main storylines are in focus: on one hand, there are histories of Russia (in general or in a certain period) and, on the other, histories of regions.

Constructed by considering these dimensions, the sample comprises 22 textbooks (Annexes 1 and 2 contain comprehensive information). It includes eight regional textbooks, and choosing these regions constituted the most important challenge of the study's design. We decided to include textbooks from Bashkortostan, Tatarstan, Chechnya, Irkutskaya Oblast, and Rostovskaya Oblast. The last two regions are intermediate between the center and the alternative centers, with no openly articulated separatist tendencies. Irkutskaya and Rostovskaya Oblasts are not autonomous regions, but represent parts of Russia that obviously differ from the center. Rostov-na-Donu is the administrative center of the Southern Federal Region and Irkutsk is one of the largest centers of Eastern Siberia.

Bashkortostan, Tatarstan, and Chechnya are alternative centers. First, they were autonomous republics of the Soviet Union, and now they are entities of the Russian Federation with the legal status of a republic. This implies the broadest possible autonomy, including to enact state legislation and determine state languages. Chechnya and Tatarstan are crucial for the study because they are the most separatist Russian entities, though their separatisms differ. It was these two, as well as Ingushetia, that refused to sign the Federal Treaty in 1992 and thereby did not recognize their subordination to the Russian Federation. In the early 2000s, however, their trajectories came to differ. At that time, Tatarstan was negotiating with the Federal government, whereas Chechnya was involved in a war with Russia. As of today, these regions are entities of the Russian Federation by law. Finally, Bashkortostan was chosen as an interesting contrasting case of an ethnic regional center in relation to Chechnya and Tatarstan. In 1990, Bashkortostan declared its sovereignty, but chose to sign the Federal Treaty in 1992.

Among the eight textbooks from the regions, four are regional histories: two of Tatarstan, one of Bashkortostan, and one of Chechnya. Hence, we examine regional histories of the alternative centers, treating Bashkortostan as a putative alternative center. The other four textbooks are histories of Russia, one from Irkutskaya Oblast, one from Rostovskaya Oblast, and two from Bashkortostan.

The sample does not take into account two distinctions that could well be important for further studies. First, we do not classify textbooks by the year of the edition (though our sample includes textbooks from 1995 to 2012) because, given the size of our sample, we are unable to obtain valid results if we add one more criterion for comparison. Second, we analyze textbooks written only in Russian even though many of the regional textbooks are in regional languages. However, even given these limitations, inevitable in qualitative research of such a scope, the sample considers distinctions that are crucial for the Russian context. Therefore, it will be possible to characterize and generalize about the narrative of perestroika in Russian textbooks.

The methods chosen are discourse and content analyses. The discourse analysis of the textbooks strives to lay bare the hidden logic of the historical narrative (what the authors identify as the "driving forces" of history). The goal is to reveal the discourse(s) of the textbooks studied. This could be defined as critical discourse analysis, according to the classification by Jørgensen and Phillips, which helps in studying "the relations between discourse and social and cultural developments in different social domains" (60). Critical discourse analysis proposes a dialectical relationship between the discourse itself and its social context: discourse is regarded as a form of social practice, which both constitutes the social world and is constituted by other social practices. This method seems to be suitable for the analysis of our data, as it helps us find the middle way between the characteristics of abstract discourses considered fairly autonomous from the social world, on one hand, and the motives and social practices of particular textbook authors, on the other. Thus, we look into complex relations between the textbooks' contents and contexts. As recommended by Jørgensen and Phillips (Chapter 3), we identify different elements of narrative, topics, and attitudes in the textbooks, and then relate them to the revealed discourses so that various elements can all belong to one discourse, and one element can be found in different discourses.

The content analysis mainly verifies the findings of discourse analysis and is used to illustrate it using generalized qualitative data. Qualitative content analysis includes the analysis of definitions of perestroika and the titles of textbook sections devoted to perestroika.

Below follows the analysis presented as characteristic of the revealed discourses with a focus on several crucial points: the preconditions for perestroika, the key actors and the logic of narration, the collapse of the Soviet Union as presumably the main outcome of perestroika, and the "portrait" of Gorbachev (as the major political actor). Description of the Chernobyl catastrophe as one of the most famous and tragic events of the period, communist ideology, and the preconditions for separatism are likewise covered. All these topics are sensitive to ideological biases, and illustrate differences in the evaluation of perestroika and of the history of Russia. The topics are highly relevant to the further comparisons of the post-Soviet countries taken up in this book.

Discourses of Perestroika in Russian Textbooks

Three distinct discourses are discernible in Russian history textbooks: the "domino principle," "feudal Machiavellianism," and the "national awakening" discourses. The second and third discourses are represented by the textbooks of Chechnya and Tatarstan, respectively. The domino principle discourse is prevalent in all of the university textbooks produced in the center, as well as in the school textbooks. In what follows, we refer to it as the "main discourse" and to the others as "deviant discourses." These labels refer only to quantitative representations of each discourse in our sample, by no means implying that one discourse is preferable to another (or even dominant in a certain region). The narrative of the perestroika process is, moreover, as coherent (or incoherent) in the school textbooks as in the university ones. The school textbooks do not differ from one another in this respect. Histories of Russia from Bashkortostan, Rostov-na-Donu, and Irkutsk—the intermediate centers—are consistent with the domino principle discourse. Among the histories of regions, the history of Bashkortostan (the contrasting case) is written within the framework of the domino principle discourse, but with the addition of "meanwhile in Bashkortostan" to make room for the regional perspective. Attention is paid to the awakening of national consciousness, but overall, the main perestroika narrative is the same as that of the center.

The Domino Principle Discourse

The basic discourse of perestroika that characterizes 19 out of 22 Russian textbooks is the domino principle. This principle implies that the primary steps in reforming socialism led to unexpected consequences that, in the end, resulted in the collapse of the Soviet Union. The preconditions for perestroika in this discourse are generally seen in the deep and latent economic, political, and cultural crises of Soviet society. The authors typically argue that perestroika was "the last chance for the system" (Danilov and Kosulina 232, translation by the authors), providing the possibility of reformation. The elite initiated the change, but the process later escalated out of control: "perestroika gained autonomy from its initiators" (Barsenkov and Vdovin 609, translation by the authors); "the real power began to slip out of the hands of the party apparatus" (Bobyleva 126, translation by the authors); "perestroika's results in many ways did not match the original intention of its creators" (Kislitsin 562, translation by the authors); and "the results of the reforms were far from the expected ones" (Zagladin, Minakov, Kozlenko and Petrov 373, translation by the authors). In the economic sphere, the reforms are characterized as inefficient; in the political sphere, unexpected results of the policy of "glasnost" are presented. Unlike in Belarus, but as in Ukraine (see chapters 4 and 3, respectively), in the Russian textbooks, it is possible to trace a single logic driving the perestroika process, a clear narrative that is independent of the individual authors of the textbooks. This narrative proceeds from an all-Soviet perspective with the Soviet Union being the main character, mentioned 839 times in 19 textbooks articulating the domino principle discourse; the next most mentioned term is Russia/the Russian Soviet Federative Socialist Republic (RSFSR), with 269 mentions; the United States is the most frequently mentioned foreign country with 105 mentions.

In 19 textbooks, the average number of pages about perestroika is about 19 in the high school textbooks and about 16 in the university textbooks. The ratio of pages about perestroika to the total number of pages is slightly higher in school textbooks at 4.5 percent, versus 3.5 percent in the university ones. One can distinguish several recurring topics and a typical sequence of narrative within this discourse. The text is usually divided into a prologue, which covers economic development, political reformation, foreign policy, ethnic conflict, and cultural aspects, followed by an epilogue. The prologue covers events that preceded perestroika and its general preconditions, whereas the epilogue covers the collapse of the Soviet Union, the putsch, and the end of perestroika. Both school and university textbooks pay most attention to the economic and political domains (20-30 percent of the space). The main difference between school and university textbooks is that foreign affairs are much less featured in the university textbooks. Note, however, that the focus here is on history textbooks, whereas foreign affairs and/or world history is the topic of other disciplines.

Fifteen of the nineteen textbooks within the domino principle discourse provide an explicit definition of perestroika. The most common or typical definition of perestroika is that it was an attempt by the political elite to reform all the spheres of society. However, three textbooks (Levandovskii and Shchetinov; Levandovskiy, Shchetinov and Mironenko; Lapteva) define perestroika differently: as a stage of Soviet history, characterized by attempts to overcome crisis and stop disintegration. Therefore, the definition of perestroika is ambivalent: as a set of reforms deliberately taken by the political elite, but also as a historical stage characterized by these reforms and their consequences. The latter is the more comprehensive definition, encompassing not only the reforms but also their outcomes and the responses to them. A typical chapter title is "Perestroika in the Soviet Union: 1985-1991," illustrating that perestroika is presented as an integral part of the Soviet Union's history.

The most often mentioned individual in the textbooks belonging to the domino discourse is, unsurprisingly, the last Soviet president Mikhail Gorbachev, with 389 mentions. The second most frequently mentioned figure (159 times) is Boris Ieltsin, the president of the Russian Federation. It is these two politicians, and not economists, writers, or workers, who are described as the main actors of perestroika. Other personalities are mentioned only rarely. Among those who are mentioned more than fifteen times, all are political actors of perestroika or played a role in shaping the preconditions for its start.

Hence, Mikhail Gorbachev is the main political figure in the domino principle discourse. The textbooks initially focus on Gorbachev as a young, new political leader in the Communist Party. They characterize him as "energetic" (Barsenkov and Vdovin 588; Dmitrienko 585; Levandovskiy, Shchetinov and Mironenko 299; Orlov, Georgiev, Georgieva and Sivokhina 480, translation by the authors), "active and resolute" (Lapteva 317, translation by the authors), and as an "initiator" (Orlov, Georgiev,

Georgieva and Sivokhina 480, translation by the authors), and point to the wide popularity and authority Gorbachev had at the beginning of perestroika. These are not personal qualities, however, but instead could be interpreted as Gorbachev's public image, which differs strikingly from that of the old political leaders. Only two authors deliberately describe Gorbachev's personal qualities: "unusual for the Soviet leader style of behavior" (Valiullin and Zaripova 189, translation by the authors) and "charming" (Barsenkov and Vdovin 589, translation by the authors).

Characterized during perestroika by his actions as the head of state and a representative of the political elite, often synonymous with "the Soviet Union" or "the government of the Soviet Union," he personifies centrist and reformist political forces. Reproached for reform inconsistencies, when the final stages of perestroika are described, most textbooks ascribe a passive role to Gorbachev (though previously characterizing him as energetic), and point to the disappointment and loss of trust in him: "the president chose the path of the observer, and thus predetermined his own fate" (Dmitrienko 590, translation by the authors). Gorbachev's withdrawal coincides with the Soviet collapse and the end of perestroika. In general, the evaluation of Gorbachev's image is marked by disappointment at the fall of a potential hero, who devolved from being a promising young leader to a passive and indecisive political figure.

As for collective actors, the Communist Party of the Soviet Union is mentioned most often (368 times). The State Committee for Extraordinary Situations (GKCHP) is another collective actor, with 90 mentions. GKCHP was the organization that, at the end of perestroika, represented the conservative part of the political elite, connected with the collapse of the Soviet Union. Other organizations play minor roles, and the vast majority of them are political parties and social movements of the perestroika epoch. When it comes to interpreting individual and collective agency in the Russian mainstream textbooks, there is a distinct perspective that focuses on the elite and the establishment rather than also on the challengers from broader society. It is Gorbachev and the Communist Party that are in absolute focus.

Mentions of the Chernobyl nuclear plant catastrophe, which turned the entire city of Pripjat into a ghost town and affected all the neighboring countries, occur in 14 out of 19 textbooks. Depicted as an accident (*avariya*) or a catastrophe (*katastrofa*), the tragedy is singled out as the most significant incident of the period. The description of Chernobyl is presented within the narrative of economic reforms (*uskorenie*, i.e., "acceleration"). The effects of Chernobyl are presented as damaging for Belarus, Ukraine, and Russia (Danilov, Kosulina and Brandt 312; Kirillov 607) and for the authorities' prestige (Valiullin and Zaripova 189; Barsenkov and Vdovin 595) that caused people's deaths (Kirillov 607; Valiullin and Zaripova 189) and economic loss (Zagladin, Minakov, Kozlenko and Petrov 371; Barsenkov and Vdovin 595), and became a reason for political distrust (Orlov, Georgiev, Georgieva and Sivokhina 490; Konukov 110). In general, the incident is used to illustrate the Soviet reforms' drawbacks and unexpected results (similar to the treatment in Ukrainian textbooks, but less emotional).

The most often mentioned events of the domino principle discourse are connected with the political life and actors of the second half and end of perestroika. In focus is on the Soviet level in general, the August Coup (putsch) of 1991, the denunciation of the Union Treaty of 1922, and the creation of the Treaty of the Commonwealth of Independent States. The abolition of article 6 of the Soviet Constitution that guaranteed the leading role of the Communist Party of the USSR (CPSU) is mentioned as well. Moreover, the declaration of Russia's Independence and the parade of sovereignties are recurrently mentioned, and national conflicts in the eight parts of the Soviet Union are emphasized with various frequencies. We note the same focus on political actors and events at the Union level as well, with significant attention paid to separatism in both Russia and the national republics.

Almost all of the authors of the textbooks sharing the domino principle discourse argue that perestroika started as an initiative to renovate socialism in accordance with communist ideology: "perestroika was designed as a reform of the Soviet model of socialism" (Lapteva 818, translation by the authors). Later, when the initiated reforms appeared inconsistent and half-hearted, the Communist Party met with growing opposition from liberals and democrats and turned to conservative reactionaries. Defending the status quo, reactionary tendencies evolved, but the liberal-democrats came out the winners. Portraying the leftists as disunited, almost all the textbooks point to important splits within the Communist Party itself. As for the ideological side, communist ideology itself is not generally in focus, except when it comes to primary attempts to reform socialism in "a Marxist-Leninist spirit." Instead, the focus is on the rise of new values. In the Ukrainian textbooks, these are nationalist values. In Belarus and in the main discourse of the Russian textbooks, new humanist, democratic, and universal values are reported as having spread through glasnost. Earlier regarded as capitalist and Western (the growth of nationalist values in Russia concerns only the national republics), in the Russian context these values are characterized mostly in a positive way, unlike in the Belarusian textbooks where the assessments are much more ambivalent (see chapter 4). However, some textbooks refer to "the desire to earn more money" (Aleksashkina, Danilov and Kosulina 329, translation by the authors) and "passion for profit" (Levandovskiy, Shchetinov and Mironenko 310, translation by the authors) as a "dark side" of the new values.

Most of the textbooks identify the separatist tensions in the national republics as starting with increased democratization and glasnost. The "relaxation" of political life along with economic decline led to more open displays of previously hidden conflicts. Old latent controversies that were suppressed during the Soviet regime were revived: "inconsistency of national policy has generated controversy in interethnic relations. In conditions of glasnost these conflicts escalated into open conflicts" (Orlov, Georgiev, Georgieva and Sivokhina 490, translation by the authors). Furthermore, the hesitancy of the center to allow greater autonomy is also proposed as partly accounting for separatist tendencies, and nationalism is considered a type of intervening mechanism between structural conditions (i.e., the reactivation of old controversies) and the struggle of the elites (i.e., center vs. periphery). Nationalism replaced the "ideological vacuum" that arose in the national republics: the "undermining [of] the authority of the CPSU leadership under the conditions of glasnost" and weakening of [the] impact of the communist ideology promoted the growth of ideas of nationalism" (Zagladin, Minakov, Kozlenko and Petrov 328, translation by the authors).

Describing the relations between the Soviet Union and its largest republic, the RSFSR, most authors merely mention the fact that Russia became independent in 1990. Only three textbooks (Semin 489; Levandovskii, Shchetinov and Mironenko 307; Barsenkov and Vdovin 616) provide additional opinions on this issue, implying that the RSFSR was one of the Soviet republics and, as such, was subordinated to the center and affected by its destructive policies even more than were the other republics. Russians were not nationalists, however, and only reacted to nationalist movements in the other republics. Indeed, and interestingly, the authors do not point to nationalist values in connection with Russia, as opposed to the national republics: "nationalist parties and movements that rejected the communist ideology objectively became allies of forces working for rapid market reforms and democratization in Russia itself" (Zagladin, Minakov, Kozlenko and Petrov 398–399, translation by the authors), which holds the values of democracy and the market economy. Hence, Russian textbooks differ from those of the other countries examined here, in that in all the other countries, the textbooks point to national movements within the republics. Boris Ieltsin remarkably personifies the new, all-Soviet democratic forces in Russia, while for Belarus, he symbolizes regional separatism.

Therefore, in the domino principle discourse, the preconditions for separatism in the RSFSR and in the national republics are partly the same and partly different. In both cases, the authors refer to the injurious policies of the center to which the struggle between the elites contributed. Nevertheless, when discussing the national republics, the authors point to old ethnic controversies that "unthawed" during perestroika, and found their expression in the nationalist movements. In the case of the RSFSR, the authors instead emphasized the economic aspects of the center's hurtful policies and the replacement of communism with liberal-democratic ideology, nationalism being mentioned only in relation to movements in the national republics. Therefore, the RSFSR represents the radical alternative to reforms planned for the entire Soviet Union, and its position could be regarded as "quasi-separatist."

The Soviet collapse is seen as the main outcome of perestroika in the domino principle discourse. There are different descriptions of this event. The basic descriptors appear rather neutral: the end of the existence (*konets sushchestvovanija*) and the disintegration (*raspad/disintegratsia*) of the Soviet Union or Soviet society. However, auxiliary descriptors are also used, such as breakdown (*razval*), collapse (*krah*), dismantling (*demontazh*), and death (*konchina*). These embed different rhetorical meanings, mostly of a negative and even pitiful sort. Presenting the collapse as the result of a process that ran out of control is common. Here, the interpretative framework still provides some room for different assessments of the inevitable failure of perestroika, and the possibility of the actors changing the course of the process. Were the reforms doomed from the outset or was there a chance to save the Soviet Union?

There are traces of two sub-discourses within the domino principle discourse. They are mostly evident in the textbooks by Dmitrienko and by Levandovskii and Shchetinov, respectively. The first is a Marxist-like interpretation of the preconditions for perestroika, holding that the system spontaneously transformed in response to growing alienation: "Soviet man, alienated from the distribution of the produced product, became a performer ... to perform forced labor" (Dmitrienko 584, translation by the authors). This is a classic description of the historical inevitability of events from a Marxist perspective. Although, surprisingly, the author points to several possibilities for elites to influence the situation, nevertheless: "the aspiration to maintain the Communist

Party apparatus' control over the course of events did not allow the making of historic decisions that could change the country's destiny" (Dmitrienko 524, translation by the authors). This interpretation is in line with the main discourse (i.e., that the unexpected collapse was facilitated by the incompetence of the elite) but with a stronger focus on the objective causes of perestroika's failure. Here, there are reminiscences of Soviet-era history writing when the authors tended to neglect the opportunities open to the actors.

The second sub-discourse points instead to a kind of actor-driven Machiavellianism, describing rival, self-interested elites, while ordinary people wait for decisions "from above." "The main objective was to stop the disintegration of the system of 'state socialism' and protect the interests of the ruling elite—the nomenklatura that formed these politicians and nominated them to the top (where the former part of the objective was subordinated to the latter one, and pretty soon the former was abandoned)" (Levandovskii and Shchetinov 311, translation by the authors). History is depicted as a game between political elites in which the people are silent. The logic of the narrative is similar to that of the first sub-discourse, but assigns responsibility to the actions of the politicians. The reforms are treated as a missed opportunity. However, in both sub-discourses the causes (preconditions) are internal, not external, as the conspiracy theories articulated in the Belarusian textbooks imply, as will be discussed below.

The domino principle discourse is characterized by an etatist, top–down perspective: it focuses on the state, and endows political elites with the ability to act while ordinary citizens' actions are presented as reactions to political struggles at the all-Soviet and regional levels. As will be shown, Ukrainian historiography presents a strikingly different understanding in which civil society plays a significant role (see further in Chapter 3). The regional level, however, does not embrace Russia (the RSFSR), as its history is associated with Soviet history and its political elite coincides with the USSR's elite. As a result, the Russian people are described as doubly passive: they react to the reforms at the all-Soviet level and to ethnic conflicts initiated by regional political elites and supported by common people at the national-republic level. The main discourse thus ignores both constructive initiatives from below and destructive manifestations of Russian nationalism.

Feudal Machiavellianism Discourse

Turning to the alternative discourses developed in Chechnya and Tatarstan, the history of Chechnya presents a striking contrast to the domino principle. Within this narrative, perestroika, defined as "a course of reforms," "opened a new period of struggle within the republican elite in Chechen-Ingushetia" (Akhmadov and Hasmagomadov 942, translation by the authors). The further narrative is not primarily about perestroika, but about the struggle among the elites concerning relations with the center and among the leaders of Chechnya and Ingushetia. The narrative is at the level of the Chechen-Ingush Autonomous Soviet Socialist Republic (ChIASSR), which is the most mentioned state/sub-state entity (others are the Soviet Union, Ingushetia, Russia, North Ossetia, and Chechnya). The history of Chechnya does not even mention the collapse of the Soviet Union; rather, the event described is the collapse of the ChIASSR. This implies that there was no unified Soviet people, but only the Chechen people under Soviet rule. Chechnya is portrayed as a "feudal principality" that had a chance to gain more autonomy because of the weakening of the "suzerain," i.e., the Soviet Union, characterized as a "totalitarian empire" (Akhmadov and Khasmagomadov 937, translation by the authors). Perestroika merely plays the role of a "trigger" for the elites' struggle and for populist actions. The ratio of pages about perestroika in the history of Chechnya (5.7 percent) is larger than in the main discourse. The narrative structure, in comparison with that of the domino principle discourse, differs strikingly: the Chechen textbook points only to ethnic issues, describing the struggle of different groups inside the region.

The main actors in the feudal Machiavellianism discourse are the local political leaders. Surprisingly, Gorbachev is mentioned only once as "a new leader of the country" who initiated perestroika (Akhmadov and Khasmagomadov 942, translation by the authors). There are other regional heroes instead, and Dzhokhar Dudaev and Doku Zavgaev are the most prominent local actors mentioned in the history textbook. The most mentioned organization is the CPSU, but the textbook focuses mostly on parties and social movements at the regional level (altogether they are mentioned more often than all-Soviet organizations), viewing history through a less top–down lens. In the history of Chechnya, the putsch is the only Soviet-level event touched on, and even Chernobyl is ignored. The emphasis is completely on the political struggle, and on the ethnic conflicts in ChIASSR. Concerning ideological and separatist issues, the feudal Machiavellianism discourse unsurprisingly features only at the level of the Chechen-Ingush republic and characterizes only Chechen-Ingush separatism. Its preconditions are depicted as old controversies ("Chechens and Ingush had made clear that they were stepchildren in this state"; Akhmadov and Khasmagomadov 941, translation by the authors) in combination with "contradictions between Russian, Chechen, and Ingush strata related to a constant struggle for the redistribution of the top positions," which in turn "provoked tensions in interethnic relations at the everyday level" (Akhmadov and Khasmagomadov 941, translation by the authors). During perestroika, all these issues resulted in Chechen–Ingush–Russian conflicts in which, it is claimed, "the Russian and Russian-speaking part of the population of Chechen-Ingushetia displayed total political passivity" (Akhmadov and Khasmagomadov 947, translation by the authors).

The logic followed here is close to that of the domino principle discourse: it points to old controversies activated during perestroika and to the center–periphery struggle. The difference is in the focus on ethnic conflict and elite struggle *within* the region that led to the split between Chechnya and Ingushetia. The Feudal Machiavellianism discourse also shares with the main discourse a focus on the activity of political elites, not ordinary citizens, and characterizes the Russian population as passive in comparison with other mobilized ethnic groups. However, this passivity is assessed negatively in the history of Chechnya, while the main discourse depicts it in a more positive light, as an absence of destructive nationalism. Aside from that, in the Chechen textbook the role of the religious (Islamic) movement within the nationalist movement is highly significant, and attention is paid to the religious (Islamic) revival. Correspondingly, the ideology of communism is described in negative terms, and as the target of "anticommunist and Islamic slogans" in ChIASSR (Akhmadov and Khasmagomadov 946, translation by the authors). Communism is ignored (as in the main discourse); its adversary, however, is not democratic ideology or humanist values but Islamic ideology.

National Awakening Discourse

The two textbooks on the history of Tatarstan also articulate a distinctly different discourse from that of the domino principle. However, this discourse has some characteristics of the main discourse: the narrative of the perestroika process starts with the standard narrative of economic and political events, but with the addition of "meanwhile in Tatarstan" (one textbook does not even define perestroika, while the other one calls it "a program to bring the country out of crisis"; Sabirova and Sharapov 305, translation by the authors). The textbooks argue that "by the mid 1980s, the power crisis in the Union had reached a critical point" (Sabirova and Sharapov 305, translation by the authors) and that "serious economic reforms were becoming inescapable" (Sultanbekov 233, translation by the authors), but take note of "the half-heartedness of the reforms" (Sultanbekov 234, translation by the authors). Later, the treatment of perestroika "dissolves" into a description of national revival in Tatarstan that focuses on the relations between the center and the region. The collapse of the Soviet Union is mentioned in a surprisingly episodic way: Soviet disintegration "has changed the conditions of Tatarstan's struggle for sovereignty" (Sultanbekov 244, translation by the authors); "the Soviet Union went through juridical disintegration, and

Tatarstan was to stand up for its sovereignty in the face of Russia, the Soviet Union's successor" (Sabirova and Sharapov 318, translation by the authors).

The history of Tatarstan could be called a "national awakening," in which the story of the unexpected changes of perestroika in the Soviet Union becomes the story of Tatarstan's revival. Tatarstan is first a part of the Soviet Union but, through perestroika and the developments following it, the territory "wakes up" and begins its struggle for sovereignty: "the people in the Russian regions and national republics were inclined to support the opposition and demanded reforms" (Sabirova and Sharapov 305, translation by the authors). The focus of the narrative shifts from the all-Soviet to the local level. Accordingly, the two history textbooks from Tatarstan characterize Tatar separatism as a struggle for sovereignty. They point to the importance of glasnost for "the wide and sharp discussion of the problems of national–cultural development" (Sultanbekov 237, translation by the authors) with a focus on its enlightening function. Thus, the rediscovery of national history and culture is presented as the main precondition for separatism, while the "alarm clock" for the national awakening are the policies of glasnost and democratization. The histories of Tatarstan mention Tatarstan most often, followed by the Soviet Union and Russia at almost the same frequency; in this, they resemble the discourse found in the Ukrainian textbooks, but without the negative assessment of the past, and the "Romanian" approach described in the Moldovan chapter.

As for the ratio of pages devoted to perestroika (about 3 percent), it is close to the ratio for the main discourse, but the range of topics treated in these pages is more limited, only political, economic, and ethnic issues being included. With only two textbooks to analyze, we cannot generalize, though it is worth noting that the narrative structure differs from the predominant one in the domino principle discourse.

Individual actors mentioned in the national awakening discourse are from both the Soviet and local levels. The Tatarstan history textbooks give most visibility to Mintimer Shaimiev, a political leader of Tatarstan, and to Gorbachev, but pay different amounts of attention to the "political game" in the Soviet Union in general. Nevertheless, when the narrative deals with Tatarstan, Shaimiev is the unreserved leader; Gorbachev is treated as a formal figure and one of the political players in Tatarstan's struggle for sovereignty, but without being accorded historical importance. At the collective level, the most mentioned organizations are the Tatar Public Center (TPC, the political movement for Tatar Independence) and the CPSU, as well as local organizations at the Tatarstan level or that are otherwise important for Tatarstan's Independence movement. Major events take place at the Soviet and the regional levels, and events at the latter level relate to the separatist movement. Chernobyl is once again ignored.

The nationalist movement is discussed in terms of a civil, people-driven movement from below, not a struggle of elites supported by local authorities: "one part of the citizens of Tatarstan, brought up in the 'international-autocratic' spirit, initially was in a certain sense shocked by the emergence of a national organization on the political scene, uncommon in the Soviet era. ... Soon most citizens of Tatarstan (Tartars, Russians, and other nationalities) came to treat the TPC and its program with understanding" (Sabirova and Sharapov 308, translation by the authors). Nationalism does not have negative connotations. Communism is seen as a political force and an ideology, while the focus is on the democratic alternative to communism. The characterization of democratic forces differs from that of the main discourse, however. The national revival is presented as a civil, people-oriented, and democratic movement emphasizing national culture and public discussion (open not only to Tatars but to all citizens of Tatarstan) of the "reduced role of the Tatar language, poor condition of national schools, and limited opportunities for media and Tatar publishing" (Sultanbekov 237, translation by the authors). Religious revival plays a secondary role here, and the narrative of Islam is combined with that of Christianity.

The national awakening discourse offers a perspective that differs from other two discourses found in Russian textbooks. It starts from the top–down narrative of political reforms, but then shifts to the people's mobilization prompted by the revival of national (regional) culture: not only politics, but also culture matters (as in Ukraine). Moreover, the history textbooks of Tatarstan do not focus on ethnic conflict, but instead tell of the national revival. What they lack, however, is an account of the economically and socially driven activity of the people, and of the negative consequences of the separatist movement.

History Textbooks in Russia

The most obvious and surprising thing about the domino principle discourse, the main storyline in the Russian historiography, is its invariable focus on the all-Soviet level. Compared with the Chechen and Tatar textbooks (and textbooks of the other countries analyzed here), it is clear that the Russian textbooks could focus on the RSFSR or on the shift from the Soviet Union to Russia. However, the history presented is that of the Soviet Union as the Fatherland and predecessor of contemporary Russia. Russia is the successor of *one* constantly changing state, whereas in the other cases in this book, *different* states are mentioned (e.g., the Golden Horde and the Russian Empire in the case of Tatarstan, or the Grand Duchy of Lithuania, the Kingdom of Poland, and the Russian Empire for Belarus).

The current borders of the Russian regions and the principles of ethno-territorial division are a heritage of the Soviet past. Regional diversity is the key to Russian history writing about the turbulent years of perestroika and the institutional transformations at that time. A framework of Soviet and post-Soviet nation-building casts light on differences and similarities.

In the Russian textbooks, three discourses are detectable in the narrative of the period of perestroika and the changes it brought. They possess common elements, as seen in the characterization of the regionally based separatism in the domino principle and feudal Machiavellianism discourses. Descriptions of the beginnings of perestroika in the domino principle and national awakening discourses are similar in content. At the same time, all three discourses contain their own unique narrative logics and provide significantly different outlooks on how to understand and evaluate perestroika. Therefore, they constitute three separate discourses.

Feudal Machiavellianism characterizes the history of Chechnya. The narrative focuses on the elites' struggle inside the region, conditioned by the needs of the common people. Perestroika plays a role as a "trigger" that starts this process, but is surprisingly absent in the textbooks. A colonial perspective is evident here, which permeates the history writing. The main actors are groups within the local political elite.

In the histories of Tatarstan, the narrative of national awakening predominates. The narrative once again shifts from the Soviet Union as such to Tatarstan in particular, with perestroika as the "alarm clock" of Tatarstan's awakening. In this case, the main actors are not only the central and regional political elites, as in Chechnya, but also the people of Tatarstan. They initiate the national movement, with support from the local authorities. Tatar history writing is the only example among the Russian cases that applies a grassroots perspective to the developments.

How do the textbooks present Russia (i.e., the RSFSR)? The narratives point to the Soviet Union and the national republics as "real" and having their own existence. The Soviet Union is the entity that disintegrated during perestroika and its existence is beyond the level of ethnicity, a civil nation in the sense of the common life. The national republics are active entities that underwent national revival and therefore withdrew from the Soviet Union during perestroika. A quite different trajectory is characteristic of the RSFSR, however. Speculating on ethnic tensions, all the Russian textbooks start with the situation in the national republics and describe the Russian responses to them. Russia is portrayed as at the center of the developments, reacting and trying to find a coherent path, but not out of ethnic or national concerns. Russian "quasi-separatism," a characteristic strain in textbooks of the main discourse, implies radical democratic and market reforms for the Soviet Union in general and not specifically for Russia itself.

Therefore, the textbooks featuring the domino principle discourse regard Russia itself as an equal region subordinated to the center, while from the point of view of the national republics — as in Chechnya — Russia *is* the center. What is common to all these discourses is the reification of distinctions between center and periphery and between different nations. However, the characteristics of Russia as an agent in its own right remain unclear, and Russian ethnicity, as presented in the textbooks, is depicted as "reactive ethnicity." Moreover, in the case of Russia, the unclear relations between state, nation, and ethnicity characterize the educational standards, as considered above.

How can this be explained? Perhaps the authors of main discourse textbooks regard the events and processes of perestroika through the lens of the contemporary political composition of Russia. There are structural analogies between the Soviet Union, its "national republics," and the RSFSR, on one hand, and the Russian Federation, its "national regions," and the rest of Russia, on the other. These analogies help us conceive of Russian history as a continuous state history extending from the Soviet Union to the Russian Federation. It is worth mentioning that continuity with the Soviet Union is also constructed in the Belarusian textbooks, but by different means — by the "invention of transition," i.e., by concealing the break. As a result, the continuity is structural in the Russian case, while for Belarus it is substantial.

Besides, the political structure of the Russian Federation and contemporary Russian identity were formed by Soviet nation-building policies. These policies entailed the institutionalization (and sometimes invention) of ethnic nations at sub-state levels in the form of union republics and autonomous republics. However, the status of the RSFSR was ambiguous. Since it presented a threat as a possible alternative center, it was less institutionalized as a nation, and acted more as the "cement" that held the Soviet Union and its exemplary republic together. Thus, the RSFSR did not have a regional Communist Party that could be a place of elite formation. Though the RSFSR was itself characterized by the greatest regional diversity, the Russian language was the official language of the entire Soviet Union. As a result, Russians came to associate themselves, and be associated by others, with the Soviet Union in general.

The deviant discourses also construct their own identities conforming to this post-Soviet framework. Polyethnic Tatarstan seeks the greatest possible autonomy in the Russian Federation. Its textbooks emphasize a civil nationalism that presents the republic as a state-like entity uniting all citizens of Tatarstan, not only Tatars. As for the monoethnic Chechnya, its discourse does not point to any state-like entity but rather refers to quasi-feudal relations with the center and concentrates on tensions inside the region. Both Chechnya (as part of ChIASSR) and Tatarstan were autonomous republics of the RSFSR. This is why the Ukrainian and Moldovan textbooks resemble the Tatar ones: they reveal the same logic of self-identification through dissociation from the Soviet past in the form of national revival.

Representations of perestroika in the textbooks reveal different logics and strategies of nation-building in the post-Soviet space that are path dependent on Soviet nation-building and on the transformations of the 1990s. These logics imply self-identification through continuity with (for Belarus and Russia) or through dissociation from (for Chechnya, and partly for Moldova, Tatarstan, and Ukraine) the Soviet Union. Moreover, they assume certain relations to contemporary Russia, characterized by how relations played out within the Soviet Union.

Annex 1. School Textbooks in Russia

Aleksashkina, Liudmila N., Aleksandr A. Danilov, i Liudmila G. Kosulina. *Rossiia i Mir v XX – Nachale XXI Veka [Russia and the World in the 20th and to the Beginning of the 21st Centuries]*. Moskva, Prosveshchenie, 2010.

Danilov, Aleksandr A. i Liudmila G. Kosulina. *Istoriia Rossii. XX Vek [History of Russia. The 20th Century]*. Moskva, Prosveshchenie, 1995.

Danilov, Aleksandr A., Liudmila G. Kosulina, i Maksim Iu. Brandt. *Istoriia Rossii. XX – Nachalo XXI Veka [History of Russia. The 20th – Beginning of the 21st Century]*. Moskva, Prosveshchenie, 2012.

Danilov, Aleksandr A., Liudmila G. Kosulina, i Aleksandr V. Pyzhikov. *Istoriia Rossii XX – Nachalo XXI veka [History of Russia. The 20th – beginning of the 21st century]*. Moskva, Prosveshchenie, 2003.

Levandovskii, Andrei A., i Iurii A. Shchetinov. *Rossiia v XX Veke [Russia in the 20th Century]*. Moskva, Prosveshchenie, 1997.

Levandovskii, Andrei A., Iurii A. Shchetinov, and Sergei V. Mironenko. *Istoriia Rossii. XX - Nachalo XXI Veka [History of Russia. The 20th – Beginning of the 21st Century]*. Moskva, Prosveshchenie, 2011.

Zagladin, Nikita V., Sergei T. Minakov, Sergei I. Kozlenko. i Iurii A. Petrov. *Istoriia Rossii. XX - Nachalo XXI Veka [History of Russia: The 20th Century]*. Moskva, Russkoe slovo, 2007.

Zagladin, Nikita V., Sergei T. Minakov, Sergei I. Kozlenko. i Iurii A. Petrov. *Istoriia Rossii. XX - Nachalo XXI Veka [History of Russia: The 20th Century – Beginning of the 21st Century]*. Moskva, Russkoe slovo, 2007.

Annex 2. University Textbooks in Russia

Akhmadov, Iavus Z., i Edilbek H. Khasmagomadov. *Istoriia Chechni v XIX-XX Vekakh [History of Chechnya in the 19th – 20th Centuries]*. Moskva, Plius, 2005.

Barsenkov, Aleksandr S., i Aleksandr I. Vdovin. *Istoriia Rossii. 1917-2009 [History of Russia. 1917-2009]*. Moskva, Aspekt-Press, 2010.

Bobyleva, Ol'ga M. *Otechestvennaia Istoriia [History of the Fatherland]*. Irkutsk, IrGUPS, 2010.

Dmitrienko, Vladimir P., redaktor. *Istoriia Rossii. XX Vek [History of Russia. the 20th Century]*. Moskva, AST, 1998.

Kirillov, Viktor V. *Istoriia Rossii [History of Russia]*. Moskva, ID Iurait, 2011.

Kislitsin, Sergei A. *Istoriia Rossii v Voprosakh i Otvetakh [History of Russia in Questions and Answers]*. Rostov-na-Donu, Feniks. 1997.

Konukov, Talgat S., redaktor. *Istoriia Otechestva. Chast' II (Seredina XIX – Konets XX Veka) [History of the Fatherland. Part II (mid-19th – end of the 20th Century)]*. Ufa, UfGATU, 1995.

Lapteva, Elena V. *Istoriia Rossii [History of Russia]*. Moskva, Akademicheskii proekt, 2009.

Orlov, Aleksandr S., Vladimir A. Georgiev, Nataliia G. Georgieva, i Tat'iana A. Sivokhina, *Istoriia Rossii [History of Russia]*. Moskva, Prospekt, 1997.

Sabirova, Daniia K., i Iakub Sh. Sharapov. *Istoriia Tatarstana s Drevneyshikh Vremen do Nashikh Dnei [History of Tatarstan from Ancient Times until Present]*. Moskva, KnoRus, 2009.

Semin, Vladimir P. *Otechestvennaia Istoriia [History of Fatherland]*. Moskva, Akademicheskii proekt, Gaudeamus, 2008.

Sultanbekov, Bulat F., redaktor. *Istoriia Tatarstana [History of Tatarstan]*. Kazan, TaRikh, 2001.

Valiullin, Kadim B., i Rezeda K. Zaripova. *Istoriia Rossii. XX Vek [History of Russia. The 20th Century]*. Ufa, RIO BashGU, 2002.

Ianguzin, Rim Z., redaktor. *Istoriia Bashkortostana (1917-1990) [History of Bashkortostan (1917–1990)]*. Ufa, BasshGU, 1997.

Waking Up a "Sleeping Beauty": Rethinking Ukrainian Perestroika

Alla Marchenko, Yuliya Yurchuk, and Andrey Kashin

Introduction

The role of perestroika in contemporary Ukraine recalls the story of "Sleeping Beauty," in line with the current tendencies to rethink the role of the Soviet Union in state politics and history. After an enforced and prolonged "sleep" under decades of Soviet dictatorship, the Ukrainian nation awoke through the politics of perestroika to a new life as a free and independent state. Perestroika is set in a Soviet context of failed modernization, and represents a new page in the history of Ukraine with unexpected outcomes. Freedom, for both Ukraine and Ukrainians, is what perestroika brings. This is the major narrative of the history textbooks, which clearly endorse Ukrainian national identity, repressed during Soviet rule. Remarkably, in contrast to developments in World War II and the nationalist movements in Ukraine, perestroika is not a controversial topic in the analyzed textbooks. The overall narrative of how to make sense of perestroika, its causes, consequences, and unfolding, have changed little over the years since independence in 1991.

Although curricula are developed and submitted by the central governing body to all the schools and universities in Ukraine, and the textbooks in use follow centralized recommendations, the real content of education also depends on many other factors, such as teachers' interpretations and evaluations, as well as the individual students' backgrounds and previous knowledge (Richardson 109–132; Rodgers, *(Re) inventing the Past* 40–55; Rodgers, *Division, Difference and Diversity* 210–236). Hence, this study does not shed light on all the nuances of a complex entanglement of the various sociopolitical processes involved: state educational politics, the process of textbook writing and publishing, teaching strategies, and students' reception—to name just a few. However, the present analysis does examine the main approaches to perestroika as formulated in school and university history textbooks.

Teaching History in Ukraine

In Ukraine, history is taught over a period of seven years in what is considered secondary school, i.e., from grades 5 to 11, and one semester in university is devoted to the topic as an obligatory humanist discipline. The main peculiarity of history as a secondary school subject is its standardization in all schools in the country. The courses are approved by the Ministry of Education, Science, Youth, and Sport of Ukraine (MESYSU), which also recommends the textbooks (in 2011–2012 four books were recommended). This recommendation is usually reflected in the inclusion of the short-listed textbooks in the school course syllabi (see the lists of textbooks in the annexes to this chapter). In university, history is not as regulated, so the various course syllabi include a larger number and variety of textbooks.

According to the distribution of academic hours among history themes, it is evident that the perestroika period of 1985–1991 constitutes an important historical milestone for Ukraine, and the course approved by the MESYSU for secondary schools pays considerable attention to the period. For example, when analyzing the distribution of class hours, the assignment for teaching about the perestroika period gets almost as many hours as does teaching about the 20 years of Soviet stagnation in the 11th grade (1965–1984). Perestroika takes up as much space as does the Great Patriotic War (1941–1945), which formerly functioned as the primary founding myth in the creation of Soviet identity.

Eleven school textbooks used in the 11th grade in 1991–2011 are included in this analysis. The total number of university textbooks analyzed is 35, including all the textbooks on Ukrainian history for students of different specializations approved by the Ministry of Science and Education of Ukraine, published in 1991–

2011. The political history of Ukraine as well as the history of the state and law are covered in this material.

The most obvious difference between the school and the university textbooks concerns the "balanced-biased" axis. The textbooks for school students are balanced in tone and avoid sharp critiques when describing personalities or events. Characteristic of the literature intended for university students is the degree of subjectivity on the part of the author, articulated through criticism or through outright positive attitudes towards certain personalities, entities, and events. The status of Crimea as an autonomous republic within the Ukrainian state represents the boundary of this research: because of the vast range of textbooks analyzed and the limited scope of this study, we did not include the history textbooks used in Crimea, some of which were written in the Crimean Tatar language.

Perestroika and the Ukrainian Nation

Perestroika is a distinct period, dealt with in separate chapters or sections within the textbooks, having its own periodization, key actors, entities, and events. It lasted only about seven years, but the amount of material about perestroika ranges from less than one percent to almost 16 percent of the textbooks. In contrast to, for example, Belarusian textbooks, where this period remains ambiguous and transitional, perestroika in Ukraine belongs squarely to the history of the Soviet Union.

How perestroika affected national state-building in Ukraine affects the attitudes expressed in the textbooks. For example, the chapter title "Perestroika: The Beginning of a New Ukrainian Revolution" provides a basis for analogies with previous efforts to establish a Ukrainian state and for connecting the awakening through perestroika with previous nation-building processes (e.g., the creation of the Ukrainian National Republic in 1917–1918).

There are occasional expressions, although clearly representing a minority position, that express some degree of sorrow or resentment, hinting at a discourse in which longing for paternalism still plays a role, some sources even referring to "the wreckage of perestroika" (*krakh* in Ukrainian) (Boiko, *Istoriia Ukrainy* (2nd ed.) 565; Kudriachenko 397). However, perestroika was an inevitable process triggered by the very nature of the Soviet system, so much so that even the description of the main actor associated with perestroika, Mikhail Gorbachev, is superficial and formal. This clearly differs from the kind of Machiavellianism described in some of the Russian textbooks, which depict history as the elites' playing field against the background of a silent population.

Historians prefer to narrate meanings in the form of stories that have a clear beginning, middle, and end (White 5-27). Here, we "borrow" the narrative structure of Charles Perrault's version of "Sleeping Beauty" and apply it to Ukrainian history, to more vividly illuminate the storyline written into the textbooks. Doing so allows us to understand how each element of the narrative, scattered throughout the texts, still subjugates the narrative logic to the same storyline—and may be read within individual textbooks as well (Propp).

"Sleeping Beauty" is set in a kingdom of fabulous richness and beauty. In a similar vein, the authors of the textbooks in question present Ukraine's history in terms of "once upon a time," before Ukraine was "occupied." In the story of Sleeping Beauty, an evil magician plays a crucial—and destructive—role. Allegedly dead and not invited to the baptismal party of the fair princess, he reappears. This parallels the Tsarist Russian Empire, which seemed to be extinguished, but was then resurrected in the form of the Soviet Union. The wicked magician curses the princess with a deep sleep that continues for many years. Similarly, the dependent status of Ukraine during the seven decades of the Soviet Union could metaphorically be looked upon as a deep sleep that blinded its inhabitants to their own potential.

Presented in the textbooks as a profoundly endogenous process, a deep systemic crisis is said to have provoked perestroika. The popular line of presenting the causes of perestroika does not really refer to any external context, and does not consider perestroika's place within developments in other parts of Eastern and Central Europe. The only direct reference to the role of the transformations in Central Europe is in one of the university textbooks, which states that these popular protests made a "considerable impact upon Ukraine's sovereignty" (Svitlychna 296, translation by the authors).

Whereas some authors (e.g., Kulchytskyi and Tyshchyk) mention that the driving force behind perestroika was rooted in a systemic crisis suffered by the entire socialist world, the predominant context is still internally Soviet. Generally, most references to external conditions and forces concern the former USSR, where the developments in the three Baltic republics and in Russia are the most frequently mentioned. The European countries and the United States are treated as neutral, or even pro-Soviet. There are mentions of visits by George Bush and Margaret Thatcher, world leaders who declared their displeasure at the collapse of the Soviet Union in 1991 (Kulchytskyi and Lebedieva; Kulchytskyi and Shapoval). The emerging picture of the context in which the last period of the USSR played out is that of a vacuum. Whether this tendency to downplay the international context is typical only of the presentation of this period, or whether it is a recurring feature of Ukrainian historiography, remains beyond the scope of this chapter.

Problems in the economic sphere, internal policies, and international relations are all considered to have influenced and been influenced by the "systemic crisis." Some of the textbooks define and refer to the system as "feudal socialism" or the "dead end of history" (Turchenko 227, translation by the authors). The economic situation and the shortcomings of the system in this respect are the most significant causes in the narrative of the severe long-term crisis. However, no particular person is to blame, and the authors avoid problematic questions of the Ukrainian people's own involvement in building and indeed reinforcing the Soviet system. The role of the people instead increases in the presentation of the final stages of perestroika, when the destruction of the system is associated with a grassroots movement with positive effects.

The textbooks reflect the fact that all perestroika processes and reforms were implemented in Ukraine with a certain time lag.

Initiated in Russia, the "major" republic of the Soviet Union, they were later "transposed" to Ukraine. Some textbooks also emphasize the reluctance of the leaders of the Ukrainian SSR to change immediately, as they were waiting for "prior stability" before acting (Pometun and Hupan 196, 198, translation by the authors). One example is the process of freeing victims of political repression, which started in 1986 in the Soviet Union as such; in Ukraine, people convicted of anti-Soviet activities gained their freedom much later (Turchenko 247–248). This situation was typical until Volodymyr Shcherbitskiy, the First Secretary of the Central Committee of the Communist Party of Ukraine (from 1972 to September 1989), resigned.

Featured in a subordinate role, the textbooks highlight the Ukrainian political elite's extreme dependence on the central authority as well as their "provincialism." The leaders of the Ukrainian republic were afraid to undertake any independent decisions and actions. Internal developments in Ukraine were limited to listing Communist Party plenums and congresses, and the textbook authors assess these as mostly declarative. The obsolete nature of the Soviet system shows in the negatively phrased presentations and pejorative connotations, as many of the described decisions/actions were ineffective. The Chernobyl accident and the non-drinking campaign are evaluated in extremely negative terms, the latter connected with the rise of underground brewing and the development of the covert sale of alcohol, which had negative effects on the economy.

Presented to the students as a social catalyst, the Chernobyl catastrophe of 1986 finally made the Ukrainian political leaders act more autonomously towards Moscow. Chernobyl illustrates not only the dark side of the Soviet past, but also the "old" Ukraine's inability to act without guidelines from the "central" leaders in Moscow (who covered up the tragedy's real scope): "Chernobyl became a symbol of Ukraine's national humiliation. It turned out that the decision to cover up the consequences of the catastrophe was made in Moscow" (Turchenko 245, translation by the authors).

Chernobyl was a catastrophe arising from mismanagement, though it is positively interpreted for its role in Ukraine's liberation. The catastrophe takes on the character of an "alarm clock", awakening the Ukrainians from their passivity, and bringing them into consciousness while provoking reactions: "Ukraine could be awakened only by an explosion" (Zaitsev 423, translation by the authors).

Used as a metaphor for the total Russification of Ukrainian culture, this "mental Chernobyl" underlines its catastrophic effects. Highlighting the subordinated status of Ukrainian culture and language, the concept of nation fits the "ethnic" dimension: "At the end of the 1980s ... the situation was such that the number of Ukrainian schools [i.e., taught in Ukrainian] in the Canadian city of Edmonton was larger than in Donetsk, Dnipropetrovsk, and Kharkiv together" (Lytvyn 632, translation by the authors).

The metaphor of a "mental Chernobyl" emphasizes the need for Ukrainian Independence to guarantee that another such disaster (understood as "anti-Ukrainian") would not happen again. In such a way, the thematic motifs of independence and dependence are intertwined with the issue of existential security. Understood as a colonial object, the center denied the Ukrainian nation its own agency, and only through independence could the Ukrainians become agents of history. In this regard, narratives of independence and colonialism work together in the same nationalization discourse that stresses the need for the revival, indeed the awakening, of the nation. Chernobyl (and related events) is transformed into a symbol, a tragedy comparable in its effect on the national consciousness to the exposure of the Molotov-Ribbentrop treaty in the Baltic countries. Compared with Belarus, where Chernobyl represents the culmination point of perestroika, in Ukraine it is instead a trigger for the national transformations to come.

Interestingly, the most positively evaluated event of this period is the shift towards the policies of glasnost, not associated with any official political line, but in answer to the needs of the people and the general situation in society. In this, Ukraine stands out among the studied countries in this book: the importance given to growing opportunities for popular mobilization and organization reveals Ukraine's more pluralist outlook. The concept of "glasnost" is described in the textbooks as a policy opposed to Soviet ideology (Deshchynskyi, Tersky, Khoma, Taraban 313, translation by the authors), demonstrating the difference between "us" and "them." The role of glasnost in exposing the previously taboo and dark eras of the Soviet regime—not least the Holodomor of 1932-1933 and the brutal political repressions of the 1950s—is taken as a sign that glasnost was neither communist nor Soviet. Through glasnost, the most vicious times and actions of the Soviet regime in Ukraine were made public. Former political prisoners such as Levko Lukianenko, Viacheslav Chornovil, and Stepan Khmara managed to become active actors in the struggle for the Ukrainian language and independence during perestroika, pointedly illustrating the contrasts of the initial and late Soviet periods.

The authors of the textbooks emphasize that the Soviet ideology was totalitarian, and hostile to Ukraine. Contrasting the nation of Ukraine to the USSR clearly demonstrates this hostility. The authors of the textbooks employ metonymies, "the USSR center," "system," and "Moscow," for example, to strengthen their narrative position. They juxtapose phenomena of Soviet and national realities with the aim of building the image of the antagonistic "other." Unlike in, for example, Belarusian textbooks, Ukrainian textbooks consistently deny the Soviet ideology within the frame of the dominant nationalization discourse.

Returning to the Sleeping Beauty storyline, it is reasonable to emphasize that the narrative in the textbooks is that all events happened naturally: the "prince" came exactly on time, embodying the forces of perestroika. The process is one of moving from an initial "top-down" stage to a stage taken over by the people, described as a grassroots movement from the "bottom up." The implementation of perestroika "from above" that started in 1985 included the efforts of the communist leaders to initiate political and economic reforms with the aim of maintaining the old system. The "bottom-up" stage, reached in 1988-1989, involved the mobilization of the entire nation, and some historians qualify this stage as one of "revolution," no longer "perestroika." It was no longer a reactive response of holding on to the old order, but a proactive force for profound change. The textbooks say more or less the same thing in this regard, and the storyline is coherent.

Perestroika became a collective image balancing different sets of reformers with various intentions (from the USSR's stylization to Ukraine's Independence), including those who changed their political position right away in line with Ukraine's change of political status. This contextualization of the perestroika period in Ukraine is completely different from how it is presented in Russian textbooks, in which it coincides with the history of the USSR (not the Russian Republic specifically). Chapter titles (e.g., "A new page of Ukraine's history") show that perestroika forms a bridge between the dismal Soviet past and the Ukrainian future, with a "before" and an "after" context. Previous Soviet legacies conditioned perestroika processes and events, for example, the gerontocracy and Russification during the "stagnation" (*zastoy*) period, and through the planned and unproductive economy.

Key Personalities

A predominant tendency in the Ukrainian history textbooks is to depersonalize events, processes, and organizations, much as in the Belarusian ones. Individual choices or decisions are often ignored in terms of, for example, how they affected specific outcomes. Such depersonalization is especially evident in how nation-building is presented.

However, when focusing on the general USSR level, this tendency is somewhat disrupted, since marked attention is paid to the most central personality of all, Mikhail Gorbachev. It is fairly typical, for example, to call the entire period "Gorbachev's perestroika": Gorbachev is mentioned eight times per book on average, while all other politicians are paid considerably less attention. Mikhail Gorbachev is the most important actor of the period, who coined the term "perestroika" in public discourse (even some of the sections'/subsections' titles are taken from Gorbachev's book *Perestroika: New Thinking for Our Country and the*

World. Only a few books give hints as to other forces behind Gorbachev: leaders of the Communist Party or external influences in the form of conspiracy theories. "Gorbachev fell under the influence of Western countries, which were not interested in the reformation of the USSR" (Lytvyn, Kolesnyk, Sliusarenko 347, translation by the authors).

Juxtaposing Gorbachev to the Communist Party establishment of the previous period helps emphasize that the party leadership was a gerontocracy — even called the "oligarchy of 'Kremlin elders'" (Kulchytskyi and Lebedieva 213, translation by the authors). Gorbachev's relative youth and good international reputation makes him appear a congenial symbol of both perestroika and of the overall renewal of Soviet society. This is a tendency maintained in the textbooks from the early 1990s until the present. The positive aspects of Gorbachev are supplemented by his renewal of de-Stalinization and his support for freedom of speech through the policies of glasnost: "He was distinguished from the other party leaders by his emphasis on democracy and energy, and his desire and readiness for radical changes in society" (Husiev, Kazmyrchuk, Kapeliushnyi, Cherevychnyi: 398, translation by the authors).

However, Mikhail Gorbachev does not appear to be the most positively evaluated personality: Boris Ieltsin, Eduard Shevardnadze, and many of the local Ukrainian leaders in fact are evaluated as better overall. The negative aspects of Gorbachev's personality depend on his inconsistency. He lost control of the situation during the second stage of perestroika (recalling his positioning in the domino principle discourse widespread in Russian textbooks), which caused Gorbachev's own personal tragedy.

In Ukraine, even though depersonalization is predominant, an exception is made for Volodymyr Shcherbytskyi, the person who held the leading political position in Soviet Ukraine during its last years and the third most important personality by the quantity of references in the textbooks. Presented as a man who resisted the ideas of perestroika, many of the problems of the first perestroika stages arose from his mismanagement. "Unlike

Moscow, where the dynamics of the political processes in this period took place with great intensity, stagnation prevailed in Ukraine. First of all, the stagnation is associated with the first secretary of the Communist Party of the Republic, Shcherbytsky, who was seen as one of the 'pillars of stagnation' in mass consciousness" (Turchenko, Panchenko, Tymchenko 245, translation by the authors).

Shcherbytskyi and his entourage are typically described in terms of "bureaucracy, protectionism, reluctance to take responsibility in solving the new, complicated tasks of society's transformation" (Voronianskyi 480, translation by the authors). Shcherbytskyi's team tried to do everything to prevent political change in Ukraine and continued to display devotion to communist ideology, as manifested in the words and actions of the Communist Party of the USSR (CPSU) and the Communist Party of Ukraine (CPU). In this narrative, the party is "the Other" and "the root of all evil." These negative attitudes are even more noticeable considering how often the CPSU and CPU are mentioned in historical writing. Descriptions refer to communist forces at the beginning of the 1990s as reactionary and unable to change anything, an attitude that later shifts towards the perception of the overall "evil" nature of communism.

Consequences of Perestroika

The narrative of perestroika in the early 1990s is set in the context of failed modernization. At the same time, it is a new page in the history of Ukraine with unexpected outcomes. Thus, the main message concluding the perestroika chapter was that perestroika itself was a matter of "entering the future with hopes for the better," with its main value said to be freedom. An aphorism recurs in the textbooks: "If you do not know what to give a human, give him freedom" (Ostrovskyi 74, translation by the authors). This narrative of uncertainty soon gave way to a rather homogenous picture of the consequences of perestroika.

In the later textbooks, there are usually no explicit evaluations of the USSR's collapse, which implicitly reinforces the idea of its self-evidently positive impact on Ukraine. The inseparable connection between the USSR's collapse and the emergence of Ukrainian Independence is alluded to both in section titles and in singling out independence as the major outcome of perestroika. The collapse of the USSR is described as an unavoidable result of the ideological and economic failures of Soviet rule. As discussed above, this is a typical strategy of describing everything connected with the perestroika period in Ukraine as internal to the USSR as such. The explicit connections made between the collapse of the USSR and the subsequent independence of Ukraine contribute to depreciating the role of national actors in the process, making independence something "given" rather than "gained."

A crucial point in the Ukrainian historiography of perestroika is the absence of any criticism of the process of independence. Assessing independence as an event of great importance (the authors ask students to evaluate "the historical significance of the Declaration of Independence of Ukraine" in almost all blocks of questions for self-checking), it is seen as the logical result of the progress of Ukrainian history up to this point in time. "The everlasting striving of the Ukrainian nation for freedom and an independent state has been realized" (Deshchynskyi, Terskyi, Khoma, Taraban 315, translation by the authors).

To make a parallel to the presentation of the causes of perestroika, the consequences of perestroika are similarly treated as internal. Such long-term results as intensive de-Stalinization and glasnost, international disarmament, and the ending of the Cold War do not receive any significant attention. For example, the Nobel Peace Prize Committee recognized Gorbachev for his contributions to world peace but, according to the textbooks, he should be appreciated only for the indirect role he played in Ukraine's Independence.

The analysis of the consequences of perestroika fits the nationalization discourse that highlights the civic, rather than the ethnic, dimension. The top bureaucrats in Soviet Ukraine, although they could well be of Ukrainian origin, were opposed to the ordinary people of Ukraine and did not work for their interests. In contrast, Ukraine's Independence favors *all* the inhabitants of the territory, regardless of ethnic origin, and is a major, indisputable achievement of the period. The nation in its civic meaning, therefore, has the highest value of the period, and national independence is attributed the indisputable status of "normality." Glasnost and democratization are valuable byproducts of perestroika: "One of the main achievements of the first stage of the democratization of society has been glasnost and its further transformation into freedom of speech" (Slyvka 391, translation by the authors).

What about the representation of key spheres during perestroika in Ukraine? Experimental elections in 1987 were unprecedented in the history of the USSR and led to further political pluralism and to the emergence of civic organizations that would be transformed into political parties. Similar transformations took place in the economic sphere as well. Starting in 1987, managers of industrial enterprises were elected, not installed (Turchenko 226).

Emphasizing the Verkhovna Rada's (the Ukrainian Parliament) historical role in the elections and in the local councils of Ukraine in March 1990 also highlights the obsolete nature of the still existing Soviet system. The outcome made way for new political forces in the then republican parliament and in some of the local councils, while putting representatives of the Communist Party in untypical opposition positions at the local political level.

The most common thematic motif in political life is that of transition and crisis, which is alluded to in most titles and subtitles of sections dealing with political developments. "Attempts to Reform the Totalitarian System" (Slyvka 380, translation by the authors) and "Attempts to Find the Way Out of a System Crisis" (Turchenko 223, translation by the authors) exemplify this motif. The second thematic motif related to political developments is that of Ukraine obtaining independence, for example, the "Acquisition of Sovereignty by Ukraine" (Zaruba 359, translation by the authors). Initially, political life in Ukraine lacked vigor, but its radical elements developed at a later stage of perestroika, as political expressions grew diverse and flexible through the processes of democratization and openness inherent in the glasnost reforms. The result was the complete destruction of the Soviet political system, replaced by a number of diverse national systems.

Perestroika in Regional Perspective

Ukraine's regional diversity is another feature of the Ukrainian context acknowledged by the textbooks. Reactions to the social and political changes launched by perestroika varied considerably in form and scope depending on the region. Here, special attention is paid to the depiction of the regional composition of Ukraine to shed light on how the textbook authors metaphorically tackle the classic question posed by Ernest Renan in 1882: "*Qu'est-ce qu'une nation?*" (What is a nation?) (1992). The authors all work within one schema that dictates how the narratives of perestroika are framed, a schema that subjects all the events to the idea of national liberation, and of (re)gaining statehood and independence. This schema is a "nationalization discourse" representing an ethnic and a civic understanding of the nation. An inclusive civic understanding of the nation prevails over an ethnic one. Emphasizing the unity of the country's citizens, regardless of their ethnic origin, the citizenship legislation drafted at independence is an important expression of intent. All citizens' common striving for independence is underlined. For both East and West Ukraine, however, national independence emerged from the turbulent period of the late 1980s, despite the variations in their regional histories.

Nevertheless, in presenting perestroika, the unity of the Ukrainian regions is underlined. All the authors state that the citizens of Ukraine almost unanimously approved the Declaration of independence during the referendum in December 1991. Pictured as one of the most inspiring moments in Ukrainian history, the "day of national honor for Ukrainian citizens" (Turchenko 267, translation by the authors) is a significant point in the nationalization discourse and in creating the civic meaning of the nation.

At the same time, when dealing with the formative moment that disrupted the flow of Soviet history, the textbook authors nevertheless tend to depict Western Ukraine as the main driver of the transformation, whereas mostly economic considerations drove civic engagement in highly industrialized Eastern Ukraine. Galicia, with its unchallenged capital Lviv, is not only a territory, but also a celebrated part of Eastern or Central Europe, and has symbolic value for those who, over the centuries, have claimed it as theirs: Austrians, Poles, and Ukrainians. Whereas Galicia, on one hand, is a territory distinguished by Western virtues such as engagement, a tradition of popular government, and active civil society, on the other hand, it has a history of backwardness and corruption under Habsburg rule (Amar 320). After Ukrainian Independence, the construction or invention of Galicia has continued in Western Ukraine, and allusions to Galicia's ancient connection to European civilization are one expression of this "nostalgia" (Stefanowska 181–193).

Lviv, the capital of Galicia, is the "cradle" of national rebirth, so that the most rigorous actions against the Soviet regime and by the Soviet regime against the people took place in this Western Ukrainian city with its Austro-Hungarian and Polish legacies (e.g., demonstrations, dispersals, and repression). In contrast to that of Ukraine at large, Lviv's post-war development has been towards becoming more Ukrainian. Roman Szporluk emphasizes that Lviv was actually *less* Russified when the Soviet Union collapsed than was Latvia's Riga or Estonia's Tallinn. In comparison with Chisenau, Moldova's capital, the same applies, Moldova being one of the Soviet republics incorporated in the 1940s where Russification attempts were made and, to a certain degree, succeeded (Szporluk 304).

Hence, one of Lviv's characteristics was its non-Russification (Amar 12). Lviv's "soul" has been one of culture and creation, and the attempts to impose heavy industrialization under Soviet rule after 1944 clashed with the city's self-image and even its non-industrial ethos (Åberg 285–301).

Along with the pronounced civic element within the nationalization discourse, there exists a strong "ethnic" dimension in the realms of language and religion. The concept of Russification (in terms of extra support for the use of the Russian language in various spheres of public life) is one of the most exploited themes in the descriptions of actual inequality among the Soviet republics. The religious situation during perestroika is described as a "revival," emphasizing that the national churches, i.e., the Ukrainian Greek Catholic Church and the Ukrainian Autocephalous Church, finally obtained the chance to function openly again in society. These facts demonstrate that, in Ukraine, perestroika is seen through the lens of a nationalization discourse in which the nation is perceived in both civic and ethnic terms.

The exceptions to this unifying picture are found in a few of the textbooks that instead emphasize the differences between the "radically national West and the pro-Russian East" (Voronianskyi 477, 479, translation by the authors). One example is a textbook published after the Orange Revolution in 2004, an event that represented the culmination of the discourse that elaborates on the opposition between the East and the West. Throughout the Orange Revolution and the preceding presidential campaign, the main electoral supporters of the then presidential candidates Viktor Ianukovych and Viktor Iushchenko presented themselves as opposed across an East–West divide. Such a divisive approach to presenting the political landscape of Ukrainian society was fostered by the mass media and political discourse after the Orange Revolution.

However, certain past events are not aligned with the discourse that stresses the uniformity of the regions. Instead, these moments of history reveal the difficulties experienced by Ukraine during its final years in the USSR. For example, a discussion of the possible transformation of Ukraine into a federal state is lacking in most textbooks. Although this idea did not receive support from most politicians, even the existence of debate on the issue tends to be downplayed in the textbooks, we assume in order to stress Ukraine's unity. Debate about the federal status of Ukraine in fact touched on several regions, i.e., the Eastern–Southern Region

(Donbas, as well as the undefined "South") and the Western Region (Zakarpathia), which were labeled as "separatist" (Lanovyk and Lazarovych 497; Lazarovych 551; Slyvka 402; Verstiuk, Haran, Gurzhii 365-366, translation by the authors).

"Nevertheless, there were fears of the misuse of this idea by the opponents of an independent Ukraine; Kravchuk and Lukianenko were against Chornovil's idea [i.e., of federalization]" (Verstiuk, Haran, Gurzhii 366, translation by the authors). However, "federalization" in Chornovil's conception is closer to the concept of decentralization and of giving more power to the regions than to federalization, in the sense of totally changing the political and economic structure of the state. Later on, Chornovil himself rejected his earlier ideas about federalization and advocated decentralization (as mentioned in several books, e.g., Androshchuk).

Similar apparently deliberate omissions occur regarding certain external forces violating Ukraine's integrity. While the textbooks cover the Moldova-Ukraine and the Hungary-Ukraine territorial disputes (Bilotserkivskyi; Temko and Tupchiienko; Verstiuk, Haran, Gurzhii), no information is given about the Ukraine-Russian boundaries, which suggests that they are regarded as indisputable. Crimea is paid no special attention, although the perestroika period was a turning point in the life of different nationalities within the USSR. In Ukraine in particular, perestroika made possible the repatriation of the Crimean Tatars from their forced exile since the 1940s in Uzbekistan. Although the consequences of repatriation were obvious long after perestroika, the lack of attention to the issue indicates a wish to downplay divisions.

One of the most telling quotations in this regard is that "party functionaries of Crimea were in a hurry to conduct a referendum before the Crimean Tatars returned and before the law on referendums was adopted" (Verstiuk, Haran, Gurzhii 365-366, translation by the authors). This means that the Crimean Tatars were treated as political forces without central backing in the new independent Ukraine, even in terms of the Crimean referendum on the future of the USSR (as implied in the quotation).

Perestroika and the Ukrainian Economy

The most vivid thematic motifs of the economic sphere are transition and crisis, for example, described in terms of "Ukraine's Worsening Economic Situation" (Turchenko, Panchenko, Tymchenko 267, translation by the authors). Stressing the "colonial" status of Ukraine's economy in Soviet times and during perestroika serves to shift the blame and responsibility for what happened in post-Soviet Ukraine to its previous status as part of the USSR. The economic hardships that Ukraine suffered are analyzed so as to present the major culprit as the lack of experience of living without Moscow's paternalism: Ukraine was a key part of the USSR, but a key part kept in chains.

Gorbachev's statements that he "cannot imagine the USSR without Ukraine" (Turchenko, Panchenko, Tymchenko 267, translation by the authors) referred to Ukraine as a producer of intermediate products and semi-finished goods, intended to keep Ukraine dependent on production in other republics of the USSR. The situation was complicated by the fact that about 80 percent of the total industrial production in the republic had no complete technological cycle. This was the result of a policy of the center to create a "single economic complex," which suppressed the desire of the republic to exit the USSR (Turchenko, Panchenko, Tymchenko 227, translation by the authors).

An incident mentioned in a positive light in most of the textbooks is the coalminers' strike in the Donbas region in Eastern Ukraine. Most of the historians analyze it solely within an economic framework, but some politicize the activities and consequences of the miners' movement: "Mass actions by the miners shook the foundations of the totalitarian system. For the first time during the Soviet period, workers who were considered to be the leading force of society openly showed that their interests differed from the interests of the Communist Party, the totalitarian state" (Turchenko 237, translation by the authors).

Contrasting ordinary people to the top bureaucracy casts the protests as a form of reaction to the inability to "repair" the system. The Communist Party was deaf to "the voice of the people" and continued to amass economic privileges for itself, which is yet another example of the differentiation between a united "nation" and a segregated "top." Ordinary Ukrainian people opposed the communist functionaries, who are not included in the category of "us" in the nationalization discourse. Through such positioning, the "communist element" becomes profoundly alien to the national one, while the national is associated with anti-communist sentiments: "In these conditions, the party leadership cared primarily about themselves. On 1 October 1989, the Central Committee decided to increase the salaries of party functionaries by 50–100 percent. At the same time, they kept all the benefits that they had, sometimes for a nominal fee" (Turchenko 238, translation by the authors).

Consequently, all the negative features of the independent economy are traced back to the Soviet era. While the Russian, Belarusian, and Moldovan textbooks also point to the economic hardships of the period, the most dramatic juxtaposing of the Soviet and post-Soviet eras occurs in Ukrainian textbooks. The narrative of the economic and political processes is black and white, stressing the background of deep crisis and collapse created by the Soviet system. In contrast, the civic and cultural spheres are places where positive changes took place.

Perestroika as Cultural Awakening

The textbooks focus, as noted above, on developments within the political and economic spheres during the perestroika period, areas dominated by the top-level functionaries of the state. Civic and cultural activities were instead inspired "from below," in reaction to a wide range of problems. The textbooks interpret perestroika as having been transformed into a movement "from below" that came to be "owned" by the people themselves. Most of the events and entities of this second period are connected to Ukraine proper, evaluated positively, in contrast to the previous, "top-down" stage. The discourse of nationalization structures these representations, which allows the Ukrainian people to be distanced from the Soviet system as such, while glorifying the Ukrainian input to the dissolution of this system. The discourse of "national awakening" in Tatarstan, mentioned in the chapter on perestroika in Russian textbooks, bears similarities to the Ukrainian situation.

Most events during perestroika are not explicitly evaluated by the individual authors. The authors clearly state their attitudes only towards the events that have obvious and indisputable meaning for the majority of Ukrainians: the Chernobyl accident, the turn to glasnost, and the uncovering of previous "blank spots" (mostly connected with repressions and political persecutions) in Ukrainian history. The same goes for personalities and entities.

Descriptions of the rebirth of a civic sphere covering the issues of national activism and the emergence and functioning of various organizations "from below" appear in almost every analyzed textbook, including those that do not distinguish perestroika as a separate period. Formulations such as the "growth of sociopolitical activity," the "emergence of a national liberation movement," and the "radical activation of sociopolitical movements in Ukraine" are used. Civic activism definitely plays a part in the history of Ukrainian perestroika and its outcomes. The cultural sphere, however, is not prominent in most school and university textbooks, with the interesting exceptions of those used in Western Ukraine. Activities of general, worldwide importance, such as the publication of the *UNESCO Courier* in Ukrainian starting in the spring of 1990, are mentioned only in Western Ukrainian textbooks (Zaitsev). Otherwise, information about culture is found in the sections about politics and civic activities, and explicitly emphasizes national issues. By linking the civic sphere to cultural issues, it is possible to regard section titles as vividly illustrating the democratic turn in civic activity and culture, as well as the concept of national revival. The national revival relates to the activities of Ukrainian writers (within the Union of Writers of Ukraine), which is not surprising given that the "activists of the sixties" (*shestidesiatniki*) are the "forerunners of perestroika" in post-Soviet public discourse.

Regarding the later stages of perestroika, references are made to anti-regime activities in every region. Nevertheless, the initiator and the main force behind the liberation are still Lviv and Western Ukraine. During Euromaidan in 2013 and 2014, the Revolution of Dignity, Lviv continued to provide great support to the nationalist ideals of the protest, and as of the beginning of December 2013, 55 percent of Euromaidan protesters were from Western Ukraine ("Maidan-2013).

The advocates of perestroika in Ukraine were notable for their strong nationalist orientation and for their struggle for the supremacy of the Ukrainian language. Since writers were driving the process, cultural revival was self-evident, and the value of the Ukrainian language and history were reaffirmed; writers such as Ivan Dziuba, Ivan Drach, Lina Kostenko, and Dmytro Pavlychko were important figures in this process.

The textbooks mention organizational circles of the "intelligentsia," such as the Ukrainian Cultural Club, the Ukrainian Language Society (named after Taras Shevchenko), the Ukrainian Helsinki Union, and Zeleniy Svit (Green World). At a certain stage, the civic movement turned into a political one, organized as the Narodniy Rukh Ukrainy (People's Movement of Ukraine), initially with "for perestroika" appended, and led by the writer Ivan Drach. The assessment of the Rukh is positive, and it and the Communist Party of the Soviet Union are the most frequently mentioned entities, though seen in very different lights.

Among the personalities associated with the cultural revival, the writers Ivan Drach, Levko Lukianenko, and Viacheslav Chornovil receive attention. Chornovil became the leader of the Narodniy Rukh Ukrainy. A political dissident who spent many years in prison, Lukyanenko is the most frequently mentioned of the nationalist leaders, usually evaluated positively and referred to as having many years of "experience" in prison. Other national leaders of that period have lower profiles.

Other forces also led the cultural revival. The Revolution on the Granite in October 1990 has become a symbol *sui generis*, converted into a metaphor of the struggle of the progressive youth of Ukraine against the totalitarian state: "Their demands reflected the moods of millions of people" (Turchenko, Panchenko, Tymchenko 250, translation by the authors).

The topic of cultural revival is closely connected to the "ethnic" dimension of the nation, which underlines the exclusive role of a single language and ethnic roots in the formation of national identity. This exclusiveness is not explicit, though it is evident from the relative amount of material about the Ukrainian language, history, and culture. Nevertheless, declarations that Ukraine is a multinational state are also found, even in one of the first textbooks produced in independent Ukraine: "There is more room to breathe in the Ukrainian house, a house for people of more than a hundred nationalities" (Koval, Kulchytskyi, Kurnosov, Sarbei 353, translation by the authors). Such an understanding of the nation constructs it as a "distinctive moral community" with specific cultural resources that can be described as cultural nationalism (Hutchinson and Guibernau 40).

One aspect of the cultural revival in Ukraine emphasized in the textbooks concerns religion. Religious revival is associated mainly with the activities of the national churches, the most pronounced example being the Ukrainian Greek Catholic Church of Galicia and Western Ukraine, a church that suffered severely during Soviet times. The thousandth anniversary of the *Rus* baptism that was celebrated in Kyiv is taken as a point of departure for the religious revival, interpreted as an event threatening the center of the USSR and simultaneously uniting people around something different from communist ideology: it is a moment of "spiritual emancipation" (Pometun and Hupan 220, translation by the authors).

In contrast, the Russian Orthodox Church is closely connected to the Soviet authorities and the KGB, functioning under all political conditions and therefore not particularly associated with the achievements of perestroika. In Russian historiography, the Russian Orthodox Church appears along with the growing religious freedom provided by perestroika. Some authors even consider this church to be an active factor in the

Russification of Ukraine (Husiev, Kazmyrchuk, Kapeliushnyi, Cherevychnyi 407; Lytvyn 670); therefore, they distinguish between the "external" Russian and the "internal" national churches.

The religious situation in Ukraine during perestroika is presented as a "revival," a "coming back" in which perestroika acted as the turning point. This supports our initial idea of contrasting the national to the Soviet in the nationalization discourse. Some textbooks, however, point to quantitative data disproving the myth of revival and actually emphasize that Russification still existed during the perestroika period, though this perception is not in line with mainstream thinking. In some instances, we have even found allusions to religious processes during perestroika as spreading the seeds of discord in the religious sphere that still persist in contemporary Ukraine (Ostrovskyi, Startsev, Starkov, Smirnov).

The most significant activity in the cultural sphere was the "human chain" from Kyiv to Lviv, honoring the unification of the Western and Eastern parts of Ukraine. The celebration of 500 years of Ukrainian Cossackdom is another important milestone and, like the human chain, had the aim of integrating the people of Ukraine. These events were prerequisites for building Ukraine's unity with respect to its previous contradictory history in the civic dimension of the nationalization discourse.

Most authors focus their attention on the internal forces promoting national self-consciousness, and only a few texts contain information on external influences. The role of the Ukrainian diaspora, the dissemination of foreign literature, and the broadcasts of Radio Freedom and Voice of America are examples of such influences (Turchenko 246).

Ukraine: Awakening to Disappointment — and National Identity

After 23 years of Ukrainian Independence, perestroika is coming alive again. The social protests of Euromaidan in 2013 and 2014, leading to the dismissal of President Viktor Ianukovych, increased civic engagement and national ideals in all of Ukraine's regions. Many of the issues covered in the Ukrainian history textbooks are not yet settled. They continue to shape the Ukrainian state and nation, its relations with Russia, and its place in the world.

The issue of Ukraine's "federalization" has been revived. Polls conducted in the spring of 2014 ("Electoral Orientations of Ukrainians") in connection with the Revolution of Dignity showed that the population of Ukraine generally supported a unified Ukrainian state. Nevertheless, violent events and recurrent media speculation about "federalization" have once more actualized the tensions between the center and the regions. The future of the Crimean Tatars came into focus in 2014, when they opposed the annexation of Crimea by the Russian Federation. According to official Ukrainian rhetoric, the Tatars are victims of Russian imperial politics, which is in line with another theme prevalent in the textbooks: the victimization of Ukraine and its people.

The topic of Russification is touched on in the stated declarative nature of the laws concerning language politics, framed as "loyalty to the center" (Turchenko 244, translation by the authors). The status of the Ukrainian and Russian languages became one of the main symptoms of the strained relationship between the old and new elites. Language issues were particularly obvious in the 2010s, when a law on regional languages was adopted ("regional language" usually meant Russian) and was used as a tool for dividing the nation during the "information war" of 2013–2014. Questions of a "common history" between Russia and Ukraine were raised in public discourse in the 2010s, including by some professional historians who discussed the idea of a single textbook covering the histories of both countries. The dichotomy of continuity–discontinuity was actualized again as a consequence of the media agenda and issues connected with Ukraine's integrity: the annexation of Crimea by Russia, anti-terrorism operations in Eastern Ukraine in 2014, and the ongoing war in Eastern Ukraine.

Despite the considerable transformation of the political landscape of Ukraine since the 1990s, the evaluations, interpretations, and depictions of perestroika in the political, economic, civic, and cultural spheres have not changed significantly. In the early 1990s, history textbooks overflowed with details showing the necessity of perestroika in the context of the socialist world, whereas the consequences of perestroika were still largely unknown and described simply as "hope for the better." This may well indicate that by the mid 1990s, both the national democratic and (post-)communist elites had already agreed on the main meaning of perestroika — i.e., independence.

The nationalization discourse has prevailed throughout the changes of political regime. The idea of cultural revival became incorporated into the "ethnic" dimension in certain fields, such as religion, language, and literature, but a "civic" conceptualization of Ukrainian statehood prevails to a significant extent. The explanation is that Ukraine, in its present territory, has diverse historical legacies, and parts of Ukraine actually had different pre-Soviet pasts and have different historical memories that still tangibly shape the process of nation-building as a whole. The ethnic dimension occurs in relation to a certain "revival" involving ethnic-related issues of "cultural nationalism," in Hutchinson's words. We assume that such a combination is a tool for the construction of a "soft" ethnic Ukrainian identity, which could prevent the seeding of conflict in a state with a multinational and "multi-historical" background. Within the prevailing nationalization discourse, we note a sub-discourse of victimization emphasizing the tragic fate of Ukraine, which is especially evident in the case of Chernobyl.

Perestroika emphasizes the discontinuity between the enforced Soviet past and the Ukrainian present, reflected in the content and structure of materials about perestroika. The late Soviet period can be divided into perestroika from "above," usually associated with the USSR in general, and perestroika "from below," associated with events and processes related to Ukraine. Through juxtaposing the negative connotations of "Soviet" with the positive connotations of "national," such a construction is underpinned. The studied material illustrates the prevalence of nationally specific realities over all-Soviet events, and the systematically positive description of actors, entities, and events related to national revival and Ukraine's self-determination.

Although the political processes are full of tensions, reflected in the present political life in Ukraine, perestroika seems to remain the historical topic that does not stir any significant tensions or conflicts among politicians, historians, and regional elites. Perestroika is intertwined with national independence and the outcome of a civic movement, Rukh, according to modern historical writing in Ukraine. Such linkages appeared in the mid 1990s when the Ukrainian elites, both communist-Soviet and national-democratic, tried to find a specific "legend," an explanatory scheme, for Ukraine and for themselves, which would differ from Moscow's interpretation of the same period.

The nationalization discourse is articulated through strategies directed either at constructing Ukraine's sameness, unity, and specificity, or at distancing Ukraine from "the Other," a role usually ascribed to the Soviet Union or the communist system. Constructive strategies are the strategy of justification, which rationalizes perestroika's results for Ukraine, its statehood, and democracy, and the strategy of emphasizing intra-national sameness, which underlines the unity of Ukraine. Differentiating strategies include dismantling of the Soviet past, through a negative perception of the communist system, as well as the strategy of shifting blame and responsibility, by depicting Ukraine as a colonial republic not responsible for the decisions made about it. The prevalence of differentiation strategies illustrates the efforts of historians to legitimize Ukraine's existence as a separate state differentiated from the unity of former Soviet republics.

Along with the aforementioned discourses, also evident is a discourse of longing for paternalism, which entails the justification of certain aspects of the Ukrainian perestroika story through invoking the necessity of a newborn state relying on "the strong hand" of the father. The longing for paternalism is reflected in recent sociological polls ("Dynamics of nostalgia for the USSR") indicating that 35 percent of the Ukrainian population (mostly from Eastern and Southern Ukraine) still feel nostalgia for the USSR.

Based on its insecure status and uneven appearance, we can identify a few strategies through which the discourse of longing for paternalism works. First, there is a strategy of "assimilation," in Wodak's terminology, the idea that "we are all in the same boat" (270), intended to emphasize Ukraine's and other post-Soviet republics' common fate. Second, there is the already mentioned strategy of shifting responsibility; in this case, it serves the goals of devaluing the national struggle for independence: independence came, but its consequences were not as positive as had been expected.

We regard this somewhat paternalistic discourse as a way to cope with the traumatic aspects of the collapse of the Soviet system and to create distance from harsh reality. The old system collapsed, but the result brought a plethora of challenges and uncertainties. Harsh economic conditions following the disintegration of the Soviet Union caught people unawares, and they were unprepared to face the new problems. Sleeping Beauty awoke to a world she could no longer recognize, as the rich and beautiful kingdom proved not to be as rich and beautiful as she had dreamt. The underlying discourse reveals a longing for utopia to a certain degree, for a past that never existed and for a future that has yet to come. The sober reality is that the princess has to learn to live in a world without the possibility of utopia.

Annex 1. School Textbooks in Ukraine

(Recommended by the Ministry of Education and Science of Ukraine)

Hupan, Nestor, Olena Pometun, Hryhorii Freiman. *Istoriia Ukrainy: 11 klas. [History of Ukraine: 11th form]*. Kyiv, Vydavnytstvo A.S.K., 2007.

Husiev, Victor, Iurii Kalintsev, Stanislav Kulchytskyi. *Istoriia Ukrainy [History of Ukraine]*. Edited by Stanislav Kulchytskyi, Kyiv, Vyshcha shkola, 2003.

Koval, Mikhail, Stanislav Kulchytskyi, Iurii Kurnosov, Vitalii Sarbei. *Istoriia Ukrainy. Probnoe uchebnoe posobye dlia 10-11 klassov srednei shkoly [History of Ukraine. Trial textbook for 10th-11th forms of secondary schools]*. Kyiv, Osvita, 1991.

Kulchytskyi, Stanislav, and Yulia Lebedieva. *Istoriia Ukrainy. 11 klas. [History of Ukraine. 11th form]*. Kyiv, Heneza, 2011.

Kulchytskyi, Stanislav, and Iurii Shapoval. *Novitnia istoriia Ukrainy (1939-2001). Pidr. dlia 11 klasu zahalonosv.navch. zakl. [History of Ukraine (1939-2001). A textbook for 11th form at secondary schools]*. Kyiv, Heneza, 2005.

Mytsyk, Iurii, Oleh Bazhan, Vitalii Vlasov. *Istoriia Ukrainy. [History of Ukraine]*. Kyiv, VD «Kyivo-Mohylianska Akademiia», 2005.

Ostrovskyi, Valerii, Vitalii Startsev, Borys Starkov, Gennadii Smirnov. *Istoriia SRSR: Pidruchnyk dlia 11 klasu serednoi shkoly [History of the USSR. A textbook for 11th form]*. Kyiv, Radianska shkola, 1991.

Ostrovskyi, Valerii. *Istoriia SRSR: materialy dlia pidruchnyka do 11 klasu. [History of the USSR. Materials for the textbook for 11th form]*. Kyiv, Radianska shkola, 1991.

Pometun, Olena, and Nestor Hupan. *Istoriia Ukrainy. 11 klas. [History of Ukraine. 11th form]*. Kyiv, Osvita, 2011.

Turchenko, Fedir, Petro Panchenko, Sergiy Tymchenko. *Novitnia Istoriia Ukrainy (1930-2001). 11 klas. [Contemporary History of Ukraine (1930-2001). 11th form]*. Kyiv, Heneza, 2001.

Turchenko, Fedir. *Istoriia Ukrainy. 11 klas. [History of Ukraine. 11th form]*. Kyiv, Heneza, 2011.

Annex 2. University Textbooks in Ukraine
(Recommended by the Ministry of Education and Science of Ukraine)

Bazhan, Oleg, Vitalii Vlasov, Oleksandr Bilousko, Iurii Mytsyk. *Istoriia Ukrainy: Navchalnyi posibnyk. [History of Ukraine. A textbook].* Kyiv, Delta, 2006.

Bilotserkivskyi, Vasyl. *Istoriia Ukrainy. Navchalnyi posibnyk. [History of Ukraine. A textbook].* Kyiv, Tsentr uchbovoi literatury, 2007.

Boiko, Oleksandr. *Istoriia Ukrainy: posibnyk dlia studentiv vyshchykh navchalnykh zakladiv [History of Ukraine: A Textbook for University Students].* Kyiv, VTs Akademiia, 1999.

Boiko, Oleksandr. *Istoriia Ukrainy: posibnyk dlia studentiv vyshchykh navchalnykh zakladiv, 2-he vyd., dop. [History of Ukraine: A Textbook for University Students, 2nd ed., expanded].* Kyiv, Akademvydav, 2004.

Bondariev, Iekhor, Volodymyr Gorbatenko, Volodymyr Hrechenko. *Politychna istoriia Ukrainy: Navch.posibnyk dlia studentiv VNZ. [Political History of Ukraine. A textbook for University Students].* Edited by Vasyl Tantsiura, Kyiv, Akademiia, 2001.

Bushyn, Mykola. *Istoriia Ukrainy: Kurs lektsii dlia studentiv neistorychnykh fakultetiv. [History of Ukraine. A lecture course for students outside history departments].* Cherkasy, Brama, 2000.

Cherkashyna, Nina. *Istoriia Ukrainy: vid davnikh chasiv do sohodennia: navch. posibnyk. [History of Ukraine: from ancient times until today. A textbook].* Kyiv, VD Profesional, 2005.

Deshchynskyi, Leontii, Sviatoslav Terskyi, Ivan Khoma, Volodymyr Taraban. *Istoriia Ukrainy ta yii derzhavnosti: navch. posibnyk. Vyd. 3-ye, pereroblene i dopovnene. [History of Ukraine and its statehood. A textbook. 3rd edition].* Lviv, Beskyd Bih, 2005.

Hrechenko, Volodymyr. *Istoriia Ukrainy. Modulnyi kurs [Tekst]: navch. posibnyk. [History of Ukraine: module course. A textbook].* Kharkiv, Torsin plus, 2009.

Hudz, Viktor. *Istoriia Ukrainy. Pidruchnyk. Vydannia druhe, dopovnene i pereroblene. [History of Ukraine. 2nd edition, improved].* Kyiv, Vydavnychyi dim Slovo, 2008.

Husiev, Victor, Hryhorii Kazmyrchuk, Valerii Kapeliushnyi, Hennadii Cherevychnyi. *Istoriia Ukrainy/Pidruchnyk dlia inozemnykh studentiv vyshchykh navchalnykh zakladiv. [History of Ukraine: A textbook for foreign University Students].* Kyiv, VPTs Kyivskyi universytet, 2008.

Kazmyrchuk, Hryhorii, Anatolii Kotsur, Olexii Verbovyi. *Istoriia Ukrainy: pidruchnyk*. [History of Ukraine. A textbook]. Edited by H. Kazmyrchuk, Kyiv, VPTs Kyivskyi universytet, 2009.

Kondratiuk, Kostiantyn, Halyna Bodnar, Volodymyr Kachmar, Viktor Kholubko. *Novitnia istoriia Ukrainy. 1914–2008 rr.: Navchalnyi posibnyk*. [New History of Ukraine. 1914-2008: A textbook]. Kyiv, Znannia, 2011.

Kudriachenko, Andrii, Halyna Kalinicheva, Anatoliy Kostyria. *Politychna istoriia Ukrainy XX stolittia: pidruchnyk dlia stud. vyshch. navch. Zakl* [Political History of Ukraine in XX century: A textbook for the University Students]. Kyiv, MAUP, 2006.

Kulchytskyi, Stanislav, and Borys Tyshchyk. *Istoriia derzhavy i prava Ukrainy. Akademichnyi kurs*. [History of the state and law in Ukraine. Academic course]. Kyiv, InIure, 2008.

Lanovyk, Bohdan, Zinoviy Matysiakevych, Roman Mateiko. *Istoriia Ukrainy: Navch. posib*. [History of Ukraine. A textbook]. Kyiv, Znannia, 1999.

Lanovyk, Bohdan, and Mykola Lazarovych. *Istoriia Ukrainy: Navch. posib. 3-te vyd., vypr. i dop*. [History of Ukraine. A textbook. 3rd edition, improved]. Kyiv, Znannia-Pres, 2006.

Lazarovych, Mykola. *Istoriia Ukrainy: Navch. posib*. [History of Ukraine. A textbook]. Kyiv, Znannia, 2008.

Lytvyn, Volodymyr. *Istoriia Ukrainy: pidruchnyk – 4-e doopratsovane ta dopovnene vydannia*. [History of Ukraine. A textbook – 4th edition, improved]. Kyiv, Naukova dumka, 2010.

Lytvyn, Volodymyr, Viktor Kolesnyk, Anatoliy Sliusarenko. *Istoriia Ukrainy: Navchalno-metodychnyi posibnyk dlia seminarskykh zaniat*. [History of Ukraine. A textbook and a guidebook for seminars] – Edited by Volodymyr Lytvyn, Kyiv, Znannia-Pres, 2006.

Melnyk, Anatolii. *Istoriia Ukrainy. Navchalnyi posibnyk*. [History of Ukraine. A textbook]. Kyiv, Tsentr uchbovoi literatury, 2008.

Muzychenko, Petro. *Istoriia derzhavy i prava Ukrainy: Navch. posib*. [History of the state and law of Ukraine. A textbook]. 6-te vyd., pererob. i dop. Kyiv: Znannia, 2007.

Ostafiichuk, Vasyl. *Istoriia Ukrainy: Suchasne bachennia: Navchalnyi posibnyk*. [History of Ukraine. Contemporary view. A textbook]. 3- tie vyd., pererob. i dop. Kyiv, Znannia-Pres, 2006.

Rybak, Ivan, and Andrii Matvieiev. *Istoriia Ukrainy u problemnomu vykladi, v osobakh, nazvakh i poniattiakh: Navch. posib*. [History of Ukraine with problem's presentations, personalities, names and concepts. A textbook]. Kyiv, Tsentr navch. Literatury, 2005.

Savchenko, Nataliia, and Myroslav Podolskyi. *Istoriia Ukrainy: modulnyi kurs. Navchalnyi posibnyk* [*History of Ukraine: a module course. A textbook*]. Kyiv, Firma 'INKOS', Tsentr navchalnoi literatury, 2006.

Shvydko, Hryhorii. *Politychna istoriia Ukrainy: navchalnyi posibnyk dlia stud. vyshch. navch. Zakladiv / 2-e vyd., pererob. i dop.* [*Political History of Ukraine: A textbook for the University Students*]. Dnipropetrovsk, Nats. hirnychyi un-t, 2005.

Svitlychna, Valentyna. *Istoriia Ukrainy: navchalnyi posibnyk. 3-є видання.* [*History of Ukraine. A textbook. 3rd edition*]. Kyiv, Karavela, 2005.

Skrypnyk, Mykola, Larysa Dombrovska, Volodymyr Krasovskii, Olexandr Dombrovskyi, Stepan Zhechev. *Istoriia Ukrainy: Navchalnyi posibnyk.* [*History of Ukraine. A textbook*]. Edited by Mykola Skrypnyk, Kyiv, Tsentr navchalnoi literatury, 2003.

Slyvka, Iurii. *Istoriia Ukrainy. Pidruchnyk dlia stud. vyshchykh navch. zakl. 4-te vyd.* [*History of Ukraine. A textbook for the University Students. - 4th edition*]. Lviv, Svit, 2003.

Tatsii, Vasyl, Anatoliy Rogozhyn, Volodymyr Honcharenko. *Istoriia derzhavy i prava Ukrainy. U dvokh tomakh.* [*History of state and law of Ukraine. In two volumes*]. Vol. 2. Kyiv: InYure, 2003.

Temko, Hryhorii, and Leonid Tupchiienko. *Istoriia Ukrainy: Posibnyk.* [*History of Ukraine. A handbook*]. Kyiv, Vydavnychyi tsentr Akademiia, 2001.

Verstiuk, Vladyslav, Olexiy Haran, Olexandr Gurzhii. *Istoriia Ukrainy.* [*History of Ukraine*] Edited by Valerii Smolii, Kyiv, Vydavnychyi dim "Alternatyvy," 1997.

Voronianskyi, Oleksandr. *Istoriia Ukrainy: navchalnyi posibnyk dlia studentiv vyshchykh navchalnykh zakladiv* [*History of Ukraine: a textbook for the University Students*]. Kharkiv, Parus, 2005.

Zaruba, Viktor. *Istoriia derzhavy i prava Ukrainy: navch. posib.* [*History of state and law of Ukraine*]. Kyiv, Istyna, 2006.

Zaitsev, Iurii, editor. *Istoriia Ukrainy.* [*History of Ukraine*]. Lviv, Svit, 1998.

The Invention of Transition: Perestroika in Belarusian History Textbooks

Marharyta Fabrykant and Andrei Dudchik

The Belarusian Context

The recent growth of interest in the Belarusian case in Eastern European and post-Soviet studies has led not only to the appearance of new monographs summarizing and elaborating on more or less established opinions (Bennett; Wilson 121-260). There have also been some attempts to rediscover the "vanished kingdoms" of the medieval proto-Belarusian past (Davies 229-308) and even challenge traditional views of contemporary Belarusian society and its identity (Buhr et al. 387-388). However, despite the increased variety of ideas, research on the Belarusian case remains confined to general issues of national identity, striving to answer the question "What is Belarus?" in the most abstract way (e.g., Pershái 379-398). The resulting multiplication of studies over the last several years is probably the most convincing, although not the only proof that such a research question is far too generally formulated to allow a single comprehensive answer (Balmaceda 42-47). A less explored and probably more difficult alternative to such generalities would be an in-depth empirical study of a specifically defined segment of the Belarusian reality using an explicitly defined and rigorously applied methodology.

Belarus is generally portrayed as the most pro-Soviet of all post-Soviet states, and as the one with the strictest ideological control. Yet the history textbooks currently used in Belarusian schools and universities differ greatly from their Soviet predecessors and, notwithstanding the alleged ideological unanimity, from one another. This chapter illustrates how these differences appear in textbook sections on perestroika, whence they come, and what they imply.

Courses in Belarusian history are taught in both Belarusian secondary schools and universities. In secondary schools, both Belarusian and world history are part of the curriculum for the entire duration of studies. In university, Belarusian history is taught as an obligatory course to all undergraduate students except those majoring in history. The latter have several courses on different historical periods with a significantly more advanced scope of study per semester. The lecturers are university-educated professional historians who usually specialize in Belarusian history. The established narrative of Belarusian history largely amounts to a distinct periodization, which is usually presented in a reified way as an objective natural sequence, not as an explanatory tool necessitated by the contemporary form of historical narrative. This periodization is based exclusively on the criterion of state-building. This history canon assumed its current form during the nationalist movement of the early 1990s, when history textbooks were being rewritten drastically and rapidly, but can be traced back to the first overviews of Belarusian history and is accepted without alternatives, albeit with varying evaluations of content (Dovnar-Zapol'skiĭ 11–18; Lastoŭski 8). The narrative sometimes recalls the foreign mainstream vision of Belarus as a cultural and geopolitical borderland (Savchenko 1–15; Shlapentokh 2–3) between Europe and Russia (Obermann 93–102; Rontoyanni 123–156; Rudling 55–58).

The Soviet history of Belarus is interesting, first, because of the relatively high status of the Belarusian Soviet Socialist Republic (BSSR). The BSSR was one of the most industrialized and technologically advanced republics in the Soviet Union, routinely referred to as "the assembly hall of the Union." Economically, the BSSR was deeply integrated into the USSR and suffered great losses from its disintegration. To some extent, this explains why technocratic discourse dominates Belarus political discussions. Another reason for the high status of the BSSR within the Soviet Union was its contribution to the victory in the Great Patriotic War (1941-1945). The social mythology of the partisan movement was widespread in Belarus and throughout the USSR (Urban 10–17), leading to the BSSR being accepted among the co-founders of the United Nations, so that participation in the Great Patriotic War is officially interpreted as the moment of birth of the modern Belarusian state. Consequently, memory of Soviet times is an important part of official Belarusian identity (Fritz 2008; Parker 97–103), and modes of the economic (Abdelal 127–149) and political (Gatrell and Baron 58–116) development of independent Belarus are highly influenced by its Soviet past.

Both secondary school and university textbooks are written by professional historians holding high-ranking academic positions at universities or in the National Academy of Sciences. Exceptions are few. To be introduced into the teaching process, both secondary school and university textbooks require the approval of the Belarusian Ministry of Education. In secondary schools, only one textbook is recommended by the Ministry of Education for a certain academic year. University lecturers enjoy more flexibility in being able to recommend any textbook, or a combination of textbooks, to their students, with the result that university courses are more diverse than secondary school ones, not only didactically, but also substantively. University lecturers may also recommend additional literature to their students, including primary sources, although the syllabi must be based on textbooks approved by the Ministry of Education. Thus, secondary school textbooks usually replace one another, while university textbooks, once officially approved, may be and usually are used simultaneously with one another.

This chapter is based on an analysis of all the textbooks on Belarusian history currently in use in Belarusian secondary schools or universities. These include six secondary school and eight university textbooks published between 1995 and 2011. All textbooks, with the exception of the one by Treshchenok contain either chapters or sections specifically dedicated to the period of perestroika. The average coverage of this period is around three percent of the total in the school textbooks, and five percent in the university textbooks. Titles and subtitles of the sections on perestroika vary to some extent, and in most of them perestroika is not explicitly mentioned. We have also studied some of the supplemental reading material at the university level, including

Western research on perestroika and the Soviet period in general; some comparison of the content of Belarusian textbooks and research on perestroika is presented here, and could be useful for representing the wider context of this issue. This gives an impression of the kind of literature that is appropriate for our research. We have used a mixed methods design, because it allows us to address two key areas of textbook research: the actual content and its relation to the wider context (Repoussi and Tutiaux-Guillon 154–170). We use quantitative content analysis because it provides a general overview of the themes raised in the large and diverse textual material and enables quantitative comparisons of textbook content (both within each country and between countries). The results of the content analysis are statistical, and one can observe the relative frequencies with which key personalities, entities, events, and countries of the perestroika period are mentioned. From a qualitative point of view, we have made use of narrative analysis and of critical and psychological discourse analysis. The narrative analysis illustrates how texts about the period of perestroika are positioned within the broader context of constructing a grand narrative of national history (Geelan 21–24).

Discourse analysis instead casts light over how history writing about perestroika is shaped by the contemporary historical and sociopolitical agenda. In particular, critical discourse analysis aims at revealing covert relations of power implicitly reaffirmed in textbooks. Psychological discourse analysis reveals the multitude of available interpretations of perestroika constructed in each textbook, in an attempt to provide a socially acceptable and coherent image of perestroika (Jørgensen and Phillips 96–137). Here, we use critical discourse analysis to analyze the textbook chapters on perestroika in light of what might be expected from the wider macro-social context. In its outcome, critical discourse analysis reveals the covert ways in which textbooks support the existing social order. Psychological discourse analysis is conducted via placing textbook material in the micro-social context in which it is used by the authors in presenting their own positions and/or eliciting specific replies from the target audience.

The Collapse of the Soviet Union: Causes and Consequences

The collapse of the Soviet Union is seen as the main event of the whole Soviet history, its last stage, and as the beginning of the independent Republic of Belarus. The collapse is regarded by the authors as the final phase not only of the period of perestroika as such, but of the entire Soviet history. It is seen as the evolutionary result of previous developments. There is no consensus about the causes of this collapse in the textbooks, and the events are still vivid in collective and individual memory.

Most of the authors point out the complex nature of the collapse. They agree that there was a crisis of the whole system, while some doubt whether it need have been fatal, in contrast to, for example, the Ukrainian textbook authors, who are quite sure that the collapse, once it had happened, was inevitable. A number of causes of the collapse are presented. Objectively, the Soviet system was in a difficult state, and words such as "crisis" and *zaniapad* (decline) are often used to describe it. A radical gap in the goals and values between the ruling elite and most of the population is also said to have existed. The reformers of the party elite suffered from incompetence and made fatal mistakes in realizing perestroika policies as a result. Moreover, there were pervasive conflicts at different levels of the Soviet system ("the war of sovereignty"; Kastsiūk et al. 422), conflicts between the Soviets and the CPSU (Koshelev 368), and the actions of destructive forces inside and outside the Soviet Union.

Some authors claim that the Belarusian situation was not as bad as that in the Union as a whole when it came to, for example, the economy: "All these problems existed in Belarus, although during the twelfth five-year plan (1986-1990) the state of the Belarusian economy, in comparison to some other republics, was quite stable" (Chigrinov 434, translation by the authors).

Comparisons are made between the Belarusian economy and that of the more developed countries in the West. Kastsiuk compares the amount of agricultural production in the BSSR and the USA to show that the state of affairs was not so critical in the former (Kastsiuk 431). However, the crisis throughout the Union influenced the Belarusian economy, which was closely incorporated into the Soviet one. As the results of the narrative analysis indicate, the main logic is unfolded in terms of a movement from the entire Soviet Union to the BSSR as one of its parts. In general, the Belarusian texts do not adhere to the "anticolonial" line of interpretation, as seen in the Ukrainian textbooks, but to the "imperial" vision of perestroika. The imperial narrative of perestroika places specifically Belarusian events at the periphery and treats them as secondary effects of shared Soviet history. The authors of Ukrainian and Russian textbooks instead tend to place their own nations' experiences at the center.

Most of the causes are anchored in a line of thought that attributes the major blame to the bad state of the Soviet "system." However, there is also an interpretation that considers the events in terms of conspiracy theories, which are presented in textbooks as fully legitimate alongside other explanations. The West is presented as hostile towards the Soviet Union at all times, and the long struggle against the Soviet Union — the Cold War — bears the brunt of the blame:

> All the time during the transformation of the Communist Party into the ruling party [Note: the special status of the Communist Party as the only official party is assumed] and the establishment of Soviet Russia and then the Soviet Union, the capitalist West constantly conducted "war" to effect its destruction. This war took different forms ... (Novik and Martsul' 386, translation by the authors).

The collapse of the Soviet Union is interpreted as the result of a long struggle of "capitalistic powers" (this very important and complex concept, encompassing capitalist states, secret services, and various organizations, was borrowed from official Soviet rhetoric of the Cold War) against the Soviet Union, using non-violent means (cf. modern conceptions of soft power with the use of a long-term strategy of indirect action; see Combs 31–39 and Nye 33–72). In the textbook for universities published in 1998, the author Evgeniĭ Novik, in line with radical conspiracy thinking, quoted fragments from Dulles's plan—a well-known conspiracy theory about Allen Dulles, the head of the CIA, as the mastermind of an alleged plan to destroy the Soviet Union (Ball 1–22). This plan was a fake document, according to which the CIA had developed a plan to destroy the Soviet Union during the Cold War by secretly corrupting the cultural heritage and moral values of the Soviet people. The policies of perestroika are thus interpreted as the main instrument for realizing this plan with the support of anti-Soviet powers inside the country: "during perestroika there were conditions for the full implementation of the "program" of A. Dulles" (Novik and Martsul' 386, translation by the authors). Novik, one of the most influential official historians who authored a series of history textbooks, uses the political cliché of *mirovaya zakulisa* (world behind the scenes, world cabal), interpreted as:

> the non-governmental political organizations of the richest and most influential people in the world, whose aim is to achieve the full integration of the global transition from a number of states, peoples, nations, and cultures to a uniform world, led by a world government. They are also known as Masonic or *mondialist* ... organizations. (Novik 484; translation by the authors).

Included here are the Bilderberg Group and the Trilateral Commission. The use of the French word "*mondialisme*" instead of the more popular globalism is interesting. Popularization of the term *mondialisme* is connected to the ideas of the French "New Right" ("*Nouvelle Droite*") movement, some ideas of which were popularized by the Russian ideologist of neo-Eurasianism Alexander Dugin (see Laruelle 115–119). For example, the version of the putsch as a provocation by the "world cabal" is presented as follows: "A third group of researchers believes that ... *gekachepisty* [Note: this Russian term is derived from the acronym GKChP, i.e., the State Committee on the State of Emergency, and refers to the members of the Committee] were just pawns in the great frame-up, prepared and carried out by the 'world behind the scenes'" (Novik 483-484, translation by the authors).

The contextual analysis shows that some variants of this explanation are present even in the works of both post-Soviet and Western authors. Conspiracy theories as such are popular among post-Soviet readers (Ortmann 551-564). The collapse of the Soviet Union came so unexpectedly to both its citizens and to Soviet and Western experts, that the usual explanations do not appear sufficient; some special explanation is needed. Since the process of decision-making in Soviet society was not transparent, and many sources are still secret and inaccessible to researchers, this gives rise to speculation that feeds conspiracy theories, which remain alive. These conspiracy theories are in some ways aligned with the spirit of perestroika's policy of glasnost with its flow of previously unknown information about the negative aspects of the Soviet past and of critique of official views of the past events (see Sherlock; Kennedy). There is also the peculiarity of official Soviet language that presupposes the practice of "reading between the lines" (Ploss 211-216).

The appearance of an independent Belarusian state is usually presented in textbooks as one of the main consequences of the collapse of the Soviet Union, but not the most important one. Independence is depicted as having played out in the shadow of the global event that the collapse was (in marked contrast to Ukrainian historiography). Many of the textbooks do not draw any direct line between the end of perestroika itself, the collapse of the Soviet Union, and the beginning of an independent Republic of Belarus. Continuity between the Belarusian Socialistic Soviet Republic (BSSR) and the Republic of Belarus is instead presumed. The Republic of Belarus is in fact interpreted as BSSR but now at a new stage of its development, inevitable after the collapse of the Soviet Union: a "new period in the history of Belarus has started — the period of full independence" (Chigrinov 401, translation by the authors).

The word "sovereignty" appears in the headings of some of the textbooks, and is defined in the lists of most important concepts (Sharova 272). The state of "real" or "full" national sovereignty is usually described by pointing to the attainment of a number of attributes of sovereignty: armed forces, institutions of power, customs authorities, a banking system, and the like. Membership in the system of international organizations is also regarded as an important element of national sovereignty. Symbols of sovereignty, such as a new flag and a coat of arms, are usually described. The problem of the distribution or redistribution of sovereignty is analyzed in terms of the relations between republican and central powers in the Soviet Union and the relations between the former Soviet republics in the Commonwealth of Independent States (CIS), which was created after the collapse of Soviet Union.

The narrative of perestroika describes the main political and economic events. Only a few disconnected mentions of everyday life are presented in the textbooks and they do not correlate to the general narrative, for example: "Drinking and absenteeism at the workplace were ordinary among working people, leading to decreased labor productivity. Telling anecdotes became one way of actively expressing displeasure" (Novik 189, translation by the authors). In this quotation, everyday life is seen in the context of economic processes (not as a separate field, as in Ries 15-41, for example), as in official Soviet rhetoric. The inevitability of change is noted: "Perestroika was only a matter of time. Many problems had accumulated in society, and superficial change would be not enough" (Kovkel' and IArmusik 580, translation by the authors). The policy of perestroika initiated by Gorbachev and his team is interpreted as a reaction to crisis of the Soviet system (cf. Brown 135-156).

Interestingly, Vol'ha Liāntsèvich compares the purely economic reforms in China with perestroika in the Soviet Union, which was oriented towards "substantial changes in all spheres at the same time" (Liāntsèvich 123, translation by the authors). Comparisons of the changes in the USSR and China were popular among foreign researchers as well (Gurtov 1-258; Sun 237-257).

Democratization is also identified as one of the important consequences of perestroika, though evaluations of the democratization process differ (Dawisha 223-281). The appearance of real political pluralism, a multiparty system, and open elections is interpreted by some as one of the major achievements of the initiators of perestroika. This is also true of authors with a neutral attitude towards the Soviet system and, with the exception of the textbook by Bokhan and Poletaeva, it is their neutral vision that is presented in school textbooks. However, for most textbook authors, who are more pro-Soviet, democratization is instead seen as a destructive consequence inspired by foreign ideas directed not only against the Communist Party, but against the Soviet Union as such. This is clearly indicated by the terms "democracy" and "democratization" being placed within scare quotation marks to show the textbooks authors' skepticism and distrust. As a rule, they are treated as synonyms for "Western" (or pro-Western) and "capitalist."

Nationalist Movements and National Independence

Ethnicity is a contested issue in Belarus. Unlike Russia, Belarus has no division analogous to the juxtaposition of *"russkie"* and *"rossiiāne,"* and being a Belarusian may refer to civic or ethnic identity (Brubaker 47–49; Denber 107–120; Greenfeld 189–275; Malešević 67–82). According to data from the national survey of 2009 (Zinovskiĭ et al. 8–10), most Belarusians regard their own Belarusianness as a separate matter of self-identity, rather than a hard-and-fast ethnicity permeating everyday life and consistent with behavior, although beliefs regarding ethnicity and nationality in general may differ, as is usual in transitional societies. The nationalist movement itself changed significantly during the 20th century. The first wave early in the century was mostly left wing, because both Russification and Polonization operated primarily via high culture and left the lower classes almost untouched (cf. Meadwell 19–51). Belarusian nationalists of the first wave strove simultaneously to reformulate the issue of social justice in national terms, create an unquestionably Belarusian high culture, and realize, or at least formulate, their own political program (Smith 73–77). The second national revival movement of the late 1980s and early 1990s had a ready political agenda in the form of anti-Sovietism and did not include any systematic attempts to go beyond it and formulate its own political and economic program. All key figures of the second Belarusian national revival came from academic and artistic culture, having no managerial experience or outlook (Savchenko 150–156). This description should be compared with the general analysis of the institutional post-communist transformation (Mishler 418–451).

The problem of nationalities in the Soviet Union (Connor) and the subsequent national revival, recognized as of paramount importance for the period in many former Soviet republics, are discussed in the textbooks on at least two levels: as national revival in the Soviet Union in general and in Belarus in particular. The general position on the phenomenon of national revival is neutral or even positive, with a negative attitude articulated towards the Popular Fronts as political organizations. The activities of the Popular Fronts are condemned for politicizing cultural problems:

> Popular Fronts, based on the ecological and cultural movements, appeared in many republics of the Union. Some *extremists* [emphasis added], longing for political power and property, joined political life in addition to the honest politicians who adhered to their own principles, and who quickly became national heroes. They explained all the people's troubles in terms of the actions of the Soviet Union's government and its exploitive internationalism. Many people became possessed with a nationalistic mood ... The real help and benefits of the Union were forgotten. (Koshelev 368; translation by the authors)

The Popular Fronts and their cooperation with the republican political elites are interpreted as one of the driving forces of the disintegration of the Soviet Union that finally led to its collapse.

Describing the Belarusian national movement becomes even more complicated. The authors usually differentiate between the national revival and the politics of "Belarusification," on one hand, and the national political movements, on the other, often referring to the Popular Front "revival" (including the Belarusian People's Front, the BNF). If national revival is mentioned with neutral or even positive connotations, as in "a peculiarity was increasing interest in the nation's history, culture, and language" (Kovkel and Yarmusik 574, translation by the authors), the nationalists are evaluated either neutrally by the authors relatively sympathetic towards the national revival movement, who refrain from explicit evaluations, or negatively by those who are pro-Soviet. For example: "It [i.e., the national revival movement] was not just a cultural-educational movement, but undoubtedly also political. It was a common political struggle disguised with slogans about the revival of national culture" (Novik 19, translation by the authors).

The national revival project in Belarus constitutes a social trauma for its active participants and supporters because it has proved to be unsuccessful, as well as for its opponents, who are diverse in their views and agree only in condemning the top-down nation-building of the early 1990s as wrong for moral or pragmatic reasons. The opponents view themselves in light of the national revival as suffering from symbolic violence, such as the enforced linguistic Belarusification (see Fabrykant and Buhr for details).

The emergence of the independent Republic of Belarus is arguably the most difficult outcome of perestroika to describe. Most textbooks convey neutral to positive attitudes towards the Soviet Union and neutral to negative attitudes towards perestroika, but positive or at least "tolerant" attitudes towards the country. This differs from the more negative attitudes towards the Soviet past and positive attitudes towards perestroika typical of the other country cases, with some exceptions found in Moldovan textbooks (see the chapter on Moldova for details). However, to simultaneously construct a positive attitude towards the Soviet Union and an independent Belarus, which appeared in the Soviet Union's ruins and largely due to its fall, is obviously not easy. Nor is it easy to combine a positive evaluation of the current independent Belarusian state with a simultaneous condemnation of the early nationalist movements (Bekus 133–138; Leshchenko 333–352; Wilson 121–139).

THE INVENTION OF TRANSITION   103

In striking contrast to the Ukrainian narrative (see the chapter on Ukraine for details), content related to national independence is quite difficult to find in most Belarusian textbooks. The emergence of the Republic of Belarus in the place of the BSSR of the Soviet Union is simply not presented as the start of a new period. Rather, it is positioned somewhere in the period starting in 1985, the beginning of perestroika, and the indefinite present. As in the Russian textbooks in which the appearance of the Russian Federation figures, the appearance of the Republic of Belarus resembles that of an official announcement, with next to no glorification of the event or reflection on its historical meaning:

> On 25-26 August the extraordinary session of the Supreme Council of the BSSR passed the law "On giving a constitutional status to the declaration of the Supreme Council of the BSSR about the state sovereignty of the Belarusian Soviet Socialist Republic," a resolution ensuring the political and economic independence of the Byelorussian SSR. On 19 September 1991, the Supreme Council passed a law on the name of the Byelorussian SSR, according to which it began to be called The Republic of Belarus. (Novik 387; translation by the authors)

Nevertheless, this is one of the few events that is illustrated, usually with national symbols and images of both the initial flag and coat of arms as well as their contemporary versions, which were accepted by most voters in a national referendum in 1995 (Novik and Martsul' 384-385). Considering that both older versions are associated with anti-Soviet nationalism and that the newer versions are almost exact copies of the Soviet Belarusian flag and coat of arms, but without the sickle and hammer, placing these visual symbols side by side and equal in size is a clear sign of the desire for deliberate neutrality in presenting these to students.

The style of the narrative of how independence was gained has several features that emphasize this neutrality. First, the appearance of an independent Belarus is presented not as an achievement but as something inevitable, that is to be neither celebrated nor regretted but merely taken into account. The gaining of independence is not attributed to specifically individual or collective actions. The narrative is intricately constructed in such a way as to make the appearance of an independent Belarus appear irrelevant in relation to the fall of the Soviet Union and taking the form of the three-party agreement signed in Viskuli, although the causal relationship appears obvious. However, in most textbooks, the official dissolution of the Soviet Union is presented with lengthy reflections on its inherent meaning, and the issue of Belarusian Independence is raised only later. Thus, Belarusian history textbooks present a rare example, literally a textbook case, of a non-nationalist narrative of the way to national independence.

A different aspect is when the textbooks deal with the nationalist movement in the Belarus of the late 1980s in which people participated who today form part of the contemporary political opposition. Although the type of content used to describe this movement is largely the same in all the textbooks, the scope of coverage varies. The more recently published textbooks give the subject considerably less coverage than do those of the late 1990s and early 2000s (e.g., the two editions of the most influential textbook by Novik et al., whose editor-in-chief has the highest status among the historians in the Belarusian academic hierarchy). This is fully consistent with the ongoing marginalization of the opposition parties in Belarus and follows the politically rational choice that a weak opponent is better ignored and left unnoticed than criticized and condemned.

In contrast, the earlier versions contain whole sections dedicated to the nationalist movement. Described as a series of small, informal clubs promoting national and mostly folk culture that suddenly appeared in various parts of the country, this narrative and versions of it in other textbooks contain lists of the names of these clubs, though their leaders or other members are not mentioned. This impersonality gives the impression that these clubs more or less appeared out of thin air. The alleged "double face" of these clubs is pointed out in some of the textbooks, stating that they posed as apolitical organizations promoting harmless cultural heritage while being constructed from the start as political movements in disguise. This pattern implicitly rejects the Czech historian Miroslav Hroch's theory of nationalist movements in Central and Eastern Europe, which postulates a neutral and natural development from individual initiatives to restore and partly invent folk cultural heritage for popularization and eventual transformation into mass political movements.

In no textbook is it stated or implied that this early nationalist movement, or even the later political party, the Belarusian People's Front, aimed at Belarusian Independence. Instead, the Belarusian nationalist movement is presented not as pro-Belarusian, but as a variant of the general anti-Soviet movement, similar to those in other republics (Lyantsevich 125). In many textbooks, they are explicitly portrayed as actors in the world anti-Soviet conspiracy to overthrow the Soviet Union, with detailed descriptions of how financial help from the West was used. Novik writes:

> The opposition, with the support of the West, tried to disorganize the Soviet Union and destroy the existing regime. Many foundations, centers, councils, and associations were organized to avoid the accusations of intervention in the Soviet Union's inner politics. Officially they were private, non-governmental organizations, but they were in fact controlled by Western secret services. Oppositional organizations in the Soviet Union received material and financial support from abroad: fax machines, Xerox machines, computers, printers, telex machines, video cameras, and other equipment, as well as money for the financing of scientific research, preparation of textbooks, dictionaries, encyclopedias, etc. (193, translation by the authors).

The textbooks offer no specific description of the kinds of activities undertaken by the participants in the nationalist movement or of any actual causal relationship between their actions and the fall of the Soviet Union (cf. Epstein 152–167). It appears that the mere existence of such groups is supposed to have threatened the stability of the Soviet state. Needless to say, nationalists are given no credit for the eventual gaining of independence. Moreover, the narrative of the nationalist movement is abruptly terminated with the end of the Soviet Union, so that it seems that it somehow ceased to exist once Belarus became independent.

Popular Fronts in various Soviet republics are claimed to have been created to provide support for perestroika at the local level, but it is nowhere suggested that the voicing of nationalist ideas was somehow related to the policy of glasnost, allowing public interaction between different opinions on political issues. In the public sphere of today, contemporary Belarusian nationalists are frequently vilified by their opponents as direct successors of the collaborationists in World War II. In the university textbook of 1995, and its featuring of Leanid Lych in particular, a prominent nationalist activist among its authors, the nationalist movement of the perestroika period is portrayed exclusively in the context of late Soviet history. However, for the nationalists themselves, their continuity with predecessors from the late 19th and early 20th centuries was of utmost importance. The first wave was the Belarusian national revival and the second was the movement of the late 20th century.

In general, the coverage of separatism and the reasons for it included in Belarusian history textbooks appears full of gaps partly covered up by the uniform discourse of objectification. The reason for this spotty coverage is the lack of a discourse that would tie it together by setting it within a meaningful contextual narrative of national independence and the nationalist movement. The essence of nationality as such, and of the Belarusian national identity in particular, is by far the most widely debated political issue in the contemporary Belarusian public sphere, but is mostly addressed in unquestioned ethno-nationalist terms (Brubaker 23–54; Fox 283–307; Gledhill 347–368). Another interesting feature of contemporary Belarusian nationalism is its increased hostility towards the liberal, democratic West. Closer affiliation with the new right-wing ideology combining *"zapadnorussism"* (West-Russianism) with Neo-Eurasianism has been a consequence (Laruelle 4–6; Fabrykant and Buhr 103–105).

There has been a rapid shift away from the romantic idealism of perestroika and the early post-Soviet years to the disappointed acceptance of realpolitik and a readiness to manipulate Belarusian public opinion instead of enlightening and reforming it (Buhr et al. 387–388). In the textbooks, this state of general confusion and intense search for simple answers is mirrored in the consequential exclusion of romantic nationalism. The one crucial actor of national history, the nation itself, is absent from the grand narrative of Belarusian history as presented in Belarusian history textbooks, particularly in the chapters on perestroika. In a way, this lack of an explicit definition of the nation in a textbook on national history recalls Ankersmit's notion of narrative logic in which the story alone implicitly creates its protagonist (Ankersmit 14). However, this mode of narrative is hardly compatible with the didactic purpose of providing an explicit conceptual framework for the historical process. Belarusian history textbooks paradoxically appear to encourage independent thinking about the national issue precisely by not teaching the theoretical apparatus necessary for this reflection.

Communism and Communist Ideology

Historical writing about any period of Soviet history is difficult to imagine without extensive reflections on the role of communist ideology. On one hand, the Soviet Union was created as a pioneering project to realize the allegedly only true understanding of history. The initial legitimization of the Soviet state rested on its being understood not as an end in itself, but as a grand tool for building a new, classless communist society. On the other hand, the Soviet project, according to its proponents, was bound to be successful because the embedded ideology provided not only the historical goal, but also the necessary means for its achievement. This was not merely an insider's perspective. Much Sovietology was based on drawing conclusions regarding historical reality from judgments as to the truthful or false character of communist ideology (e.g., Kramer; Cipkowski).

In particular, this was true of the period of perestroika. One key question regarding this new policy was the extent to which it was consistent with the initial purpose of the Soviet state. Perestroika, especially in its early stages, was portrayed not only as an innovation, but also as a return to the true communist principles that formerly had been obscured, primarily as a result of the disastrous Stalinist regime. Slogans such as "more democracy, more socialism" declared the allegiance of perestroika to socialism. The ideologically acceptable imperfection of socialism opened up space for reforms and even for alternative projects, such as "socialism with a human face."

In textbooks this could permit alternative or at least more flexible interpretations. We would therefore expect any post-Soviet textbook on perestroika to contain a specific analysis of communist ideology and the role it played during the period. Attitudes towards communism and its relationship with perestroika, however, differ considerably both across and within countries. In the Belarusian case, these inner disparities of opinion are not emphasized. Belarus, probably more than any other newly independent post-Soviet state, officially claimed its intention to preserve historical continuity and reject the possibility of a violent break with the Soviet past. For this reason, we expect the treatment of perestroika in Belarusian textbooks to contain careful explanations of communist ideology and its relationship with contemporary Belarusian state ideology.

Surprisingly, that is not the case. Communism is mentioned rarely, compared with the ideological innovations of perestroika, such as glasnost or the market economy. Moreover, when the words "communism" or "communist" occur at all, they are almost always as parts of official names, most frequently those of the Communist Party of the Soviet Union and its section, the Communist Party of Belarus, which are the two most frequently mentioned institutions and organizations. The context of these occurrences suggests that the word "communist" is merely neutral and conventional and does not imply any reflection on the extent to which the Communist Party represented authentic communist ideology. For example, the narrative of the ban of the Communist Party in the newly independent states immediately after the fall of the Soviet Union is connected to the Communist Party of the Soviet Union as possessing a monopoly of power. The event is understood as the termination of a one-party system, not as a ban on the communist ideology the party represented.

The failure of the putsch sped up the fall of the CPSU and CPB. In relation to these events, on 25 August 1991, the Supreme Council, most members of which were communists, passed the resolution "On the temporary stoppage of activity by the CPSS-CPB in the territory of Belarus." (Fomin 80; translation by the authors)

This common feature of Belarusian history textbooks represents an emerging distancing from late Soviet history.

Unlike in Russian textbooks, the inner contradictions between the Communist Party and its satellites are never referred to in the Belarusian ones. Contrary to what might have been expected, key political actors of the period are never characterized as true communists or the opposite. The textbook authors who condemn Gorbachev and, more typically, Ieltsin for "treason," most notably Treshchenok (281, translation by the authors), understand this as treason against the people and their wish to remain Soviet citizens or treason against the Soviet Union itself and its great, although unspecified, historical mission. It is never interpreted as treason against communist ideology as such.

Similarly, the countries mentioned in the context of Soviet history after the Cold War are never characterized as pro- or anti-communist. Communism is assigned the role of a historically specific phenomenon instead of being a source of meta-historical interpretation from a universalist perspective. One reason for this peculiarity lies in the overall structure of the master narrative of contemporary Belarusian historiography. Adherence to communist ideology and its primary importance for the political agenda and everyday life was a characteristic trait of all Soviet historiography that vanished almost completely from the post-Soviet Belarus. Emphasizing the role of communism would result in the construction of an inner continuity between Soviet history and the discontinuous history of the contemporary Republic of Belarus. Suggesting in such a way that the Soviet and post-Soviet periods belong to different narratives, instead of being parts of the same story, is incompatible with the notion of having preserved everything worthy from the Soviet past. What exactly should be evaluated as "worthy" and to what extent it should encompasses communist ideology is not explicated and remains unclear.

The lack of emphasis on communism as an ideology does not mean, however, that the treatment of perestroika in Belarusian history textbooks does not take into account the ideological dimension of the Soviet past. Our analysis shows that the notion of power based on ideology is implied in many textbooks, although this ideology is not presented as communism, nor is it given any other name, despite the ongoing search for the official ideology of the Belarusian state. This discursive construction mostly occurs in textbooks expressing a negative evaluation of perestroika. In this regard, the whole period is characterized as one of social degradation caused by the clash between old and new ideologies and the gradual replacement of the former by the latter. This foundation of past ideology appears to consist of two features.

First, the ideals and aspirations of the Soviet people are implied to be predominantly spiritual. Communism, as the official ideology of the Soviet Union, is evaluated in the Belarusian textbooks not in terms of its economic or political consequences, as in the Moldovan textbooks, but as a thing in itself, in accordance with the popular ethno-nationalist notion of the unique eastern Slavic spirituality (*dukhovnost'*). The free market economy is characterized as inseparable from greed, ruthless egoism, and attaching excessive significance to material possessions:

> In society, there emerged capitalist tendencies, propaganda of enrichment by all means. ... Propaganda of the cult of gain and personal profit appeared, as did violence, which in Soviet times was considered degrading for people and society. (Novik 190–191; translation by the authors)

It is implied that economic liberalization led to this shift from lofty idealism to mundane materialism. Contrary to the case in Russia, the image of anti-communism in Belarusian textbooks is implicit and presented not as a national revival movement in the Soviet periphery, but as a new anti-spiritualism allegedly starting from the center. Interestingly, the spirituality that was supposedly destroyed by perestroika is defined not in and of itself, but negatively, as something contrary to the spirit of liberalism in its classical, early 19th-century sense. The picture of the condemned opponent appears to be much clearer than that of the cause of the struggle. This is characteristic of a nostalgic discourse representing not so much support for any particular ideology, as for a generalized craving for the anti-pragmatic world of ideals as an alternative to the materialist economic reality in which Belarus now finds itself.

This emphasis on spirituality is particularly noteworthy if one considers that communism was, according to its own self-presentation, consequently and uncompromisingly materialist. By its adherents, communism was claimed to be a non-spiritual ideology based on its objective scientific approach (Cherniaev). The quest for spirituality can therefore be seen as a compensatory reaction to economic failure or insufficient success at both the macro-social and individual levels. It can also be seen as a desire to reestablish the "one and only truth" in place of the unusual and inconvenient pluralism of opinions (e.g., Novik 193). Understanding the free market economy in terms of the catchphrase "greed is good" was also predominant in the West in the 1980s, where it prompted reactions akin to the above-noted quest for spirituality (e.g., New Age beliefs, downshifting, and environmentalism). However, in the post-Soviet case, such notions have survived long past their period of universal popularity, finding their way into contemporary textbooks.

Another feature of this discursively constructed Soviet ideology is its collectivism, which is understood in two ways. The alleged spirituality is portrayed as universal, spontaneous, freely emanating from the people, and providing a source of solidarity based on an unquestioned unity of opinions and internalized values. Spirituality in this sense is important not only to give society direction and a sense of meaning, but also as a socially shared field of meanings that holds society together. Collectivism is presented as an end in itself and one of the inalterable components of spirituality. This definition of collectivism runs contrary to the notions of individualism and collectivism in contemporary social sciences, where these are neutral concepts capturing major patterns of orientation. The textbooks present individualist and collectivist societies as absolutes and implicitly relate individualism to a lack of spirituality. Collectivism in general, and particularly the idea that the collective need only display sufficient grandeur to be worthy of theoretical consideration, may be considered close to the original essence of communism.

The discursive construction of communism as the ideology of the Soviet state and society therefore consists of a collectivist pathos combined with an abstract notion of spirituality. Although the period of perestroika is almost universally constructed as traumatic and emotionally engaging, communism does not seem to invoke any sense of emotional attachment. Unlike other parts of the Soviet cultural legacy, whether real or imagined, communism is presented as belonging to the past, not as something that the authors would like to pass on to the next generation.

This lukewarm and detached attitude towards communism is in pronounced contrast to the strong opinions on the fall of the Soviet Union. In Treshchenok's textbook, which openly praises the Soviet Union (271) — we should remember that no textbook presents the Soviet Union or communism as distinctly negative — this glorification rests on the image of the largest state in the world with considerable military power and a longevity lasting several generations.

The Soviet Union is praised not for the truth and historical righteousness of its communist ideology but for its greatness in terms of power. The underlying message is that perestroika and its outcome have produced a sense of powerlessness, but not of moral inferiority, in those who opposed perestroika. The contemporary Republic of Belarus is portrayed as a strong state but, unlike the Soviet Union, it did not require the emergence of an ideological project such as communism. Preserving a sense of continuity between the Soviet and post-Soviet Belarus entails omitting from the narrative of perestroika any analysis of the meanings and transformations of communism.

Representations of Gorbachev in Textbook Chapters on Perestroika

The key feature differentiating narrative from other types of discourse is arguably not events but characters. Moreover, "good narrative" implies a clear hierarchy of characters, particularly the visibility of the protagonist(s) as opposed to secondary characters in the background. In Belarusian history textbooks, however, characters and people are not prominent, and there is a tendency towards general depersonalization (similar to that found in the Ukrainian textbooks). We consider this to be an important peculiarity of Belarusian history-writing. Descriptions of social and economic processes—which indicate a structural approach to history—are usually at the center of the narrative with relatively little attention paid to the people. One would expect the situation to be much the same in the narrative of the period of perestroika, with descriptions of events being featured and little attention paid to people, including to Mikhail Gorbachev, the head of the Soviet Union and one of the leading politicians of this period.

The quantitative content analysis confirms this to a certain extent: the vast majority of people are mentioned only briefly, once or twice as a rule. The only significant exception is Gorbachev, and photos of him are presented in some textbooks, which is highly unusual. Fully 48 percent of all space devoted to personalities is related to Gorbachev, with the two second most frequently mentioned personalities, Boris Ieltsin and Stanislau Shushkevich, receiving much less attention. Taking into account the general depersonalization of the Belarusian historical narrative, this relatively high interest in Gorbachev is unusual and noteworthy. The many mentions of Gorbachev in the texts do not indicate an interest in his personality, and his biography, for example, is presented in only one textbook on world history (Kosmach et al. 127). There are no quotations from his speeches, and the evaluations are mostly of his actions rather than his personal qualities. The evaluations range from positively neutral to skeptical, but without radical extremes, bringing Belarusian history textbooks closer to international academic literature (e.g.,

Oppenhiem 18-23). In Belarusian textbooks, even though his pro-Soviet critics condemn his actions as a "betrayal," he is not portrayed as a traitor as such (Novik and Martsul 382, translation by the authors). His actions are usually discussed, sometimes by emphasizing their "collective" nature, as in references to the "Gorbachev team," a "group of energetic executives" (Koshelev 367, translation by the authors), the "Gorbachev administration" (Bryhadzin et al. 459, translation by the authors), and "new KPSS leaders headed by M. Gorbachov" (KPSS being Communist Party of the Soviet Union) (Chigrinov 432, translation by the authors). It seems that Gorbachev's name is sometimes used to symbolize decisions and actions taken by a certain fraction within the party elite. The importance of his personal services and faults is not emphasized, similar to the view presented in international studies (e.g., Brown 29-68). There is, however, a significant difference between the presentation of Gorbachev in the texts of the school and university textbooks. The style and tone in the school textbooks is more neutral and more objective, while the university textbooks engage in evaluation, mostly negative and sometimes voiced rather strongly. This difference, in turn, reflects a functional difference. The secondary school course is supposed to give the students the necessary primary competence in the mere facts and their general evaluation. University textbooks target a more intellectually engaged audience and are designed to simultaneously develop and restrain critical thinking by providing ready-made examples of the authors' own reasoning. For example, Novik and Martsul' interpret Gorbachev's actions as a betrayal: "Gorbachev's renunciation of the office of the General Secretary of the CPSU and the signing of the decree of the illegal stoppage of CPSU activity ... were ideological and a political betrayal (intentional or unintentional), unparalleled in history" (Novik and Martsul' 382, translation by the authors).

The attitude towards and the evaluation of Gorbachev's actions depends strongly on the general attitude of the particular author(s) towards the entire Soviet project and the collapse of the Soviet Union, authors with a pro-Soviet orientation being much more critical. This goes for mainstream pro-Soviet conservatism expressed in the approval of the Soviet Union and the *"zapadnorussism"* regarding the Soviet Union as the successor of Tsarist Russia (Treshchenok 55-59). Similarities between critique of Gorbachev and critique of perestroika itself are only implied, but not presented directly, partly because the authors' own personalities are projected onto their opinions about the narrated events just as strongly as are Gorbachev's personality traits. For example, some authors criticize Gorbachev's personal qualities and interpret his weaknesses as among the reasons perestroika failed and the Soviet Union collapsed. Sometimes such an evaluation is presented outright, sometimes through comparisons with other significant figures. For example, Treshchenok compares Gorbachev with Alexander Kerensky, the political leader and Prime Minister during the time of the Russian Revolution in 1917:

M. Gorbachev is very similar to the weak-willed chatterbox of the period when

> the Russian Empire collapsed — Alexander Kerensky — but lacking his education and the gloss of an advocate ... Publicity became Gorbachev's only achievement." (Treshchenok 283; translation by the authors).

It is interesting that certain important peculiarities of perestroika (e.g., glasnost) and its realization are closely connected to Gorbachev's personal qualities (cf. Gorbachev 21-23; Grachev 214-233). At the same time, the start of perestroika itself is less connected to his personal intentions, but is described more as an objective and even naturally developing process, deliberate at first, but then rapidly running out of control. In such a way, the description bears resemblance to the "domino principle" identified in the Russian textbooks.

The key element of Gorbachev's political biography is his struggle for power within the Soviet Union and the communist party in general. Gorbachev is presented as an unsuccessful political leader, and a tragicomic one to boot. The narrative style is skeptical: "Gorbachev was full of good intentions, but it was just those intentions that paved the road to hell" (Treshchenok 283, translation by the authors). This description of his actions could well be interpreted as a negative example of political behavior and power struggle, in which possible analogies could be found in Roman (Suetonius) and Renaissance (Machiavelli) traditions.

According to some textbooks, support for Gorbachev's politics of change was considerable in the Communist Party but, contrary to the clichés popularized by official Soviet propaganda, not unanimous: "Gorbachev was supported by the majority of ordinary party members and some representatives of the party establishment" (Kosmach et al. 127, translation by the authors). He failed in his attempts to balance different groups within the Communist Party and the resistance towards his politics increased: "The inconsistency of Gorbachev, who tried to maneuver between the communist-conservatives and communists-liberals, led to the formation of a new radical political movement" (Koshelev 367, translation by the authors). Gorbachev had to maneuver and tried to compromise, which could explain the inconsistency of his actions. Gorbachev's abandonment of his initial position as the Secretary of the Communist Party and the introduction of the institution of the presidency is regarded not as a case of democratization, but as a tactical move in the power struggle within the party. The constant decline of the Party's influence led to the decline of Gorbachev's own political career, despite his personal efforts. Gorbachev's participation in the last period and collapse of the Soviet Union is presented as almost passive. Once again, like the description of the collapse as evolving according to the domino principle in the Russian textbooks, once the process started to unfold it was seen as self-reinforcing.

Gorbachev's main political opposition is personalized in the form of Boris Ieltsin. The conflict between the two is described as embodying the conflict between the powers of the Soviet Union and the powers of the republics, though it is sometimes seen as a more or less personal clash. Boris Ieltsin's qualities are contrasted to those of Gorbachev: "M. Gorbachev's successful rival—B. Ieltsin—did not have any meaningful intentions at all, only a passionate desire for absolute personal power... Unlike Gorbachev, B. Ieltsin did not have a weak will. On the contrary, he was an aggressive and assertive politician" (Treshchenok 283–284, translation by the authors). Gorbachev's personal qualities as a political leader were insignificant, according to the textbooks.

This and other comparisons, such as the previously mentioned comparison with Kerensky, are part of a widespread tradition of comparing Gorbachev with other significant past and present figures, and are significant in narratives about Gorbachev in the textbooks (see Graebner 114–136; Malici 47–84; Matlock 106–129; Shakibi 143–185). It introduces some characteristics of Gorbachev and evaluates his role and actions, but indirectly and mainly negatively, emphasizing the absence of some qualities.

Soviet society is presented as rather heterogeneous, with a few mentions of social groups that are not explicitly defined, such as the occasionally mentioned nomenklatura (bureaucratic establishment/elite), *trudiāshchiesiā* (working people), and *intelligentsiiā* (intellectuals) (Novik 187). The nomenklatura and intellectuals are among the most frequently mentioned groups, and they are described rather critically. The nomenklatura are criticized by both pro-national and pro-Soviet authors: "Party leaders were reborn and, under pseudo-democratic hype, finally retrained ... as advocates of the privatization of commonly created property. Another part of the nomenklatura comprised dogmatic functionaries with no historical perspective... There were no people of the future among them" (Treshchenok 282, translation by the authors). It is possible to compare this critique to the traditional Russian criticism of intellectuals, from the famous collection of essays entitled *Vekhi* (Berdiāev 6–36) to modern works (Gudkov and Dubin 12–27; Kustarev 8–32), as a reactionary and anti-social force, as opposed to the positive evaluation of the intellectual's role in Central Europe (Eyal and Szelenyi 29–56), and to the anti-Soviet tradition of research into the nomenklatura (Voslensky 356–444) as a new exploitative group (which differs from internal Soviet criticism of its particular representatives). The style of description and critical analysis is rather similar in both cases.

To sum up, Mikhail Gorbachev is the most frequently mentioned person, not only among politicians, but among all other famous Soviet people of this period. At the same time, he is not presented as a great historical actor shaping the course of history. Rather, it is his position as the political leader of a team, which was the initiator of the transformation, that is in focus, as is the Communist Party as the leading political power in the country and the Soviet Union as a great power with a number of significant internal problems.

Representations of the Chernobyl Disaster

The Chernobyl disaster was undoubtedly one of the most significant events in the Soviet history of the perestroika period, in view of both its immediately recognized uniqueness and its consequences. Besides, unlike any other event of the period, this catastrophe mostly affected Belarusian territory. This fact, recognized worldwide, and primarily by the Belarusians themselves, makes the Chernobyl disaster one of the few events of the Soviet epoch specifically belonging to Belarusian history without the typically shared and more or less evenly distributed relevance to all former Soviet republics. Moreover, the causes of this disaster and the event itself belong to the Soviet Union and are results of decisions made by the central government, while the long-term consequences have had to be endured by an independent Belarus alone. In this sense, the Chernobyl disaster plays a unique role in Belarusian history in creating both continuity and discontinuity between the Soviet and post-Soviet periods. Within the general narrative framework, the Chernobyl disaster would be expected to play the role of a culmination, the key event in the chain of both causes and effects.

At the level of mere content, however, the Chernobyl disaster is given much less coverage than would be expected. The event is mentioned in only one of all the school history textbooks currently in use in Belarus, and only in the form of a brief factual report stressing its consequences and making no suggestions as to the possible causes: "Resettlement, treatment, the improvement of people's health, and the creation of the proper conditions for working and living in the affected territory are still problems for the national economy even today" (Sharova 274, translation by the authors). The emphasis is on the past, not the present, and the problem is described as an after-effect, not as a pertinent current issue.

University textbooks present more variety both in the types of content considered relevant to the Chernobyl disaster and in their contexts. Many textbooks convey an impression of the event's significance without sacrificing the general tone of objectivity by reporting facts and figures without making generalizations:

> The research conducted in July identified 11 districts in the Homel' region and five in the Mahilioŭ region affected with cesium-137. The overall territory with a density of 15 ki/km² amounted to 5568 km². In that territory, there were 428 settlements with a [combined] population of over 100,000 inhabitants." (Kastsiŭk 577; translation by the authors).

Such material may confuse students, because the reason for learning it is unclear, and a more analytical reading requires expert knowledge not possessed by most of the target audience. The Chernobyl disaster is never mentioned as an internal historical event, but figures solely in the sections on Belarus in global politics. The disaster is presented as a point of diplomatic negotiation, and Belarus's international partners in this process, both countries and institutions, are evaluated depending on their readiness to recognize the sufferings of Belarusians and offer financial help to overcome the consequences of the catastrophe:

> During a session of the UN General Assembly, certain influential Western countries, in order to get rid of the Chernobyl problem, proposed transferring it from the international to the regional level. In this case, Belarus would have to solve the problem on its own. It would be deprived of help from the world community. (Novik and Martsul' 445; translation by the authors).

In this way, the Chernobyl disaster is presented only in terms of its consequences, not the occurrence itself, and is moved outside the Soviet history of Belarus.

However, in the second, revised edition of this textbook, the contextualization undergoes a drastic change. The Chernobyl disaster is addressed in the general text about perestroika, which is no longer divided into political, economic, and cultural sections, and is presented among perestroika's various drawbacks. Moreover, from a unique catastrophe of worldwide significance, the event is re-contextualized as one of many disasters of comparable significance. It is narrated in a paragraph that comes after one dedicated to the anti-alcohol campaign and is given approximately half the coverage. The main emphasis is shifted from the event's long-term consequences for the Republic of Belarus to its immediate and indirect impact on the Soviet Union. The necessity to sacrifice a large part of the budget to coping with the catastrophe is evaluated as an additional factor worsening the economic situation. The implication in the broader context of the chapter on perestroika in this textbook is that, at least to some extent, the Soviet Union's complicated economic situation was due not to ineffective economic policy or even fundamentally wrong underlying assumptions, but to random occurrences, such as an explosion at a nuclear power station. The underlying reason for this minimal and spotty coverage of the Chernobyl disaster lies in the difficulties arising from its relationship with perestroika.

Perestroika may refer to: 1) the policy that was originally proclaimed; 2) its implementation, including unintended or foreseen but undeclared consequences; and 3) the period as such and everything that occurred when the policy was being discussed and implemented. In the third sense, the Chernobyl disaster clearly constitutes part of the perestroika narrative, but this interpretation adds little to our understanding of either Chernobyl or perestroika. The other two options may place the catastrophe within the narrative sequence of reforms directly related to perestroika, or else present it as an outcome of earlier periods of Soviet history (cf. Kordonskiĭ 44–46). The latter option, which is omnipresent in Ukrainian textbooks, would lay the responsibility on the Soviet regime, while the former option sees the policy of perestroika as having eventually led to the termination of the Soviet era (Sedaitis and Butterfield 24–39).

Interestingly, neither mode of narrative is represented in Belarusian history textbooks. Instead, we find a narrative configuration that is not obvious, in which the Chernobyl disaster is related to perestroika not as its outcome, but as its precursor, and not literally, but symbolically as a bad omen of a generally disastrous plan:

> The ill omen at the start of perestroika was the catastrophic disaster at the Chernobyl nuclear power station in Ukraine on 26 April 1986. ... The physical and moral health of the nation received a tremendous blow, the consequences of which have been poorly coped with and will have a prolonged impact on later generations. The collapse of the Soviet Union, in fact, left the Republic alone with this calamity, which imposed an enormous burden on its economy. (Treshchenok 279; translation by the authors).

This quotation shows that the Chernobyl disaster is endowed with a variety of meanings in Belarusian university textbooks, but does not yet occupy a fixed place in the shared narrative of perestroika in Belarus.

The fact that the Chernobyl disaster is not easily positioned in the historical narrative of perestroika in Belarus can be further explained with regard to the two hidden power relationships behind the issue. First, in the late 1980s, almost immediately after the event, it had become, together with the uncovering of the mass graves of the victims of Stalinism near Minsk, the second shared emblem of anti-Soviet and nationalist sentiments. Leaders of the Belarusian Popular Front, the main opposition force of the period, almost immediately attributed both direct and symbolic responsibility for the event to the central government (Abdelal 127–149). Unlike other afflictions of Belarus under the Soviet regime lamented by nationalists, the Chernobyl disaster affected everyone regardless of his or her political views and, more importantly, was perceived as such, giving the opposition a powerful tool for influencing public opinion. Unsurprisingly, long after the fall of the Soviet Union, the main annual mass demonstrations of the opposition articulated the "The Chernobyl Way" message and were conducted on the anniversary of the catastrophe. As such, the whole Chernobyl issue, regardless of its interpretation, was appropriated in the Belarusian context by the opposition political discourse, so that giving it more than absolutely necessary coverage in officially approved textbooks would be the symbolic equivalent of inviting opponents to one's own ground and decreasing one's own sphere of control.

The second reason for the paucity of coverage of the Chernobyl disaster in Belarusian textbooks lies in its being at once biological and sociopolitical. The significant part of the discursively constructed and shared meaning of the Chernobyl disaster lies in switching the boundary between nature and society in terms of causes, consequences, and underlying reasons, employing the whole range of discursive instruments of biopolitics. For example, in a university textbook written in the early 1990s, when the short-lived popularity of ethnic nationalism had peaked in Belarus, the chapter dedicated to the issue bears a telling title: "Chernobyl as a Threat to the Gene Pool of the Belarusian People." This claim is further developed in the main body of the text:

> The citizens of the republic of Belarus live and work under strenuous and even extreme conditions caused by the Chernobyl disaster. The gene pool of the Belarusian nation is under the threat of death. (Kastsiūk et al. 445; translation by the authors).

Equating the people with the nation and presupposing the existence of a common and nationally unique gene pool are the two pivotal indicators of the biological version of primordialism. However, the chapter itself does not elaborate on these views, but instead presents the usual facts and figures without consistently generalizing on their basis. This suggests that the primordial discourse implying the biological turn of politics was imported into the Belarusian cultural space from ethno-nationalist movements in neighboring states, such as Lithuania and Ukraine. In the case of Chernobyl, this means that the biological consequences of radiation were not politicized in the mass consciousness as a symbolic or literal contamination of the national "body politic."

To sum up, the Chernobyl disaster, instead of having one obvious and shared representation, is endowed in Belarusian textbooks with a variety of meanings: as a weakness of perestroika; as a complication outside any government's reasonable control; as a non-obvious sign of the strength of the state, for example, its ability to cope with the consequences of the disaster and bear the costs; and as illustrating the vicious nature of the Soviet state (the last interpretation is found in Kastsiūk 577). None of these interpretations allows the Chernobyl disaster to be interpreted as a milestone in the gradual weakening of the Soviet Union that resulted in its fall. As in narrating other thematic series of events in the period, the reluctance to attribute the fall of the Soviet Union to its own internal logic disrupts the overall consistency and continuity required of a rhetorically convincing "good narrative." The inability to place an event within a narrative chain of causes and effects indicates the break of a narrative instead of its supposed culmination (Dudchik and Fabrykant 65–78). This may be indirect evidence that the neutral and fragmentary representations of the Chernobyl disaster in the Belarusian history textbooks signal a fresh and all too recent cultural trauma that has not yet become part of past history. Despite the chronological point of its occurrence, the Chernobyl disaster belongs to the present in the Belarusian collective memory, and its reintegration into the grand narrative of national history, and especially its relationship to the other trauma, the fall of the Soviet Union, is to be determined only in retrospect.

Conclusions

In this chapter, we have analyzed the ongoing construction of the Belarusian historical narrative in chapters of contemporary Belarusian history textbooks covering the period of perestroika. This thematic focus has proven to be particularly relevant to the Belarusian case for two reasons. In Belarus, as in some of the other post-Soviet states, perestroika marks an intermission between the Soviet past and the post-Soviet present. As such, this period is currently in the process of being moved out of the multiple and discordant memories of the past and being cast as a collectively shared narrative. Textbooks provide relevant sources illustrating how this emerging part of the national historical narrative is constructed and transmitted. Moreover, perestroika initiated the process that led to the collapse of the Soviet Union, which resulted in the emergence of the independent Republic of Belarus. However, much of the ideology of the Belarusian state even today rests on emphasizing the continuity between the Soviet Union and post-Soviet Belarus. This makes the period of perestroika an ambiguous subject to be balanced between the alleged continuity and the apparent discontinuity that characterize the interpretations.

The textbooks do not present a shared and consolidated view of the past, but a plethora of emergent opinions and rhetorical gestures. The prevailing motif is one of ambivalence. On the surface, the Soviet past appears worthy not merely of passive nostalgia, but of acute regret and a search for causes (sometimes interpreted as not obvious, deeply hidden, and still in need of explanation), even for those personally responsible for the Soviet collapse. This ambivalence was evident in the previously analyzed cases. Yet the communist ideology (with its terminology, explanatory schemes, etc.), considered the backbone and raison d'être of the Soviet state, gets at best lukewarm approval from most textbook authors, overlaid with indifference. On one hand, Gorbachev is portrayed as a weak and irresponsible person unable to cope with the challenges of the epoch. On the other hand, it is precisely his weakness that inspires interest in him and makes him into an antihero and the only distinct personality of the whole period. The Chernobyl disaster is granted the role of a key and, in some textbooks, even archetypal event of the whole perestroika period, with special relevance to Belarus. The Chernobyl catastrophe is given relatively little coverage, however, and the coverage that is given offers very little specific factual detail. Nationalists are cast as the villains of the piece—ruthlessly rational and the purposefully destructive enemies of all things Soviet. Nationalists' personalities, however, contrary to the "weak" Gorbachev, do not attract the authors' interest and appear as a faceless, abstract force, and even the ideology of nationalism is left unexplained. The ambivalence underlying these contradictions is evident in the authors' attitude towards perestroika as a finished period that is nevertheless profoundly relevant to the present, not only in terms of its consequences, but also in its not yet comprehensible causes. This hesitation, unparalleled in the other country cases, reflects the dominant Belarusian perception of the Soviet past as something that is over and cannot return, but ought to be somehow selectively preserved (in a rather abstract and rhetorical way, without elaborated specification) alongside new historical realities.

This post-Soviet mixture of old and new is frequently called a "transition," which implies a progressive movement in a certain direction, regardless of whether such a movement is actually discernible. We suggest that the representations of perestroika in Belarusian history textbooks serve the purpose of *inventing* a transition narrative as a means of passing over controversies as to whether there is continuity or discontinuity between the Soviet past and the post-Soviet present. The concept of the "invention of transition" explains the problematic relations between contemporary Belarus and its Soviet past. Officially, the Soviet period is represented as important and even formative for Belarusian nation-building. According to the official position, Belarus, more than any other post-Soviet state, preserves all the positive features of the Soviet Union, whatever they might include. At the same time, perestroika and the collapse of the Soviet Union initiated and even caused contemporary Belarusian statehood and, soon afterwards, its current political regime. The regime tends to treat the end of the Soviet epoch and the emergence of an independent Belarus as the proverbial half-empty and half-full glass, respectively.

To maintain the uneasy balance between the two conflicting visions of the same glass, the government monitors popular ideas of the change and offers its own version of its direction and concrete manifestations. We suggest that this coping strategy, i.e., channeling popular notions about social change, should be called the "invention of transition," which recalls Hobsbawm and

Ranger's famous "invention of tradition" (1–14), in which governments feed carefully constructed manifestations of national identity to the masses. The allusion to this concept points to the essential struggle to restore the formal narrative structure of historicity despite the unyielding and controversial content (including different ideological views and interpretations) of the narrative and its nebulous context with its high dependence on ongoing politics and power relations.

The Belarusian textbook chapters on perestroika yield results that were not easily foreseen even when an insider's perspective is combined with academically shared knowledge of the relevant context. The richness and diversity of the primary data and their interpretations, as well as the qualitative methodology of the study, do not encourage overly broad generalizations. Some conclusions, however, follow from the pertinent motifs of our analysis.

First, the official position on perestroika reflected in the textbooks is not nearly as uniform as one would expect, considering the public image of the Belarusian political regime. The diversity of opinions, discursive techniques, and overall narrative structures is apparent even between authors who are ideologically very similar regarding other matters. This comparative diversity in modes of expression, so different from the strictly codified way of speaking cemented by Soviet Marxist-Leninist dogma, is not easily explained away by individual psychological factors, nor can it be subdivided into clearly delineated sets of discursive constructions. Instead of a pro-Soviet and an anti-Soviet discourse, textbooks place the representation of perestroika within an unstructured field of interactions and merge various discourses. This discursive configuration reflects the open, flexible character of both Belarusian ideology and the underlying discussion of national identity issues. There is a need to react to changes in the national agenda and to imbibe newly popular ideas from abroad, mainly from post-Soviet Russia (e.g., conspiracy theories and neo-Eurasianism). This reflects the need for flexibility in generating acceptable interpretations, which is much stronger than the need to direct the interpretation towards the desired goal that is supposedly implied in the very definition of transition.

Second, the narrative of perestroika in Belarusian textbooks resembles a story at least as much as it does a history. The reasons for this story-making include the depth of the social trauma caused by the dissolution of the internalized Soviet cultural environment as well as the still open, unresolved character of many issues of the perestroika period. The narrative of perestroika in textbooks is addressed to those who were born too late to be its eyewitnesses, but constructed from within, as if the events were still being re-experienced in real time. The historical periodization in most textbooks dates the beginning of the contemporary period in Belarusian history not from the gaining of independence, but from the start of perestroika, which is presented both as an archetypal primordial beginning of history and as something all too recent in the authors' individual memories. From the unexpected diversity detected in Belarusian textbooks, one might conclude that the general idea giving sense to the national narrative is not past, but present oriented. Therefore the representations of perestroika in Belarusian history textbooks do not merely reflect a society in transition, but exemplify the discursive invention of transition as such.

Annex 1. School Textbooks in Belarus

Novik, Evgeniĭ K., editor. *Istoriiā Belarusi XIX-nachalo XXI в. [History of Belarus, XIX-beg. of XXI cent.].* Minsk, BSU, 2009.

The process of perestroika is described in a special five-page section. The narrator shows his skepticism about the described events and actions (e.g., through using scare quotation marks), which are mainly evaluated negatively. Perestroika is described as a result of objective (i.e., economic, political, and social) necessity. The politics of perestroika (as an anti-Soviet phenomenon) is mainly described in terms of a struggle for political power. The movement for Belarusian national revival is mainly described negatively and in terms of a struggle for political power.

Fomin, Vitaliĭ M., editor. *Istoriiā Belarusi 1945–2005 [History of Belarus 1945–2005, in Russian].* Minsk, BSU, 2006.

The process of perestroika is described in a special six-page section. The narrative tone is neutral. Perestroika is described as a difficult processes that led to crisis but had positive results. It is mainly the political process that is described. Democratization and its results (i.e., glasnost—the appearance of new political parties and political opposition) are described. The section presents a number of concepts, tables, and figures.

Koshelev, Vladimir, editor. *Vsemirnaiā istoriiā, XIX – nachalo XXI в. [World History, XIX-beg. of XXI cent.].* Minsk, BSU, 2009.

The process of perestroika is described in part of a section entitled "The Political Reformation of SU" (three pages). The narrator shows his skepticism about the described events and actions (e.g., through using scare quotation marks). Perestroika is described as a voluntarily started process that led to a struggle between Soviets and the party, and between the republics and the center. Special attention is paid to the national movement and fronts. Of the personalities, only that of Gorbachev (characterized mainly negatively) is presented.

Kosmach, Gennadiĭ A., Vladimir S. Koshelev, Marina A. Krasnova, , editors. *Vsemirnaiā istoriiā Noveĭshego vremeni 1945–2005 [World History of Modernity 1945–2005]*. Minsk, BSU, 2006.

The process of perestroika is described in a special six-page section. The narrative tone is neutral. Perestroika is described as a progressive and dramatic result of objective necessity, with related mistakes presented as resulting from the absence of adequate planning. The concepts of glasnost, new political thinking, and economic reform are used. Changes in the sphere of consciousness and culture are described. The Chernobyl catastrophe is described as a tragedy. Gorbachev's personality (characterized mainly negatively) is presented.

Kovkel', Ivan, and Edmund I︠A︡rmusik. *Istoriiā Belarusi s drevneĭshikh vremen do nashego vremeni [History of Belarus from Ancient Times to Our Own]*. Minsk, Aversev, 2010.

The process of perestroika is described in a four-page part of a section entitled "Social, Economic, and Political Development of Belarus, 1980–90." The narrative is rather neutral in tone. Perestroika is described as a result of objective (mainly economic) necessity. Its results are evaluated as mainly negative. It is mainly economic reforms that are analyzed. The Chernobyl catastrophe and its negative consequences for the Belarusian economy are described.

Sharova, Nataliiā. *Istoriiā Belparusi opornye konspekty dliā podgotovki k tsentralizovannomu testirovaniiū [History of Belarus: Synopsis for Preparation for Testing]*. Minsk, Aversev, 2010.

The process of perestroika is described in a special six-page section. The narrative tone is neutral. Perestroika is described as a result of objective (mainly economic) necessity. The section includes a number of concepts, tables, and figures. It is mainly economic and political reforms that are analyzed. The Chernobyl catastrophe and its negative concequences for the Belarusian economy are described.

Stashkevich, Nikolaĭ S., Georgiĭ IA. Golenchenko, Ivan I. Bogdanovich. *Istoriiā Belarusi. Posobie dliā podgotovki k tsēntralizovannomu testirovaniiū* [*History of Belarus: Workbook for Preparation for Centralized Testing*]. Minsk, Aversev, 20122.

The textbook contains a seven-page chapter dedicated to perestroika and entitled "BSSR in the Second Half of the 1980s: Perestroika Policy and its Peculiarities in BSSR." Perestroika is evaluated as an economic necessity in view of the preceding crisis of the centralized system of regulation, which, according to the authors, could no longer function, even though no feasible alternatives had been developed in sufficient detail. The political dimension of perestroika is assessed as more successful, especially because of glasnost, which is acclaimed as its major achievement. BSSR is characterized as one of the most conservative and reform-resistant Soviet republics.

Purysheva, Nataliiā, and Mikhail Starovoĭtov. *Istoriiā Belarusi. Shkol'nyĭ kurs v kratkom izlozhenii.* [*History of Belarus: School Course in Brief*]. Minsk, Tetra-Systems, 2012.

The chapter on perestroika does not mention its subject in the title, "BSSR in the Second Half of the 1980s." Perestroika is presented as something initiated by Gorbachev, with no apparent reasons explained. The content of the chapter is mainly factual, augmented with a sparse, mildly negative evaluation of perestroika (mainly its outcomes, not aims). Interestingly, the Belarusian National Front is described as an anti-Soviet and anti-state movement aimed at creating an independent Belarus "similar to European democracies, but with some national specificity.

Annex 2. University Textbooks in Belarus

Kastsiūk, Mikhail P., Ilaryion M. Ignatsenka, Uladzimir I. Vyshynski, editors. *Narysy historyi Belarusi, ch. 2* [*Essays on the History of Belarus, vol. 2*]. Minsk, Belarus, 1995.

This textbook was written by a group of historians from the Institute of History of the Belarusian National Academy of Sciences, and allegedly presents an early, moderately nationalist version of Belarusian history. The textbook contains a chapter entitled "The Difficult Path towards Radical Transformation," which is subdivided into the following sections: 1) "Economic crisis"; 2) "The Chernobyl Disaster is a Threat to the Gene Pool of the Belarusian People"; 3) "Decline of the Social Sphere"; 4) "Problems of Democratization"; 5) "On the Way to National Cultural Revival"; and 6) "Towards State Sovereignty." Perestroika is presented as the objectively inevitable collapse of an ineffective system of government, with the main emphasis on the economic and social spheres rather than on politics. The Soviet state is harshly criticized, while that of the then newly independent Belarus is moderately praised, as are some international organizations. The text contains very few dates of historical events and figures, but presents many statistical data. A special focus on Belarus' unique experience of perestroika is presented wherever possible, especially concerning the Chernobyl disaster.

Novik, IAŭhen K., and Henadz' S. Martsul', editors. *Historyiā Belarusi [History of Belarus, vol. 2. February 1917–1997]*. In Belarusian. Minsk, Universitetskae, 1998.

This textbook is edited by the administratively most influential historian of contemporary Belarus and reflects the official version of Belarusian history. The textbook contains the chapter "Belarus in the Period of Reformation: Socioeconomic, Political, and Cultural Development: International Relations; Belarusian Diaspora (1985–1997)." The last period in the history of Belarus is presented as lasting from the start of perestroika to the present, and this presentation is retained in the two subsequent editions of this textbook (from 2003 and 2007). Therefore, it is perestroika, not the appearance of the independent Republic of Belarus, that is considered the benchmark event. Part 1 of the last chapter is entitled "Sociopolitical Life: Formation of a Multiparty System" and contains the following sections: 1) "The Policy of Perestroika and Its Essence: The Appearance and Activity of Political Opposition"; 2) "Crisis of the One-party Soviet System: Causes, Essence, Results; Fall of the Soviet Union; Declaration of

Independence of the Republic of Belarus"; and 3) "Creation and Activity of Political Parties and Social Movements: Formation of a Multiparty System." Perestroika is presented as a well-intentioned but incompetently executed set of reforms, which eventually destroyed what it was meant to improve. The main emphasis is on political events, which are depicted from within, using the language of the period, especially the Cold War stance and apologetics of the Communist Party. It is important to analyze all the editions, particularly the differences between the corresponding chapters in the first and two subsequent editions. In the second and third editions, to mention only a few differences, the Cold War discourse gives place to contemporary anti-globalism in its neo-Eurasionist version; the Belarusian nationalist movements and parties and the diaspora are paid much less attention, and an attempt to present several alternative evaluations of perestroika is made. In all three editions, the common Soviet experience dominates specifically Belarusian events. For example, in the second and third editions, the Chernobyl disaster is presented as yet another complication, mainly due to the resulting massive state financial expenditure, and is given three time less coverage than the anti-alcohol campaign, while in the first edition, the Chernobyl disaster is not mentioned at all.

Chigrinov, Petr G. *Istoriiā Belarusi [History of Belarus]*. In Russian. Minsk, Polymiā, 2001.

This textbook is written for those preparing for the university entrance examination and gives an impression of attempting to reconcile the first and second sources in this list. The chapter entitled "Change of Political and Socioeconomic Course: Declaration and Formation of the Sovereign State" contains a section on perestroika entitled "Political and Socioeconomic Crisis," and a section on independent Belarus entitled "State Sovereignty and Democratization of the Political System." The period "from 1985 to the present" is preserved, but is clearly subdivided between the late-Soviet and post-Soviet subperiods. The section on perestroika attempts to pay equal attention to

THE INVENTION OF TRANSITION 133

politics, economics, and the social sphere, with a self-imposed neutrality of tone. The perestroika period is presented as a tragic time of crisis in all spheres, from the environment to economics, ideology, and institutions.

Bryhadzin, Piotr I., Uladzimir F. Ladyseŭ, Piotr I. Ziālinski, *Historyiā Belarusi, ch. 2, 19-20 st. [History of Belarus, vol. 2: "19th–20th Centuries].* Minsk, Belarusian State University, 2002.

This textbook contains a chapter entitled "Belarus on the Way to Systemic Transformations" with two sections: 1) "Gaining Independence" and 2) "The Economics, Politics, and Culture of Belarus: Tendencies of Development." This textbook emphasizes specifically Belarusian events and the Belarusian aspects of the common Soviet experience. Perestroika is described exclusively as a policy of democratization, ignoring other realities of the period. Special attention is paid to de-Stalinization and rehabilitation. Democratization is presented as an inevitable and natural process, which was initiated by the government without any clear vision, but apparently because of some objective laws of history.

Treshchenok, IAkov. *Istoriiā Belarusi, vol. 2, [History of Belarus, vol. 2].* Mogilev, Mogilev State University, 2005.

The textbook contains a chapter entitled "The Growing Crisis of the Soviet System: The Fall of the Soviet Union and the Declaration of the Sovereign Republic of Belarus; Systematic Review of Key Events (1953-1991)." The ongoing period of Belarusian history is dated from the death of Stalin, who is presented as a harsh but at least temporarily efficient "great ruler," and contrasted with his unworthy and incompetent successors. The 1960s and 1980s are considered two very similar periods of continually deepening crisis in all spheres, but without a clear demarcation between economics, politics, and ideology or an obvious criterion of crisis. The Chernobyl disaster is called an ill omen for perestroika as a whole. Unlike in other textbooks, the key role in history is attributed to "great people" (e.g., the collapse of the Soviet Union is attributed exclusively to the lack of political will among key official figures of the time) rather than to objective historical laws or specific conditions.

Chigrinov, Petr G. *Ocherki istorii Bielarusi [Essays on the History of Belarus]*. In Russian. Minsk, Vyshėĭshaia̐ shkola, 2007.

This textbook is very similar to the previous source by the same author. In particular, the title of the chapter on perestroika and its sections are roughly the same. However, this textbook is addressed not to potential, but to actual undergraduate students. Consequently, the political section contains less specific and especially less quantitative information and more evaluations, while the socioeconomic and ecological sections remain mainly the same as before. Unlike Chigrinov's previous textbook and most others, this textbook appears to merge perestroika and the contemporary period, with the "balanced and cautious" policy of the Belarusian president contrasted with the tumultuous and unstable atmosphere of the period described in the text.

Novik, Yaŭhen K., Ihar L. Kachalau, Natalya Ya. Novik, *Historyia̐ Belarusi: ad starazhytnykh chasoŭ – pa 2008 g. [History of Belarus: From Ancient Times to 2008]*. Edited by Yaŭhen Novik, Minsk, Vyshėĭshaia̐ shkola, 2009.

This textbook is a significantly shortened version of the earlier work by Novik, which represents the essence of official history in contemporary Belarus. It is particularly important because comparing it with the previous work reveals the parts of the original version that the authors consider the most important and that deserve to be preserved when half of the material is excluded. The main preliminary conclusion of such a comparison is that all parts of the chapter on perestroika have been shortened almost equally, preserving the original proportions of coverage given to various aspects, although one would expect priority to be given to names, dates, and figures over interpretation and evaluation. This textbook may be viewed as an example of the stabilization and dissemination of the official grand narrative of Belarusian history.

Kastsiuk, Michail, editor. *Historyia͡ Belarusi, vol. 6: Belaru's, 1996–2009 [History of Belarus, vol. 6: Belarus, 1996–2009]*. In Belarusian. Minsk: Sovremennai͡a shkola, Ekoperspektiva, 2011.

This textbook was written by roughly the same group of authors and edited by the same person as was the first university textbook in this list, but differs from it in many ways. Unlike the other sources, this textbook does not include perestroika in the ongoing historical period. Instead, it contains a chapter entitled "The Belarusian Socialist Soviet Republic During the Growing Crisis and Termination of the Soviet System (1971–1985)," with a final part "Belarusian Society in Times of Perestroika" with the following sections: "Economic Vector of Modernization"; 2) "Start of Political Reforms: Democratization Processes"; and 3) "Catastrophe at the Chernobyl Nuclear Power Station and its Impact on Economics, the Social Sphere, and Public Morale." The text contains many dates and figures and, especially in its first part, abounds in the portrayal of personalities, but offers very little overt interpretation and evaluation. Key events are presented from within in terms of their immediate effects, but not their overall significance. Political life in the Soviet Union of the perestroika period is presented as a set of rivalries among party officials, with no preference expressed, and mechanisms are described expertly and in detail.

Liantsėvich, Vol'ha. *Historyia͡ Belarusi [History of Belarus]*. Minsk, MIK Edition, 2012.

The material on perestroika is part of a large chapter covering half a century of Belarusian Soviet history and entitled "Soviet Belarus: Achievements and Problems of the Constructive Labor of the People (1945–1991)." Perestroika is presented as a set of mechanisms initiated in response to objective causes, but never achieving its initial goals. The whole process of relating perestroika to its prerequisites and consequences is narrated in a determinist manner.

Bokhan, IUriĭ N., Natal'ia̐ I. Poletaeva. *Istoriiā Belarusi v kontekste mirovykh tsivilizatsiĭ [History of Belarus in the Context of World Civilizations]*. In Russian. Minsk, Ekoperspektiva, 2011.

The chapter on perestroika is entitled "Attempts at Economic and Political Modernization of the Soviet Union and the BSSR in the Years of Perestroika (the Second Half of the 1980s)," making it the only Belarusian textbook that views perestroika in terms of modernization theory. Perestroika is characterized as radical, but somewhat inconsequential; in particular, its economic side is criticized for the remnants of centralized planning. Also, it is the only Belarusian textbook presenting de-Stalinization as the major achievement of perestroika.

Moldova: Perestroika between Russia, Romania, and "Moldovan-ness"

Diana Bencheci and Valerii Mosneagu

Teaching History in Moldova

The teaching of history in Moldovan schools revolves around two courses: Romanian history and world history. Two hours per week are devoted to the subject of history in grades 5-9 and three per week in grades 10-12 in secondary schools of the humanities. Universities accredited by the Ministry of Education teach history only in the faculties of history. Separate chapters are devoted to perestroika in contemporary Moldovan history textbooks, and an overall observation is that these textbooks have constituted a battlefield over identity and belonging, and the battle is far from settled. The textbooks analyzed here convey an ongoing struggle between emphasizing Moldova as a Romanian territory, underlining its Russian heritage, and pointing out a unique Moldovan identity. At times, this struggle has reached into government, specifically, the Ministry of Education, illustrating the political importance of the interpretation of history for contemporary Moldova.

Fifteen school textbooks in Romanian and world history and 13 university textbooks form the material on which this chapter is based (see Annexes 1 and 2). One of the most used world history textbooks was written by Anatol Petrencu, and it has appeared in several editions since 1995, the latest one considered here being from 2011. Petrencu is one of the most influential historians in Moldova, and has served as chair of the Association of Historians of Moldova. He is also a politician and an outspoken critic of the Communist decades in Moldova. The textbooks by the political scientist Sergiu Nazaria constitute alternatives to the world history textbooks by Petrencu. In them, perestroika is not developed as a specific topic, but can be indirectly inferred from references to the phenomenon of "opening," to the breakdown of the USSR's international relations, and to the prospects for the development of a multipolar world in the 21st century.

The Romanian history textbooks have authors with both Moldovan and Romanian backgrounds. The Moldovan historians Boris Vizer, Anton Moraru, Ion Șișcanu, and Emil and Demir Dragnev are represented, as is well-known Romanian historian Ioan Scurtu. In the school textbook edited by Moldovan historian Nicolae Enciu, which has also been published in more than one edition, only a sub-section is dedicated to perestroika, and it refers to the effects of perestroika on the political situation in Romania and to the conditions that led to revolution. All these authors propose a general vision of perestroika as a process generated from the evolution of a totalitarian regime.

The university textbooks employ a wider variety of approaches, and many of them are not textbooks but rather analytical monographs. One is by French historian and Soviet expert Nicolas Werth, who uses a set of research methods that makes the historical facts come alive. He claims that the failure of "Gorbachev's perestroika" cannot be understood without systematically considering the determinants of the decades of Stalinism that preceded the perestroika period. The book by Constantin Ion, entitled *Bessarabia under Soviet Conquest from Stalin to Gorbachov*, focuses on important historical events in the territory of contemporary Moldova. The author dedicates a special section to perestroika, entitled "Romanians and Perestroika." Certain concepts used take on dual meanings. For example, "Romanian" is identified with "Bessarabian," and the discourse of "national revival" and "national freedom" is included in the chapter "National Resurrection in Bessarabia: The Role of the Romanian Revolution and the Integration Process" (Ion 176).

Another book used at the university level is by yet another French historian, Stephane Courtois who like Werth is well known for his work on communism. Courtois presents perestroika as a well-intentioned set of reforms of political, economic, and social life. Concepts such as "popular democracy explosion," "European communist domino," and the "implosion of the Soviet Union" are the result of a wide-ranging description of the historical events that preceded perestroika (Courtois 680).

The subject of perestroika can be taught within the world history course, but not in the "national" history course, which is devoted to the history of the Romanians. The school history textbooks certified by the Ministry of Education often just formally and briefly mention perestroika and the issues that determined it, describing Mikhail Gorbachev as the political leader who launched the process. Although perestroika is not given a separate chapter in any of the world or Romanian history school textbooks, these books still contain a number of exercises and questions about the topic.

Reinterpreting Moldova in Light of Perestroika

How Moldova was incorporated into the Soviet Union in comparison with the other former Soviet republics has become part of the narrative of the causes of perestroika in many of the textbooks analyzed here. Formed in 1922, the Soviet Union comprised Russia, Ukraine, Belarus, and the Trans-Caucasian Federation. Whereas Soviet historiographies avoid going into the various ways in which these territories, including Moldovan territories, were integrated, the Moldovan textbooks depict the process in critical terms. The integration process was determined by the division of spheres of influence between Nazi Germany and the Soviet Union through the secret protocols of the 1939 non-aggression agreement called the Molotov–Ribbentrop Pact. Annexation of Moldovan territory by the Soviet Union was one result of the Pact. The incorporation of Bessarabia (Moldova) into the Soviet Union took place in a specific manner. The annexation of the Baltic States in 1940 was officially justified in terms of security, whereas in the case of Poland, whose eastern territories (among them Galicia) were incorporated into Ukraine, concerns and motivations were articulated in terms of "ethnic brotherhood." In Romania's case, the justification for Bessarabia's return to the fold was instead based on its being illegally occupied territory. It should be noted that the Soviet Union never recognized Bessarabia's voluntary entry into Romania.

In the school textbooks, the Molotov-Ribbentrop Pact is mentioned in relation to Soviet history of the late 1980s, and described in a neutral tone. The fact that the Soviet Union intended to reconquer the area that was once the Russian Empire and was lost in the collapse in 1917 is not emphasized. In contrast to the Baltic States, Bessarabia was never an independent state, but rather part of the Romanian Kingdom. Its population was undergoing the difficult process of integration into the Romanian sociopolitical, economic, cultural, religious, and linguistic milieu. Although affinities certainly existed in these areas between Moldovans and Romanians, this process was still quite complex. It was further complicated by negative political and ideological perceptions of each other, and by the administrative methods used by the Romanian authorities to enforce the process. Today, pro-Romanian Moldovan historians and politicians tend to idealize Romania before the war, presenting it as a bulwark of democracy and tolerance.

The process of combining Bessarabia with the Moldovan Autonomous Soviet Socialist Republic created what became the Moldovan Union Republic. The smaller part of that republic, the Moldovan Soviet Socialist Republic (MSSR, i.e., present-day Transnistria) was dominant, whereas the former Bessarabia, which constituted the larger territory, played a subordinate role. Today, we find the legacies of this division in the Transnistrian and Moldovan territories forming the basis of the Transnistrian territorial conflict, which involves Russia as well. This historical context has had a major impact on the interpretation of the causes and the processes of Gorbachev's perestroika in modern history textbooks in the Republic of Moldova. Perestroika was a process that affected Moldova's national history and development as a state.

Two major orientations dominating the various history textbooks directly influence the narrative of perestroika. Some historians consider the Moldovan national identity as synonymous with the Romanian. In their opinion, it could not possibly differ from the Romanian identity, because the Bessarabia territories had earlier belonged to Romania, causing them to share the same language, history, and culture. History is what determines identity, and Moldovan politicians who try to impose different values from those of Romania are demonstrating that they suffered under the attempted Russification, which dates back to Soviet times.

The essence of the textbooks that apply a Romanian historical perspective is that they ignore the phenomenon of perestroika in the specifically Moldovan context. This is largely a unionist view that sees the Republic of Moldova as nothing but a temporary state awaiting sufficient maturity to once again join Romania. In these textbooks, perestroika's effects on Romania are the only ones mentioned. Perestroika started a process of national awakening and aspirations for national freedom. Romanian historian Ioan Scurtu, together with Ion Șișcanu, who are authors of the Romanian history textbook *Istoria românilor: Epoca contemporană*, claim that perestroika was a positive experience for the Soviet political system, which was in crisis and decline at the time (Scurtu and Șișcanu, 198). It stimulated the awakening of national consciousness among the Romanians from the Moldovan Soviet Socialist Republic (Transnistria), leading to the recognition of Romanian as the official language and to the revival of the Latin script. It also meant the formalizing of the tricolor (red, yellow, and blue) flag and independence itself (27 August 1991). *Istoria românilor: Epoca contemporană* is unequivocal in describing the importance of perestroika for the national revival of the former Soviet republics.

In this way, Scurtu and Șișcanu of the 2007 edition of the 12th-grade textbook claim that perestroika was the driving force of the rediscovery of national values (Scurtu and Șișcanu, 201).

The other position is the ideology of Moldovanism. It is substantiated by the fact that Moldovans use the Russian language not only to communicate with minorities, but with one another as well. Advertisements as well as television and radio programs are all broadcast in Russian. Companies and businesses are owned by Russian capital, and Russian speakers have constantly served as leaders in Chisinau. Most citizens are bilingual, but the minorities that speak only one language speak Russian. These textbooks note that Bessarabia came under Russian domination in 1812 and was united with Romania only in the interwar period in the 1920s and 1930s, altogether for 22 years. Since 1812, people who lived in the territory of the Prut River thus underwent an intensive process of Russification (some experts would say acculturation), a process that continues to this day.

In accordance with this view, the "Romanian people" is an artificial construct. A few centuries ago, there were only Vlachos. Nothing was known of "Romania" or the "Romanian people." It is a people without identity, consisting of the fragments of nations — Moldovans, Hungarians, Gypsies, Bulgarians, Ukrainians, and Germans — who found themselves (willingly or not) in the territory of Wallachia in the newborn state named "Romania." For the Moldovan people, this "union" was a terrible misfortune, with tragic consequences that persist even today. When the new constitution was adopted in 1994, the Romanian-ness (in the ethnic rather than political sense) of the local population and its language was officially denied; the name "Moldova" was imposed, and "Moldovan" was characterized as "different from Romanian." Thus, the official position is to emphasize Moldovan-ness.

Typical of the supporters of an independent national Moldovan history is the alternative view that Moldova was historically integrated with Russia. For them, Gorbachev's perestroika not only led to the destruction of the Soviet Union, but also weakened the ties between Moldova and Russia. A negative view of the entire restructuring is accordingly articulated. The Moldovan textbook authors point out a number of challenges that Moldova is facing in order to develop an all-embracing identity acceptable to all citizens. One is the inability to build local patriotism, which stems from minimal trust in the future of the state, as observed in the serious problems of education and high rates of expatriation and double or triple citizenship among inhabitants of the Republic. Another is the instability in Moldova's relations with neighboring countries, which are exploited by the various parties in domestic politics. Each party uses its privileged relationship with one of the neighboring countries to act against opposing parties.

The world history textbooks edited during the 2001-2009 period, when the communists were in power, and those used in the Transnistrian region describe perestroika as a process that led to the destruction of a large and powerful nation with a long history of culture, science, technology, and military power. For example, this is the major approach in Sergiu Nazaria's *Istoria universală contemporană 1914-2001*:

> The country, which certainly was in need of innovation and of new and modern approaches to management, was thrown far back due to an inability to think and due to the perestroika leaders' lack of capacity. There were no real plans and the actions to transform the economic, political, and spiritual spheres were ill-conceived. (Nazaria 111, translation by the authors).

The Transnistrian Moldovan Republic is a self-proclaimed, officially unrecognized state formed in the Eastern part of the Republic of Moldova (mainly on the left bank of the Dniester River) after independence. Its proclamation of independence was accompanied by Civil War, and the conflict has not yet been resolved and is therefore termed "frozen." Transnistrian schools use Russian history textbooks, and for Transnistrian historians, perestroika is painted in dark colors. They regret not only the collapse of a great state—the Soviet Union itself—but also the isolation from Russia that this collapse has meant for Moldova and for Transnistria in particular. This is not a unique Transnistrian position, but is common among many representatives of the Russian nation and Russian-speakers who live in the area of the former Soviet Union.

The supporters of "Moldavenism" tried to remove the course on Romanian history from the school curriculum, which was introduced in the early 1990s and designed to awaken national consciousness among children and initiate ideological training in preparation for integration with Romania. However, the communist regime that came to power in 2001, which certainly had a "Moldovan" approach, did not manage to remove Romanian history from the educational curriculum despite attempts to do so. The communist government constantly promoted the exclusion of Romanian history as a subject in schools in Moldova. Therefore, starting on 1 September 2006, "integrated history" was introduced as a compulsory subject in schools. In this history, Romanians and Moldovans are presented as two separate nations with separate histories and languages, and the unification of Bessarabia with Romania is described as a "fascist occupation" by the textbooks on "Integrated History" (Enciu 154).

Integrated history consisted of three sections—world history (50 percent), national history (45 percent including local or regional history), and the local history of the place where the school is located (5 percent). The integrated history textbooks were intended especially for grades 5, 10, and 12.

The integrated history course was thus an attempt to unite national and world history. Some historians consider history to be one subject, and when national history is separated from the context of world history—as was the case in Moldova during the 1990s—confrontation occurs between "us" and "them." Hence, the name of the course "History of the Romanians" should, according to this view, be changed. The realization of the integrated history model was not, however, possible.

After three years, with the 2009 shift in power when a center-right government was installed, Romanian history returned to schools. Under the influence of European institutions, Prime Minister Vladimir Filat instructed the Ministry of Education to change the name of the Romanian history course simply to "History." However, this was not achieved either. The Minister of Education, who promised to implement the instruction, held consultations with representatives of the history community, after which he left the existing course name untouched. He was dismissed from his post and transferred to another job. The new Minister of Education was not a specialist in the area of education. According to unofficial sources, she was instructed by the Prime Minister to replace the course name "History of the Romanians."

Currently, the curriculum provides for Romanian history and world history to be taught alongside each other as two separate courses in schools.

What Caused Perestroika?

The authors of the school textbooks give detailed explanations of the factors that led to the collapse of the USSR. The inability of the communist system to modernize the economy, excessive bureaucratization, excessive planning of all production (i.e., of producer and consumption goods, created in all branches of material production over a given period, usually a year), and the lack of democratic freedoms are all pointed out.

The deplorable situation in the social and economic spheres is presented in the textbooks as leading to the initiation of perestroika. Regarding economic development, the authors are critical, as when Petrencu points out that Moldova had the worst economy in the Soviet Union. Corovoi's textbook states: "The MSSR's economic situation was deplorable. While in some regions of Russia there was a great shortage of workers, in Moldavia a surplus of labor formed after migration promoted by Moscow" (Corovoi 243, translation by the authors).

Another important reason the textbooks identify for the final collapse of the USSR was the acceptance of inequality of development between the republics: "National liberation movements were an important factor in the collapse of the Soviet empire. The competition with the free world was furthermore lost by the USSR in all spheres: economic, military, and social" (Petrencu and Chiper 112, translation by the authors).

Although different authors emphasize different factors and key elements of perestroika, the different editions by the same authors contain identical content about perestroika. The exception is the 2007 edition of the world history textbook *Istoria universală contemporană* in which Anatol Petrencu and Ioan Chiper describe the political sphere of the time. This author examines perestroika in terms of the political and economic causes of the collapse of the communist regimes:

Marxist-Leninist theory has failed because it was founded on the principles of class struggle, the dictatorship of the proletariat, enemies of the people, punishment without trial, struggle with the bourgeoisie, militaristic domination psychology, and terrorism. The anti-national policies of denationalization and Russification were oriented towards local levels and were rigidly promoted for over half a century. From the outset, it was clear that socialism in the USSR suffered from large deformations and deviations from Leninist theory, and that the main task is now to rebuild society. The vision of the new leadership was that the socialism created by Stalin continued without essential challenges until the mid 1980s. The objective of perestroika was thus to demolish that form of socialism and to implement the concept of civilized, cooperative socialism. (Petrencu and Chiper, 249, translation by the authors).

Among the key events and concepts driven by perestroika were, according to Petrencu and Chiper, "new political thinking in international relations," a "common European home," and the "collapse of the Soviet socialist system" (Petrencu and Chiper, 155, translation by the authors).

The textbooks emphasize the discourse of nationalism and the freedom movement, with the Supreme Soviet elections, held throughout the Soviet Union in March and April 1989, as the point of departure. As a result, not only communist deputies were sent to parliament. The year 1989 was a period of many manifestations of nationalism. Romanian history textbooks, for example, talk about "Moldovans protesting in favor of a union with Romania" (Moraru 487, translation by the authors).

The national history textbooks' main discourse presents a striking contrast between perestroika and the national revival processes, which are represented as very important in the former socialist countries.

At the university level, perestroika is included in chapters that refer to international relations in the 1980s and internal developments in the USSR in the 1970s and 1980s (in world history textbooks) and in chapters that refer to the proclamation of independence of the Republic of Moldova (in Romanian history and integrated history textbooks). All textbooks use narrative analysis as a way of teaching perestroika and how it played out. Textbooks for university students are naturally more complex and the volume of factual information is much greater. They alternate between positive and critical discourses, as illustrated in these two quotations:

> The democratization policy launched by Gorbachev in 1985 favored the expansion and deepening of the national freedom movement and revival in the MSSR. (Corovoi 242, translation by the authors).

> The idea of the harmonization of interethnic relations through policies of perestroika proved to be utopian. This policy resulted in the collapse of the Soviet empire, so Romanians from Bessarabia got an opportunity to try to secure national control. (Dragnev and Dragnev 106, translation by the authors).

Some works, for example, by Soulet (298) and Courtois (667), devote separate chapters to the collapse of the USSR and to perestroika. The content analyses of these textbooks show that the authors reflect not only on the direct consequences of perestroika, but also on how lingering conflicts and problems, part and parcel of the Soviet structure, that surfaced in the process played out: the process "elucidated issues that remained unresolved for decades—the Armenian enclave of Nagorno-Karabakh in Azerbaijan, the Tartars of Crimea" and so on. Werth and Courtois are historians who have devoted themselves to the critical analysis of communism in general and the Soviet Union in particular, and the use of their work in Moldovan universities implies that these perspectives are accentuated.

The university history textbooks and additional texts describe perestroika as a central element of the policy adopted by Mikhail Gorbachev to reform the society and economy of the USSR (Werth 126). This was a process that gave rise to the development of democracy and to the emergence of new and independent states. The perestroika process had different stages and sub-stages, which implied significant changes in the aims and means of change. This approach is characterized by rather lengthy and detailed descriptions of the process of perestroika. In fact, it creates the impression of a thoughtful and gradual process of social and political change in the Soviet Union undertaken under Gorbachev's leadership. Whereas in school textbooks perestroika is addressed indirectly through other concepts driven by it, such as a "new mentality," "opening," and the "common European home," in monographs and university textbooks, perestroika is described in all its manifestations, for example, as "a revolution from above with specific features of pluralism and willingness to accept foreign experience" (Cojocaru 170, translation by the authors).

For example, Werth in his article refers to the need for a comprehensive approach to the three decades of "Stalinism's consequences" (126) in order to understand what he regards as the failure of perestroika: "The size of the countries in which the crisis took place was directly linked to their national revival" (Werth 126). Werth believes that one of the causes of the failure of perestroika was the USSR's large territory, while another was Stalin's policy of the forcible assimilation of certain peoples. Hence, by the term "failure of perestroika," Werth is referring to the final result, which was the disintegration of the state.

The textbook authors present a number of tasks and exercises that express a strong, underlying view of Russia's expansionist character and the subsequent victimization of the former Soviet republics. The discourse embedded in these tasks justifies the idea of the self-determination of the Soviet people. For example, one task is formulated in the following way: "Interpret and explain the statement by Boldur: 'The Russian Empire had to be destroyed, not to secure its component nationalities, but for the high goal of building communism.'"

The structural reasons for perestroika are featured in the Moldovan school and university textbooks. However, when it comes to agency, overwhelming attention is paid to a single person: Mikhail Gorbachev. The assessment of his role and personality has a dual character. Some authors consider him a traitor. For example, Iachim notes:

> The whole world praises the democracy of Gorbachev and his ambition to build socialism with a human face, but it ended abruptly with the Soviet Union being dismembered. The people of the West consider M. Gorbachev a kind of Messiah, who saved the world from Bolshevism, and crucified himself on the cross instead of Stalin, Lenin, etc. (130, translation by the authors).

This text, used in history courses in Moldovan universities, is a kind of literary essay written in a sarcastic voice; for example, Gorbachev is called "*sovietskii tari* (soviet king), (Iachim 131) and "uncle Misa" (Enciu 158). Such a sarcastic tone is used towards other personalities of the time as well. The authors who characterize Gorbachev in negative terms consider the fact that his initiatives intended to strengthen freedom and democracy instead brought the country to collapse. He is seen as acting out of a selfish striving for power to create his own political base, which was separate from the communist conservatives and also from the radical reformers.

Others praise him and consider him to be the liberator of many peoples, the individual who abolished party control of the media and who required economic plans that initiated the transition to a market economy. Formulations such as "the most admired person in the world," "the person who assured himself a prominent place in history," and the person who "put an end to Soviet control of the 'iron curtain'" are used (Enciu and Mistreanu 158, translation by the authors). He is claimed to have deepened the concept of global security in which nuclear war cannot be used to achieve political, economic, or ideological aims.

Collapse of the Soviet Union: The Consequences of Perestroika

In both the school and university textbooks, the collapse of the USSR is represented as the culmination of perestroika and the tragic end of "a big country," but also as the birth of the Moldovan state. The point of view reflected in Moldovan textbooks is unequivocal and officially sanctioned, since each textbook has to be approved by the Ministry of Education before being published. Today's official version of perestroika is that the collapse of the USSR was a grand event for the revival of national independence and sovereignty in the Republic of Moldova.

University textbooks pay significant attention to the Soviet coup attempt of 1991. In contrast to the ambivalent position of the reformers, the powerful Communist Party and the army vehemently opposed any measure that would have changed the character and integrity of the Soviet Union, and the conservatives attacked by signing the Union Treaty. Also thoroughly presented in national history textbooks is the concept of a "common European home," developed by the Soviet leadership and in line with the "new political thinking." Enciu and Mistreanu, for example, argue in *Istoria universală, epoca contemporană* that Europe should be regarded as a whole, although it was recognized that on the continent there are countries with different social and political orders (159). Sergiu Nazaria claims that even a "normal war" would be disastrous for Europe (86). Taking account of European realities, among them the operation of dozens of nuclear plants and the existence of many chemical plants, Soviet leadership advocated cooperation between European nations (Nazaria 88). The "common European home" does not imply isolation from other parts of the globe: Europe should contribute to solving global problems such as malnutrition, underdevelopment, and indebtedness.

Following discussion of the collapse of the USSR in the university textbooks is a rich array of interactive activities, involving the analysis, evaluation, comprehension, and comparison of different points of view. In a secondary discourse, the textbooks describe the role of the Communist Party of the Soviet Union at that time, which lost much of its former power and control in the country with a new wave of reforms sweeping over the political system. The description of social and political events is enriched with treatment of topics such as "the development of socialism," "the new qualitative changes and transformations of society," "accelerating the development of society," "the strategic course of the CPSU," "the democratization of society," "people's self-management socialism," and "the improvement of socialism" (Soulet 290, translation by the authors).

The Romanian history textbooks emphasize how national culture developed during perestroika. There are descriptions of the topics covered in the literary media of the time, and of the new freedom of intellectuals to organize and demonstrate in the final stages of perestroika. There are mentions of the literary circles that emerged as alternatives to the CPSU. After the beginning of perestroika and the appearance of discussions of the Soviet Union's new project, civil society in Moldova emerged and Moldovans developed national consciousness and values that endorsed self-determination. During this time, the restoration of Romanian as the official language, which was forbidden during the Soviet occupation, became an objective.

The Romanian history textbooks describe 1989 as a historic year for the revival of Moldovan national values and national consciousness. There is an appreciation of the fight for the Moldovan language and alphabet, and the fact that public and political personalities from Moldova reached positions in the Supreme Soviet of the Soviet Union is noted.

The Romanian history textbooks pay considerable attention to Gorbachev's "alcohol reform," which was designed to fight widespread alcoholism in the Soviet Union. Prices of vodka, wine, and beer were increased significantly, while sales were limited. Those who were found drunk at work or in public areas were tried and convicted. For Moldova, it was a very painful process, because the most famous vineyards were destroyed. This campaign had a significant impact on reducing alcohol consumption but a devastating effect on the state budget, resulting in a loss of approximately 100 billion rubles through shifting the production and sales of alcohol to the black market (Moraru 529).

The end of the Cold War is another consequence of perestroika. Petrencu for example, states that the reasons for the end of the Cold War were "the economic crisis that encompassed most of the socialist states in the 1970s and the lack of political democracy in the authoritarian- bureaucratic model of socialism" (Petrencu 251, translation by the authors).

The university textbooks emphasize the importance of the "Sinatra doctrine" ("I did it my way"). This doctrine embraces the policy of non-intervention in the internal affairs of the Warsaw Pact countries and has proven to be one of the most important foreign policy reforms. In 1988, Gorbachev announced that the

Soviet Union would abandon the Brezhnev Doctrine and allow the Eastern Bloc countries to decide independently on the direction of their domestic politics. It is stated that Gorbachev felt a great sense of responsibility for the economic and social errors that had been committed in Eastern Europe in the name of socialism. He realized that the Europeanization of the Soviet Union could not proceed without the de-Sovietization of Eastern Europe. In coming to power, he was able to gradually move away from the restrictive Brezhnev policy of "limited sovereignty" or "socialist internationalism," whereby each communist party was responsible not only to its own people but also to all socialist countries.

Conclusions

Moldova has lived through an identity crisis since independence in 1991. The consciousness of its people is strongly divided, as illustrated in history education that embraces the territory's Russian history, in which Romanian and Moldovan identities are contrasted. Hence, as noted at the beginning of this chapter, Moldovan history textbooks have constituted a battlefield over identity and belonging, and the battle is far from settled. Moldova is a post-Soviet country that belongs to Western Europe, while still being part of the Commonwealth of Independent States (CIS). Reflected in the presence of both Western European cultural traditions and ties to the East, this dualism is echoed in the mentality and behavior of the population, the political elites, and the ruling establishment.

When analyzing the contents and context of perestroika as described in the school textbooks used in Moldova, including in Transnistria, we noticed that authors combine factual and academic language with a persuasive rhetoric. The school textbooks on world history and those on Romanian history treat perestroika in different ways. The narrative of perestroika in world history textbooks situates it in the peaceful international climate created by the political elites of the time. The authors connect it to the withdrawal of Soviet troops from Afghanistan, the fall of the Berlin Wall, and the Velvet Revolution in the former Czechoslovakia. The textbooks also deliver their own conclusions with reference to the restructuring that took place. As a consequence of the changes brought by perestroika, there is today a noisier affirmation of radical Islam, the emergence of new industrialized countries, a revolution in technology, economic reforms in China, and the contours of new threats brought by globalization. The amount of exposure historical events receive in the Romanian history textbooks, as well as the title given to national history as a subject, differ depending on the ruling policy of the political elite in Chisinau.

The teaching of perestroika in universities is more complex and multifaceted than it is in the schools due to the nature of the university students, who are a multicultural and multinational social group, and due to the interdisciplinary treatment of historical processes. The debates on the importance of perestroika were amplified in university textbooks published in the 1990s.

A general view presented in the Moldovan history textbooks analyzed here is that perestroika gave birth to the idea of a national revival of the Soviet people, and led to the emergence of a new political elite made up of intellectuals. This new elite established a political culture that promoted the transition to democracy. The end of perestroika that resulted from the collapse of the USSR meant the beginning of the history of the Republic of Moldova.

In any society, the influence of culture on political processes is very significant. The contemporary movement towards democracy in the former Soviet republics, including Moldova, represents a cultural process, since "democratization depends on culture and international organizations" (Diamond, 16-24). More than that, the development of the national culture of Moldova during the perestroika period had an important impact on the further democratization of the political processes. The nature of the transformations occurring in Moldova's contemporary political culture is conditioned by the transition that has already taken place.

Annex 1. School Textbooks in Moldova

Petrencu, Anatol. *Istoria universala: Epoca contemporana. [World History. Contemporary Epoch]*. Chisinau, Stiinta, 1995.

Petrencu, Anatol. *Istoria universala contemporana (1914–1998). [Contemporary World History 1914-1998]*. Manual pentru clasa 9, Chisinau, Prometeu, 1998.

Petrencu, Anatol. *Istoria universala contemporana. [Contemporary World History]*. Manual pentru clasa 9. Chisinau, Prometeu, 2000.

Petrencu, Anatol, Maia Dobzeu. *Istoria universala. Epoca contemporana. [World History, Contemporary Epoch]*. Material didactic pentru clasa 9. Chisinau, Stiinta, 2004.

Petrencu, Anatol. *Istoria universala contemporana. [World History, Contemporary Epoch]*. Chisinau, Asociatia istoricilor din Republica Moldova, 2007.

Petrencu, Anatol, Dobzeu, Maia. *Istoria universala: Epoca contemporana. [World History, Contemporary Epoch]*. Material didactic pentru clasa 9. Chisinau, Stiinţa, 2011.

Petrencu, Anatol, Chiper, Ioan. *Istoria universala. [World History]*. Manual pentru clasa 12. Chisinau, Asociatia istoricilor din Republica Moldova, 2007.

Enciu, Nicolae. *Istoria integrata. [Integrated history]*. Chisinau, Civitas, 2008

Enciu, Nicolae, Mistreanu, Tatiana. *Istoria universal: Epoca contemporana. [World History, Contemporary Epoch]*. Clasa 12. Chisinau, Civitas, 2006.

Nazaria, Sergiu. *Istoria universala contemporana (1914–2001). [Contemporary World History, 1914-2001]*. Manual pentru clasa 12. Chisinau, Civitas, 2001.

Nazaria, Sergiu, Roman, Alecsandru, Sprinceana, Mihai, Albu, Sergiu, Machedon, Ludmila Barbus, Anton, Dumbrava. *Istoria. Epoca contemporana. [History. Contemporary Epoch]*. Manual pentru clasa 9. Chisinau, Cartea Moldovei, 2006.

Scurtu, Ioan, Şişcanu, Ion. *Istoria romanilor: Epoca contemporana, [Romanian History. Contemporary Epoch]*. Manual pentru clasa 12. Chisinau, Prut international, 2007.

Dragnev, Emil, Dragnev, Demir. *Atlas de istorie universala si a romanilor. [The Atlas of Universal and Romanians History]*. Chisinau, Civitas, 2005.

Dragnev, Emil; Dragnev, Demir. *Atlas de istorie universala si a romanilor. [The Atlas of Universal and Romanians History]*. Chisinau, Civitas, 2006.

Petrencu, Anatol. *Vseoshaia istoria 1914-1996. [World History]*. Chisinau, Civitas, 1997.

Vizer, Boris. *Istoria contemporana a romanilor, Materiale experimentale pentru clasa 9. [Contemporary Romanian History. Experimental materials for 9th class]*. Chisinau, Stiinta, 1997.

Annex 2. University Textbooks in Moldova

Werth, Nicolas. *Istoria Uniunii Sovietice: de la Hrushciov la Gorbaciov (1953-1985). [History of the Soviet Union: from Khrushchev to Gorbachev (1953-1985)]*. Bucuresti, Corint, 2000.

Courtois, Stephane. *Dictionarul comunismului. [The Dictionary of Communism]*. Iasi, Polirom, 2008.

Iachim, Ion. *Istoria Rusiei, [History of Russia]*. Chisinau, Pontos, 2006.

Lucinschi, Petru. *Ultimele zile ale URSS, [The last days of the USSR]*. Bucuresti, Evenimentul romanesc, 1998.

Constantin, Ion. *Basarabia sub ocupatie sovietica de la Stalin la Gorbaciov, [Bessarabia under Soviet occupation from Stalin to Gorbachev]*. Bucuresti, Fiat Lux, 1994.

Soulet, Jean-Francois. *Istoria comparata a statelor comuniste din 1945 până în zilele noastre, [Comparative history of the Communist states from 1945 to the present day]*. Chisinau, Polirom, 1998.

Moraru, Anton. *Istoria romanilor (Basarabia și Transnistria, 1812-1993), [History of Romanians (Bessarabia and Transnistria, 1812-1993)]*. Chisinau, Universul, 1995.

Corovoi, Gheorghe. *Istoria romanilor, [History of Romanians]*. Chisinau, Civitas, 1999.

Munchaev, Shamil', Ustinov, Victor. *Istoria Sovetskogo gosudarstva, Moscva, NORMA, 2008. [History of the Soviet Union]*.

Negru, Gheorghe. *Politica etnolingvistica in RSS Moldoveneasca, [Ethnolinguistic policy in Moldavian SSR]*. Chisinau, Prut international, 2000.

Ivanescu, Sorin; Bogdan Schipor, Flavius Solomon, Alexandru Zub, *Basarabia: dilemele identitatii, [Bessarabia: the dilemmas of identity]*. Iasi, Dosoftei, 2001.

Which Future Came? Multiple Perestroika(s) as Prisms of the Soviet and the National

Li Bennich-Björkman and Sergiy Kurbatov

Now it is 2019. More than 25 years have passed since the Soviet Union dissolved, leaving fifteen republics to face an uncertain future as sovereign states. Most of them were new states with no long prior experience of statehood, and only very brief experience in a few cases, at least in the 20th century. The exceptions were the three Baltic States, which were sovereign from 1918 to 1940, and Russia itself. More than 30 years have passed since the youngish, new General Secretary of the Communist Party Mikhail Gorbachev let loose the reform processes that he called perestroika and glasnost, which led to the final destruction of a union once believed to be invincible. Although numerous predictions of the future collapse of the Soviet Union had been made from the 1950s to the 1980s, it was commonly believed that Soviet strength would prevail despite the escalating war in Afghanistan and the increased rivalry with the West over soft values and military force. However, the developments that unfolded from 1985 until the final attempt to restore the power of the Union in August 1991 liberated many previously hidden aspirations and opened old wounds, creating many expectations and emotions, most of which took the rest of the world—and the leaders in Moscow—by surprise. As Roger Grigory Suny wrote, there was almost disbelief in the West at what was happening, so that "each turn of events, each incident of hesitation or of backsliding, seemed to confirm those suspicions" (Suny 2). In the end, the Soviet Union was unable to harness its human dynamism without breaking up or at least substantially re-establishing itself according to new principles, a process that finally proved impossible. The Soviet superpower collapsed, new states were born, and new institutions established. These things happened.

How have the countries emerging amidst these historically turbulent changes chosen to commemorate and nationally embed their experiences of living through them? How have these pathbreaking changes been narrated into the national memory of each of the four countries studied, contextualized to harmonize with the overall story of each nation's fate and way forward? That question was asked at the beginning of this book. Having come this far, and based on the individual chapters on each country, several answers suggest themselves.

Competing Interpretations and Common Ground

"Is history a science or an art?" asked Henk Wesseling (265–267). "Like the novelist the historian writes a story, but in the historian's case sources are needed to justify the story," reads Wesseling's (267) concluding answer to his own question. History appeals to our mind's rational abilities, while at the same time speaking to our emotions, value systems, and ways of perceiving the past. This non-rational approach to times gone by becomes most important when the described past is close to us and there are numerous witnesses among our contemporaries. Teaching the past in this situation — as the studied textbooks do — is at once an exciting adventure and a demanding challenge.

The individual chapters have highlighted one of the most important arenas of collective memory and interpretation in modern societies: written historiography. The voices heard in the textbooks are those of officially sanctioned professional historians, who in that role possess authoritative standing as experts, but whose interpretations nevertheless depend on their nationality, ideological position, generational belonging, and, not least, gender (many of the textbook authors are men). This is most obvious in the Moldovan textbooks, in which Romanian or Romanian-inclined historians tend to emphasize cultural and linguistic ties to Romania, while historians based in the contemporary Moldovan capital Chisenau instead define a unique Moldovan-ness on which the country could build. The Russian roots of the Bessarabian territory also play a role for certain historians, leaving the newborn country with several rival options when it comes to selecting and choosing an identity.

History textbooks in the Moldovan context thus constitute an active battlefield, where identity—Romanian, "Russian," or Moldovan—is a source of struggle. The consequence is vacillation concerning what the national identity is to be, echoed in the way Moldova's political elites have balanced a desire to embrace Russian civilization at one time, against European belonging at another. Bessarabia's 19th century, when it was part of the Tsarist Russian Empire, plays a crucial role for the former elite, as do the five Soviet decades, whereas for others, it is the Romanian interwar years that constitute a specific point of reference.

In contrast to historians' ongoing struggle over identity in Moldova, the most clear-cut example of a narrative settled early on is that of Ukraine. The absence of struggle—at least of an open sort—is striking. Changes in political power, clearly reflected in Moldova's historiography, do not affect the Ukrainian historians' interpretations of perestroika and Soviet dissolution. Regardless of whether it is Leonid Kravchuk, Leonid Kuchma, Viktor Iuschenko, or Viktor Ianukovich holding the presidential powers, or the more nationalistic parties or the Party of Regions, the central narrative basically stays the same. Predominantly, it regards perestroika and Soviet dissolution through the lens of national freedom. Ukrainian-ness is not contested, but is portrayed as always having been there, concealed during the long Soviet decades, only to emerge into the open after 1991.

Moreover, the representations of perestroika and the collapse of the Soviet Union in the textbooks reveal different logics and strategies of nation-building in the post-Soviet space that illustrate path dependency with respect to nation-building in Soviet times, and with regard to the transformations of the 1990s. These logics imply self-identification through either continuity (Belarus and Russia) or dissociation (Chechnya, Moldova in part, Tatarstan, and Ukraine) with the Soviet Union.

The narrative of the breakup of the Soviet Union and its causes and consequences is connected to how the Soviet past is envisioned in these historical accounts. According to the constitution of 1977, the Soviet Union "shall be a single union, a multinational state formed on the basis of the principle of socialist federalism as a result of free self-determination of nations and the voluntary association of equal Soviet Socialist Republics." This refers back to the original constitution of 1923 that guaranteed the national equality of the republics and the right—boldly invoked in 1990 by the Lithuanians—to leave the Union. The Russian Soviet Federative Socialist Republic (RSFSR) was thus just one of fifteen republics that all possessed equal legal status; all republics were defined as sovereign, with their own constitutions and the right of free withdrawal from the Union. The actual level of this sovereignty, however, was questionable, which has given rise to colonial and imperial approaches to the Soviet past and its degree of national equality and hierarchy that distinguish the textbooks in the four countries.

These understandings of the past affect how Russian and republican relations are valued. In the colonial interpretation, Russia is regarded as the "master" republic with the overall ambition to enslave and use the others to strengthen and empower itself. The imperial interpretation instead envisions more harmonious relations with Russia, the natural leader and "father figure," looking out for and making its periphery prosperous. While the colonial interpretation sees the Soviet past as one involving the suppression of nationalities, including a privileged position for the Russian core, the imperial version interestingly regards this epoch in more integral terms, as one when all nationalities were equal. Hence, if the colonial lens suggests a zero-sum game, in which one republic gains what another loses, the imperial lens instead sees a game of simultaneous, reciprocal gain.

From the colonial perspective forcefully emphasized in Ukraine, Chechnya, and Tatarstan, the interpretation shifts to an imperial one in Belarusian textbooks, with Moldova undecidedly in between. In both the Russian and Belarusian textbooks, the tone is overwhelmingly positive in considering the past. Soviet rule brought modernization and industrialization to the populations, and the Soviet Union was a leading state internationally, through technological advances and in its progressive and egalitarian model of life. In Ukrainian textbooks, the Soviet past is instead interpreted as making the nation into a poor and inert colony, a stagnating territory held down by the center and by the co-opted local elite, who bear great responsibility for the ongoing impoverishment. Assessing the past affects the vision of what the future holds: for Belarus, it means holding onto a Soviet identity, while for Ukraine, it means distancing itself as far as possible.

However, not only difference prevails. There is common ground in the historiography of all the individual countries as to what brought about perestroika. All versions describe a profound and internally generated economic and political crisis that challenged leaders in Moscow, which in turn prompted General Secretary Mikhail Gorbachev to take action. Belarusian as well as Ukrainian textbooks critically stress that there was a radical gap between the goals and values of the ruling elite and the majority of the population, and that the reformers among the party elite suffered from incompetence and made fatal mistakes in realizing perestroika policies as a result. Here, together with the populistic appreciation of "ordinary people," we find a hidden accusation that the Soviet elite participated in a kind of collective betrayal. Only in Belarus, a country that since 1994 has returned to the most Soviet-style organization of all the former Soviet Union nations, do history textbooks invoke the clandestine aspirations of the West to bring the great Soviet state to an end via high-flying conspiracies.

The history textbooks in all four countries also commonly teach that perestroika leading to the Soviet Union's breakup was nearly inevitable: there was no going back, as forces had been let loose that were basically unstoppable. Perestroika was caused by objective processes and the necessity of changes that were obvious to everyone. Historical determinism lies around the corner, even though the choices of the political elites and—as most clearly articulated in Ukraine—of the people, pushed developments forward.

When moving on to the consequences of perestroika, the subsequent breakup of the Soviet Federation, and how the transformations should be assessed, the individual historiographies of each country point in profoundly different directions.

What Happened?

Already emphasized before the fall of communism by a number of scholars, insights into the crucial importance of local variance within the Soviet bloc accumulated in the late 1990s and the 2000s. "If the watchword of the communist era was conformity, the watchword of the post-communist world is diversity … It is hard to imagine that only a short while ago a single model of economic and political institutions dominated the region," wrote Timothy Frye (1). In the textbooks used in secondary schools and universities from 1991 to 2012 in the four studied countries, the dramatic events that played out in the 1980s and 1990s take on radically different meanings depending on the national contexts, which, indeed, emphasize their diversity. In the three former "core" republics, in the sense of being part of the original Soviet Union established in 1922, i.e., Russia, Ukraine, and Belarus, the answer to "What happened?" ranges from "not much" in Belarus to "everything" in Ukraine. In Moldova, which is discussed last, the significance of the dissolution of the Union is recognized, though ambivalently evaluated.

Russia

In Russia, history textbooks articulate the country's position as a unique nation and the successor state of the Soviet Union, with a demanding role still to fulfil. The complexities of the Russian Federation, with its manifold nationalities and a Russian nation that mobilized for independence only in the last years of the Soviet Union, push historians to try to balance the civic nature they want to ascribe to the Russian state against an equal emphasis on the diverse nationalities that make up the huge territory. The Russian Republic was the only nation in the Union that did not have a regional Communist Party until very late, in

1990, an arrangement intended to prevent Russia from developing into an alternative center to the Soviet Union as such. That is why the Soviet state promoted the institutionalization of nations in all Soviet republics except in Russia, whose actual status remained ambiguous. The role played by Russian nationalism in preparation for separating from all-Soviet power during the perestroika period is therefore a fascinating topic that is not adequately covered in history textbooks.

At the same time, the principal political leaders of the Soviet era were largely Russian by nationality or residents of Russia, which encouraged the identification of Russian interests with Soviet ones. Russians were "exported" to the republics to be part of the local party leaderships, and Russian-born "titulars" continued to fill the party state. Moreover, the regional divisions within the country comprised 16 autonomous republics (with their own constitutions and the right to veto territorial changes) and five autonomous oblasts. Russia thereby displayed the greatest regional diversity in the Soviet Union. As a result, it was less institutionalized as a national republic than were the other Soviet republics. Yuri Slezkine, who used the metaphor of "communal apartment" to describe national policy during the Soviet era, asks:

> But what about the Russians? In the center of the Soviet apartment there was a large and amorphous space not clearly defined as a room, unmarked by national paraphernalia, unclaimed by "its own" nation and inhabited by a very large number of austere but increasingly sensitive proletarians. The Russians, indeed, remained in a special position. They could be bona fide national minorities in areas assigned to somebody else, but in Russia proper they had no national rights and no national opportunities (because they had possessed and misused them before). (434)

Whereas Russian nationalism became more self-assertive during perestroika, the Russian state—the Russian Federation—incorporates many other nations that also grew in national consciousness and cohesiveness starting in the 1980s. The Russian textbooks comment mostly on the awakening of the "national republics," pointing to a number of emergent national parties and movements. Before the October Revolution in 1917, Russia was a multinational state with non-Russians accounting for 57 per cent of the population. Nevertheless, unification of the country often took place through Russification, which created economic and political problems in the national districts. The ethno-religious diversity of the state became a problem in the 19th century, which was an age of intense nation-building processes, and the ruling elites did not manage to formulate adequate solutions. "Tsarism never created a nation within the whole empire or even a sense of nation among the core Russian population... Tsarist Russia managed only too well in building a state and creating an empire; it failed, however, to construct a multiethnic 'Russian nation' within that empire" (Suny 56). This failure facilitated the Revolution and shaped the initial conditions of nation-building processes in the Soviet Union.

Traces of these potential and actual sub-national divisive developments are evident in the textbooks used in Chechnya and Tatarstan. In Chechnyan history textbooks, a cynical power game forms the core of the narrative: it constitutes elite domination with an essentially passive people being tricked out of their rights and aspirations. The Chechnyan nation thus suffers according to an interpretation that challenges the overall Russian narrative of a diverse, but civic, country. If anything, Chechnya is a victim according to Chechnyan historians. In textbooks used in Tatarstan, national awakening—in contrast to the Russian ambivalence on whether to take a civic or ethnic stand—is instead the main message. The people of Tatarstan are invigorated by the sense of a common fate and belonging, a story differing completely from the Chechynan one.

National revival occurred most vividly in the autonomous regions that claimed sovereignty in the 1990s. On 6 August 1990, in response to these developments, the Acting Chair of the Supreme Soviet of the Russian Federation Boris Ieltsin, in Kazan, the capital of Tatarstan, uttered his famous declaration: "Take as much sovereignty as you can!" (Ieltsin).

Nevertheless, in 1992, most of these autonomous regions chose to sign the Federal Treaty, acknowledging their subordination to the Russian Federation, a formal recognition process that was completed by the beginning of the 2000s. Ideas of national revival however still linger in several autonomous entities, for example, in Tatarstan. As the chapter on Russia has shown, for many of the titular nations of the Russian Federation republics, regional identity is predominant, though this does not rule out a "civic" identity as well. Most Russians in these republics consequently identify themselves in a dualistic way, equally as citizens of the Federation and as ethnic Russians.

As for the national revival of Russia itself, the 1990s saw the rise of the Russian (ethnic) nationalist movement, which peaked in 1993–1995. These nationalists differ from each other in ideological orientation: one part sought the restoration of the lost empire, while another identified ethnic Russian-ness as a goal. Since the early 2000s, some textbooks argue, nostalgia for the Soviet Union has withered away, replaced by ethno-xenophobic attitudes (particularly towards migrants).

In Russia, neither engagement nor detachment predominates in the tone of the textbooks, which are marked by a nuanced objectivity. The textbooks are surprisingly neutral and matter-of-fact, given that Russia has, since the early 2000s, seen intensified nationalistic ambitions from the political leadership and renewed value-based conflict with the West. There is no enthusiastic embracing of Russia as the successor state of the Soviet Union, but rather an articulated ambivalence that shines through. Nevertheless, contemporary Russia is—in contrast to Belarus, Ukraine, and Moldova, whose territories were under the governance of different states—the direct successor of a sole state. This state is Kyiv Rus, Moscow State, Tsarist Russia (or the Russian Empire), and the Soviet Union.

Ukraine

History textbooks tell of a Ukraine that liberated itself and finally awoke to self- realization. Ukraine is the only country of the four examined here in which nationalist mobilization has long-standing roots, and when Galicia became part of the country during World War II, this reinforced Ukrainian nationalism. The major storyline in Ukrainian textbooks is of the unanimous creation of a Ukrainian nation that had become passive and alienated during its Soviet past, but woke up to the possibility of taking charge of its own fate. Independence is assessed as an event of great importance, and in many of the textbooks students are asked, through symbolically important questions, to evaluate the historical significance of the Declaration of Independence of Ukraine.

The dismantling of the Soviet Union has meant that the unique Ukrainian nation has stepped forward into an existence of dignity and freedom. If anything, history textbooks intensify this focus when dealing with the aftermath of what was the first major popular mobilization after independence, the Orange Revolution of 2004. What had begun as protests against electoral fraud and a political leadership that had failed the people and developed into cronyism grew into a huge public action in Maidan Square in Kyiv (D'Anieri, *The Last Hurrah* 231–249; O'Brien 355–367; Reznik 750–765).

Historically, Ukraine, whose contemporary territory, with the exception of the western parts, was part of the Russian Empire from the 18th to early 20th centuries, struggled for independence after the Bolshevik Revolution in October 1917 (along with Finland, Estonia, Latvia, Lithuania, and Belarus, among others). The Civil War that broke out between the Bolsheviks and the Central Rada or Council (later the Parliament) in 1918 led to defeat for the Ukrainian side and to its full incorporation into the Soviet edifice (in contrast to Finland and the Baltic States, which managed to secure sovereignty). The Rada was unprepared for the struggle, both politically and militarily, whereas the Bolsheviks were fuelled by fanatical devotion to the cause of Soviet communism and were well equipped, organized, and disciplined. They displayed brutality, even sadism, and violence and killings accompanied the establishment of the Soviet Union as part of the natural means of conquering. The creation of a federation of republics was intended by Lenin to prevent the realization of the plan of Josef Stalin to create one state—Rossiia—that would downgrade the independent states of Ukraine, Georgia, Armenia,

Azerbaijan, and Byelorussia to autonomous republics at a subnational level. As Slezkine notes, "Lenin's acceptance of the reality of nations and 'national rights' was one of the most uncompromising positions he ever took, his theory of good ('oppressed nation') nationalism formed the conceptual foundation of the Soviet Union and his NEP-time policy of compensatory 'nation-building' (*natsional'noe stroitel'stvo*) was a spectacularly successful attempt at a state-sponsored conflation of language, 'culture', territory and quota-fed bureaucracy" (414).

This approach led to the policy of Ukrainianization, which lasted, according to George Shevelov, from 1925 to 1932:

> As a result, the effects of Ukrainianization were far from straightforward. On one hand, more people than ever mastered Ukrainian and became to some extent familiar with Ukrainian literature and culture; some of them even switched to speaking in Ukrainian. The Ukrainian language was heard more frequently in the streets of the major cities ... On the other hand, the aura of coercion and artificiality accompanying the policy aroused hostility. (Shevelov 212)

In Ukrainian history textbooks, bitterness over the Soviet past looms large. Soviet rule of the country meant destruction of the national spirit, exploitation of the country's resources, and brutality towards the population. The Holodomor of the Ukrainian peasants in 1932–1933 (the Great Famine), a national tragedy kept hidden until perestroika, is vividly recalled as one of the major disasters that has befallen the Ukrainian nation. According to the official historical narrative presented in textbooks, the Holodomor was a genocide committed against the Ukrainian nation. Although the Russian, Belarusian, and Moldovan textbooks also point to the economic hardships of the Soviet period, Ukraine stands out as being sharply criticizing the Soviet and post-Soviet eras. Harsh words are used to describe the developments in economics and politics in Soviet times, stressing the intensifying crisis over time and the collapse created by the Soviet system.

Ukrainian historiography also articulates disappointment at the lack of current economic and social progress, explaining it in relation to Ukraine's Soviet past that sadly made the country into a colony. This destroyed the preconditions for independent economic strength, and this destruction has continued to put its mark on development since independence. In contrast to the disappointment in the economy, the civic and cultural spheres are highly valued, as these are areas where genuine positive changes have occurred, and there is emotional engagement in the descriptions of these arenas of human expression.

Enthusiasm for newfound independence fills the pages of the Ukrainian textbooks. Ukraine is a civic state, embracing all its inhabitants regardless of ethnicity. This "civic" conceptualization of Ukrainian statehood is highly significant, since the different parts of Ukraine do not all share the same pre- Soviet past. Memories of that time tend to shape the process of nation-building, and there is a need to create a commonly shared vision of Ukraine's essence as a state defined by its institutions and values. The textbooks avoid seeding conflicts in a state with a multinational and "multi-historical" character.

The story of the Sleeping Beauty symbolizes Ukraine's 20th-century journey. The beautiful and resourceful Ukraine is awakened by perestroika after having slept through decades of Soviet tyranny. Interestingly, Anatol Lieven, who wrote about the Baltic revolutions of the 1990s, chose precisely the same story to describe Estonia, Latvia, and Lithuania: "One of the themes of this book therefore suggests itself to me as the story of the Sleeping Beauty, as re-written by the Wicked Witch" (xxxvi).

Belarus

Historically, Belarus declared itself independent in 1918 and then struggled for—and lost—its sovereignty. Defeated by the Bolsheviks, Belarus, along with Ukraine, was part of the original group of nations and territories that formed the Soviet Union. The many decades under Soviet rule, however, have contributed to making Belarus less, not more, nationalistic. Whereas the authors of the Ukrainian and Russian textbooks place their own nations' experiences at the center of events from a colonial perspective, the imperial narrative of perestroika and the consequent breakup places Belarusian events at the periphery, treating them as secondary effects of a shared Soviet history. Here we can identify a specific paradox: the imperial perspective is evident in the textbooks of a country that could be regarded as a colony, whereas such a perspective is absent from the textbooks of the metropolitan power itself, Russia. In striking contrast to the Ukrainian narrative, content related to any struggle for national independence is therefore quite difficult to find in most Belarusian textbooks. Belarusian historians lean towards an understanding of perestroika and its consequences as being not that important to the Belarusian nation, which continues to take its place in the larger mosaic of the many nationalities that constituted the Soviet Union. While Belarusian Independence follows in the footsteps of perestroika and the Soviet breakup, it is mainly as part of a larger pattern that involves the entire Soviet Union. Belarusian historians avoid accentuating nationalism and national identity, continuously situating Belarus within a broader community of peoples (or nationalities, which was the Soviet term). This way of emphasizing multiple nationalities is reminiscent of the Soviet rhetoric of the many peoples that constituted the Union.

Many of the Belarusian textbooks do not draw any direct line connecting the end of perestroika itself, the collapse of the Soviet Union, and the beginning of an independent Republic of Belarus. The major and mostly regrettable consequence of perestroika is seen as the breakup of the Soviet Union, which destroyed longstanding ties. The historians, in what appears a disentangled and aloof manner, deny the importance of forming a strong national identity. The contrast to neighbouring Ukraine could not be greater. Hence, not all Belarusian textbooks articulate a national identity and endorse national independence, even though nationalism has been seen as a defining idea in Western and Eastern Europe alike since the early 19th century. Belarus clearly contradicts the conclusion drawn, for example, by Suny, that "the demands of the titular nationalities of each republic became the dominant motifs in the program of both Communist and non-Communist leaders" (Suny 9), or by Beissinger on how national mobilization played a central role in the breakup of the Soviet

Union (2002, 47-102). One message of the Belarusian history textbooks is that the global events that occurred as a result of the Soviet dissolution are bigger than the emergence of Belarus itself.

In Belarus, perestroika is treated reductively, and the distinct historical break it constitutes in the historiography of the other countries does not find resonance here. Continuity, not discontinuity, is thus established. The Republic of Belarus simply constitutes the continuation of the Byelorussian Soviet Socialist Republic, but now at a new stage of its development: the period of full independence. Most of the Belarusian textbooks consider the resulting democratization of the country as negative, which is demonstrated by the fact that terms such as "democracy" and "democratization" are placed within quotation marks to indicate scepticism and distrust; as a rule, they are treated as synonymous with "Western," "pro-Western," and "capitalist." Democracy is regarded as a foreign idea, alienated from the main principles of the development of national history. As pointed out above, the notion of a deliberate, clandestine attack by the West on the Soviet Union that caused its breakup can be found in Belarusian historiography and plays into this assessment.

Perestroika, leading to the end of a great state, the Soviet Union, to which Belarus belonged, is mostly addressed in neutral or negative terms. That independence and statehood followed this tragedy is given little weight. The tragedy touched Belarus but did not change its predestined path—"unruffled" seems an appropriate adjective. Belarusian historiography is dispassionate. Whereas Ukrainian historians cherish the people, the popular front, and civic activism, the opposite is true in Belarus. Nationalistic movements are seen as polarizing society and, over time, there has been a growing tendency to neglect their role in contemporary history, illustrating, as in Moldova, a clear political purpose behind the teaching of history.

Moldova

Finally, textbooks in the Soviet latecomer Moldova clearly acknowledge the radical change and the crossroads that the fall of the Soviet Union meant for the country. It was a large rip in the historical fabric, and discontinuity is clearly a dominant theme. The Moldovan textbooks make it obvious that the history of the 19th and 20th centuries has pulled the territory in various directions. From its inclusion in Tsarist Russia as Bessarabia since 1812, it came under the Romanian flag in 1918 after the fall of the Russian Empire. Forcibly claimed from Romania by the Soviets in 1939, the Bessarabian territory was joined by Moscow to the Russian territory of Transnistria to form the Moldovan Soviet Socialist Republic. The Civil War over Transnistrian secession has led to a situation considered "frozen" and unresolved, in which Transnistria retains much of its Soviet identity and definitely ties itself to present-day Russia. It would therefore be interesting to compare the interpretations of the perestroika period in the history textbooks of Belarus and Transnistria, which has not been done here. Transnistria declared itself independent of Moldova, but has not been recognized and continues its existence as a de facto state. Since independence, Moldova's explicit struggle has been over questions of "who we were," "who we are," and "who we should be."

Open frustration, even confusion, is paired with buried resentment in a new country that is more of an artificial construct than the other three. Ukraine comes closest to Moldova in that sense, as its present territory consists of the eastern, southern, and central parts that had earlier made up the Ukrainian nation, as well as a western part that was forcibly annexed from Poland, Romania, and Czechoslovakia in 1940–1944 (e.g., Eastern Galicia, Bukovina, Volhynia, and Transcarpathia). In contrast to Moldova, however, the Ukrainian "core" territories have been home to a people — a nation — who have identified themselves as Ukrainians (or Ruthenians) for a long time. Vacillating between advocating that the new country's cultural identity is Romanian, Russian, or uniquely Moldovan, Moldova is clearly still in a process of identity formation, and the textbooks accordingly offer different interpretations of what the Moldovan nation should be, turning either towards Romania, as was advocated at independence, or towards Russia. An interesting and more open-ended soul search for something that could be exclusively Moldovan also continues, as the textbooks show, and Moldova has not yet decided its cultural path. Of the four countries, Moldova's search for an imagined community to fill its state institutions with solidarity, sense, and meaning is the toughest.

A strong and unanimous nationalism is thus manifested in Ukraine, as well as in the Russian autonomous region of Tatarstan, where the major consequence of perestroika is interpreted as national self-realization. Textbooks in Belarus display the opposite tendency, downplaying the importance of nationalism and Belarusian Independence by placing the country within a broader context of many nationalities. In Russia, the responsibility of being both successor state and the carrier of the fate of many diverse nationalities overshadows a persistent Russian nationalism. Moldovan-ness is still in formation, squeezed between Romanian and Russian alternatives.

The People and the Elites

One final question remains: is any agency evident in the historiography of these four countries, and, if so, who is shaping history according to the historiographers? The answer to that question may be the most important one for understanding present-day developments of democratization, empowerment, and state-building.

The Russian, Belarusian, and Moldovan history textbooks—like those in Chechnya—present a narrative of perestroika and the transformation into independent states as a combination of structural developments combined with the actions of political elites. They recall Natan Eidelman's popular idea in the USSR in the late 1980s that perestroika was a "revolution from above" (25). Initiated by Mikhail Gorbachev, the person paid the most attention in all of the textbooks, the reforms were carried forward and fulfilled by the local elites and representatives of the Communist Party. Belarusian textbooks, in particular, display a depersonalized way of presenting historical processes, pointing out structures rather than agency, which coincides with the element of historical determinism noted earlier: what happened is seen as inevitable and is not associated with anybody's real will or ambition.

The people, in the form of civil society and popular movements, only play an active role in the narratives of two of the studied territories: Ukraine and, to a certain extent, the Russian Republic of Tatarstan, where "civil society" is shown to be important in the national awakening. However, it is the Ukrainian history textbooks that stand out in how they ascribe agency and importance to ordinary people, who are described as carrying forward perestroika, which started as a top-down initiative, transforming it into a grassroots movement "from below." Here, the elites are far from the only actors on the historic scene.

The people have ambitions and are equipped with the desire and will to gain freedom and independence. Because of their resources, changes take place. Civil society—in terms of formal organizations and associations as well—was an integral and decisive part of perestroika in Ukraine and in the dissolution of a destructive state. For example, Rukh, the popular front in Ukraine that later split into several political parties, plays a major role. Ukrainian textbooks give the impression that it is possible to shape historical developments and that coming together as a people can make a difference, which is an implicit theme throughout the books. Of the countries studied here, it is only in Ukraine that large grassroots mobilizations have changed the political landscape since independence, not once but twice: during the Orange Revolution of 2004 and Euromaidan of 2014 (D'Anieri, *Establishing Ukraine's Fourth Republic* 3-20; Fedorenko et al. 609-630). This indicates a creed of participation in Ukraine, echoed in the historiography of contemporary times. The importance given to the growing possibilities of popular mobilization and organization reveals Ukraine's more pluralist outlook, in contrast to the other countries, and openness is emphasized as a crucial resource for society. The textbooks contrast the concept of glasnost to the Soviet ideology of silence, and highly value this openness.

The blame for Soviet inertia and backwardness lay on the elite party leaders in Ukraine, not least on the First Secretary of the

Communist Party, Volodymyr Shcherbytsky (who was among those who resisted large-scale reforms in Soviet Ukraine from 1985 to 1989). Political elites actively held back change, while people on the ground were pushing for independence. They wanted something, and they acted: through the human chain from Kyiv to Lviv, through Rukh's activities, and through the writers' and other cultural unions.

That the Orange Revolution and Euromaidan (the Revolution of Dignity) took place in Ukraine and not in Belarus, Russia, or Moldova reflects the officially articulated conviction in Ukrainian historiography that society and the people are powerful. The virtuous carriers of the national spirit stand in stark contrast to the elites who halt development. Uniquely, history textbooks in Ukraine seem to be teaching the younger generation to believe in their own power to change the country and make a positive difference. This message is not conveyed in the textbooks of any of the other three countries, where power is described as lying with the elites or is deterministically situated outside human reach. Ukrainian history textbooks instead emphasize the importance of grassroots initiatives and the direct participation of everybody in democratic transformations of society. For the future, that may prove decisive.

Works Cited

Abdelal, Rawi. "Memories of Nations and States: Institutional History and National Identity in Post-Soviet Eurasia." *Nationalities Papers*, Vol. 30, No. 3, 2002, pp. 451-484.

Akhmadov, Yavus Z., and Edil'bek H. Khasmagomadov. *Istoriia Chechni v XIX-XX Vekakh* [History of Chechnya in the 19th—20th Centuries]. Moscow, Puls, 2005.

Aleksashkina, Lyudmila N., Aleksandr A. Danilov., and Lyudmila G. Kosulina. *Rossiya i Mir v XX—Nachale XXI Veka* [Russia and the World in the 20th and to the Beginning of the 21st Centuries]. Moskva, Prosveshchenie, 2010.

Almond, Gabriel, and Sidney Verba. *The Civic Culture: Political Attitudes and Democracy in Five Nations*. Princeton, Princeton University Press, 1963.

Amar, Tarak Cyril. *The Paradox of Ukrainian Lviv: A Borderland City between Stalinists, Nazis, and Nationalists*. Ithaca and London, Cornell University Press, 2015.

Androshchuk, Oleksandr. "Chornovil ta ideia federalizatcii Ukrainy: evolutciia pogliadiv." *Narodnyi Rukh Ukrainy: istoria, ideologia ta politychna evolutciia*. [Chornovil and Idea of Federalization of Ukraine. People's Movement of Ukraine: History, Ideology and Political Evolution]. Kyiv, Institute of History of the National Academy of Sciences, 2009, pp. 22-34.

Ankersmit, Franklin Rudolf. *Narrative Logic: A Semantic Analysis of the Historian's Language*. The Hague, Martinus Nijhoff Publishers, 1983.

Applebaum, Anne. *Gulag: A History of the Soviet Camps*. New York, Doubleday, 2003.

—. *Red Famine: Stalin's War on Ukraine*. New York, Knopf Doubleday, 2017.

Assman, Jan. "Collective Memory and Cultural Identity," *New German Critique*, No. 65, 1995, pp. 125-133.

Ball, Alan. M. *Imagining America: Influence and Images in Twentieth-Century Russia*. New York and Oxford, Rowman & Littlefield Publishers, 2003.

Balmaceda, Margarita M., James I. Ciem, and Lisbeth L. Tarlow. "Introduction." *Independent Belarus: Domestic Determinants, Regional Dynamics, and Implications for the West*, ed. Margarita Mercedes Balmaceda, James I. Ciem, and Lisbeth L. Tarlow, Cambridge, MA, Harvard University Press, 2005, pp. i-xviii.

Barsenkov, Alexandr S., and Alexandr I. Vdovin. *Istoriia Rossii. 1917-2009* [History of Russia. 1917-2009]. Moscow, Aspekt-Press, 2010.

Bauman, Zygmunt. *Intimations of postmodernity*. Routledge, 2003.

Beissinger, Mark. *National Mobilization and the Fall of the USSR*. Cambridge, Cambridge University Press, 2002.

Beissinger, Mark, 2004 "Rethinking Empire in the Wake of Soviet Collapse." *Ethnic Politics After Communism*, eds. Zoltan Barany and Robert Moser, Ithaca, Cornell University Press, 2005, pp. 14-45.

Bekus, Nelly. *Struggle Over Identity: The Official and Alternative Belarusianness. The Official and Alternative Belarusianness*. Budapest, Central European University Press, 2010.

Bellah, Robert N., Richard Madsen, William, M. Sullivan, and Ann Swidler. *Habits of the Heart: Individualism and Committment in American Life*. Berkeley, University of California Press, 1985.

Bennett, Brian. *The Last Dictatorship in Europe*. New Haven, Yale University Press, 2011.

Bennich-Björkman, Li. "Post-Soviet Developments: Reflections on Complexity and Political Order." *Journal of Contemporary Central and Eastern Europe*, Vol. 26, No. 1, 2017, pp. 1-18.

Berdiaev, Nikolaĭ. "Filosofskaiā istina i intelligentskaiā pravda" [Philosophical Truth and Intelligentsia's Truth] In *Vekhi* [Landmarks], ed. Mikhail O. Gershenzon, Moscow, Ripol Klassik, 2017, pp. 6-36.

Bergman, Kjell, and Berith Jakobsson. *Ester i Göteborg: Om identitetens bevekelsegrunder* [Estonians in Gothenburg: On the Conditions for Identity]. Göteborg, Etnologiska institutionen. 1984.

Bilotserkivskyi, Vasyl. *Istoriia Ukrainy. Navchalnyi posibnyk* [History of Ukraine: A Textbook]. Kyiv, Tsentr uchbovoi literatury, 2007.

Blakkisrud, Helge, and Kolstoe, Paul. "Dynamics of de Facto Statehood: The South Caucasian de Facto States Between Secession and Sovereignty." *Southeast European and Black Sea Studies*, Vol. 12, No. 2, 2012, pp. 281-298.

Bobyleva, Ol'ga M. *Otechestvennaia Istoriia* [History of the Fatherland]. Irkutsk, IrGUPS, 2010.

Boiko, Oleksandr. *Istoriia Ukrainy: posibnyk dlia studentiv vyshchykh navchalnykh zakladiv* [History of Ukraine: Textbook for University Students]. Kyiv, VTs Akademiia, 1999.

Boiko, Oleksandr. *Istoriia Ukrainy: posibnyk dlia studentiv vyshchykh navchalnykh zakladiv, 2-he vyd., dop.* [History of Ukraine: A Textbook for University Students, 2nd ed., expanded]. Kyiv, Akademvydav, 2004.

Bokhan, IUriĭ N., Natal'iā I. Poletaeva. *Istoriiā Belarusi v kontekste mirovykh tsivilizatsiĭ* [History of Belarus in the Context of World Civilizations]. Minsk, Ekoperspektiva, 2011.

Brown, Archie. *The Gorbachev Factor*. Oxford, Oxford University Press, 1997.

Brubaker, Rogers. "Nationhood and the National Question in the Soviet Union and Post-Soviet Eurasia: An Institutionalist Account." *Theory and Society*, Vol. 23, No. 1, 1994, 47–78.

Bryhadzin, Piotr I., Uladzimir F. Ladyseŭ, Piotr I. Ziālinski, *Historyiā Belarusi, ch. 2, 19-20 st.* [History of Belarus 19th–20th Centuries vol. 2], Minsk, Belarusian State University, 2002.

Buhr, Renee L., Marharyta Fabrykant, and Steven Hoffman. "Youth and Identity in the Post-Soviet Sphere: A Comparison of Lithuania and Belarus." Conference Paper, Annual World Convention of the Association for the Study of Nationalities, 19–21 April 2012, New York, Columbia University.

Bystrytskyi, Ievhen. Chi Mozhe 'Natsionalism' Buty Naukoiu [Why 'Nationalism' Can not be a Science] *Politychna Dumka [Political Thought]*, No. 2, 1994, pp. 136–142.

Cherniaev, Anatolii. "Spirituality Destroyed." *Russian Politics and Law*, Vol. 45, No. 5, 2007, pp. 26–42.

Chigrinov, Petr G. *Istoriiā Belarusi* [History of Belarus]. Minsk, Polymiā, 2001.

Chigrinov, Petr G. *Ocherki istorii Bielarusi* [Essays on the History of Belarus]. Minsk, Vysheĭshaiā shkola, 2007.

Cipkowski, Peter. *Revolution in Eastern Europe: Understanding the Collapse of Communism in Poland, Hungary, East Germany, Czechoslovakia, Romania, and the Soviet Union*. New York, Wiley, 1991.

Cohen, Stephen F., and Katrina van den Heuvel. *Voices of Glasnost: Interviews with Gorbachev's Reformers*. New York and London, W.W. Norton, 1991.

Cojocaru, Gheorghe E., "Sfidarea problemei nationale si perestroika lui M. Gorbaciov" [Contempting the national problem and perestroika of M. Gorbachev] *Destin Rominesc*, no. 3–4, 2004, p. 170.

Coleman, James. *The Adolescent Society*. New York, The Free Press, 1961.

Combs, Dick. "Working Levels of the Soviet Regime." *Inside the Soviet Alternate Universe: The Cold War's End and the Soviet Union's Fall Reappraised*, ed. Jack F. Matlock Jr., University Park, Penn State Press, 2012, pp. 28–54.

Connor, Walker. *The National Question in Marxist-Leninist Theory and Strategy*. Princeton, Princeton University Press, 1984.

Conquest, Robert. *The Harvest of Sorrow: Soviet Collectivization and the Terror-Famine*. Oxford, Oxford University Press, 1986.

Corovoi, Gheorghe. *Istoria romanilor* [The History of Romanians]. Chisinau, Editura Civitas, 1999.

Courtois, Stephane. *Dictionarul comunismului* [The Dictionary of Communism]. Chisinau, Editura Polirom, 2008.

D'Anieri, Paul, "Establishing Ukraine's Fourth Republic: Reform After Revolution." *Beyond the Euromaidan: Comparative Perspectives on Advancing Reform in Ukraine*, eds. Henry E. Hale and Robert W. Orttung, Stanford, Stanford University Press, 2016, pp. 3-20.

D'Anieri, Paul, "The Last Hurrah: The 2004 Ukrainian Presidential Elections and the Limits of Machine Politics." *Communist and Post-Communist Studies*, Vol. 38, No. 2, 2005, pp. 231-249.

Danilov, Aleksandr A., and Lyudmila G. Kosulina. *Istoriia Rossii. XX Vek* [History of Russia. The 20th Century]. Moskva, Prosveshchenie, 1995.

Danilov, Aleksandr A., Liudmila G. Kosulina, i Maksim Iu. Brandt. *Istoriia Rossii. XX – Nachalo XXI Veka* [History of Russia. The 20th – Beginning of the 21st Century]. Moskva, Prosveshchenie, 2012.

Danilov, Aleksandr A., Liudmila G. Kosulina, i Aleksandr V. Pyzhikov. *Istoriia Rossii XX – Nachalo XXI veka* [History of Russia. The 20th – beginning of the 21st century]. Moskva, Prosveshchenie, 2003.

Darden, Keith A. *Economic Liberalism and Its Rivals: The Formation of International Institutions among the Post-Soviet States*. Cambridge, Cambridge University Press, 2009.

Dawisha Karen., editor. *Democratic Changes and Authoritarian Reactions in Russia, Ukraine, Belarus and Moldova*. Cambridge, Cambridge University Press, 1997.

Davies, Norman. *Vanished Kingdoms: The History of Half-forgotten Europe*. London, Penguin, 2012.

Denber, R., editor. *The Soviet Nationality Reader: The Disintegration in Context*. Boulder, Westview Press, 1992.

Deshchynskyi, Leontiy, Sviatoslav Tersky, Ivan Khoma, Volodymyr Taraban. *Istoriia Ukrainy ta yii derzhavnosti: navch. posibnyk*. Vyd. 3-ye, pereroblene i dopovnene. [History of Ukraine and its statehood. A textbook. 3rd edition) Lviv, Beskyd Bih, 2005.

Diamond, Larry. Proshla li "tret'ya volna" demokratizatsii? [Did the "Third Wave" of Democratization passed?]. *Polis*, 1999, pp. 1-13.

Dmitrienko, Vladimir P., ed. *Istoriia Rossii. XX Vek* [History of Russia. The 20th Century]. Moskva, AST, 1998

Dneprov, Eduard D., ed. *Modernizatsiia Rossiiskogo Obrazovaniia: Dokumenty i Materialy* [Modernization of the Russian Education: Documents and Materials]. Moskva, GU-VShE, 2002.

Dovnar-Zapolskiy, Mitrofan. "Literatura epokhi vozrozhdeniya" [Literature of the revival Epoch] In *Istoriya Bielarusi* (History of Belarus]. Minsk, Bielarus, 2005, pp. 464–506.

Dragnev, Emil, and Demir Dragnev. *Atlas de istorie universală și a romînilor.* [The Atlas of Universal and Romanians History]. Chisinau, Civitas, 2005.

Dudchik, Andrei, and Marharyta Fabrykant. "Ordinary Tragedy: 'Perestroika' of Collective Memory about Chernobyl Disaster in Belarusian History Textbooks." *Anthropology of East Europe Review*, Vol. 30, No. 1, 2012, pp. 65–81.

Dynamika Nostal'hii za SRSR [Dynamics of nostalgia for the USSR]." Results of national sociological poll conducted by the Rating Group. Sep. 2016. ratinggroup.ua/research/ukraine/c910ad1d40079f7a2a28 377c27494738.html. Accessed 02 Mar. 2018.

Eckstein, Harry. *Regarding Politics: Essays on Political Theory, Stability, and Change.* Berkeley, University of California Press, 1992.

Ėĭdel'man, Natan. *Revoliutsiia Sverkhy v Rossii* [Revolution from Above in Russia]. Moscow, Kniga, 1989.

Elektoral'ni Orientatsii Ykraintsiv [Electoral orientations of Ukrainians]. A press release from the Kyiv International Institute of Sociology's Poll. Mar. 2014. kiis.com.ua/?lang=ukr&cat=reports&id=247& page=3. Accessed 02 Mar. 2018.

Enciu, Nicolae. *Istoria integrată*. [Integrated history], Chișinău, Civitas, 2008

Enciu, Nicolae, and Tatiana Mistreanu. *Istoria universală, epoca contemporană, Clasa 12* [World History, the Contemporary Epoch, for 12th Form]. Chișinău, Civitas, 2006.

Epstein, Jay E. *Deception: The Invisible War Between the KGB & the CIA.* New York, Random House Value Publishing, 1991.

Eyal, Gil, Ivan Szelenyi, and Eleanor R. Townsley. *Making Capitalism Without Capitalists: The New Ruling Elites in Eastern Europe.* London, Verso Books, 1999.

Fabrykant, Marhartyta, and Renee, L. Buhr. "Small State Imperialism: The Place of Empire in Contemporary Nationalist Discourse." *Nations and Nationalism*, Vol. 22, No. 1, 2016, pp. 103–122.

Fairclough, Norman. *Critical Discourse Analysis.* London, Longman, 1995.

Fedorenko, Kostyantyn, Olena Rybyi and Andreas Umland, "The Ukrainian Party System before and after the 2013- 2014 Euromaidan." *Europe-Asia Studies*, Vol. 68, No. 4, 2016, pp. 609-630.

Fomin, V.M., ed. *Istoria Belarusi 1945-2005* [History of Belarus 1945-2005]. Minsk, BSU, 2006.

Foster, Stuart. "Dominant traditions in international textbook research and revision." *Education Inquiry*, Vol. 2, No. 1, 2011, pp. 5-20.

Fox, Jonathan. "Nationalism Versus Civilisations: An Assessment of Alternate Theories on the Future of Ethnic Identity and Conflict." *National Identities*, Vol. 5, No. 3, 2003, pp. 283-307.

Fritz, Verena. *State-Building: A Comparative Study of Ukraine, Lithuania, Belarus, and Russia*. Budapest, Central European University Press, 2008.

Frye, Timothy. *Building States and Markets after Communism: The Perils of Polarized Democracy*. Cambridge, Cambridge University Press, 2010.

Fukuyama, Francis. *The End of History and the Last Man*. New York, Free Press, 1992.

Gatrell, Peter, and Nick Baron. "Violent Peacetime: Reconceptualizing Displacement and Resettlement in the Soviet—East European Borderlands after the Second World War." *Warlands: Population Resettlement and State Reconstruction in the Soviet-East European Borderlands, 1945-50*, eds. Peter Gatrell and Nick Baron, London, Palgrave Macmillan, 2009, pp. 255-268.

Geelan, David, R. *Weaving Narrative Nets to Capture Classrooms: Multimethod Qualitative Approaches for Educational Research*. Dordrecht, Springer, 2007.

Gel'man, Vladimir. "The vicious circle of post-Soviet neopatrimonialism in Russia." *Post-Soviet Affairs*, Vol. 32, No. 5, 2016, pp. 455-473.

Gledhill, John. "The Power of Ethnic Nationalism: Foucault's Bio-power and the Development of Ethnic Nationalism in Eastern Europe." *National Identities*, Vol. 6, No. 4, 2004, pp. 347-368.

Grachev, Andrei. *Gorbachev's Gamble: Soviet Foreign Policy and the End of the Cold War*. New York, Wiley, 2008.

Graebner, Norman. A, Richard Dean Burns, & Joseph M. Sircausa, *Reagan, Bush, Gorbachev: Revisiting the End of the Cold War*. Westport, Praeger, 2008.

Greenfeld, Liah. *Nationalism: Five Roads to Modernity*. Cambridge, MA, Harvard University Press, 1992.

Gudkov, Lev, and Borys Dubin. *Intelligentsia* [Intellectuals]. Moscow, Izdatelstvo Ivana Limbacha, 2009.

WORKS CITED 181

Gurtov, Melvin, editor. *Transformation of Socialism: Perestroika and Reform in the Soviet Unionand China*. Boulder, Westview Press, 1990.

Halbwachs, Maurice. *La Memoire Collective*. Chicago, University of Chicago Press, (1950)/1992.

Hale, Henry. *The Foundations of Ethic Politics: Separatism of States and Nations in Eurasia and the World*. Cambridge, Cambridge University Press, 2008.

Hobsbawm, Eric, and Terence Ranger. *The Invention of Tradition*. Cambridge, Cambridge University Press, 1983.

Hutchinson, John, and Montserrat Guibernau, eds. *Understanding Nationalism*. Oxford, Polity Press, 2001.

Husiev, Victor, Yuri Kalintsev, Stanislav Kulchytski. *Istoriia Ukrainy* [History of Ukraine]. Kyiv, Vyshcha shkola, 2003.

Husiev, Victor, Hryhorii Kazmyrchuk, Valerii Kapeliushnyi, Hennadii.Cherevychnyi. *Istoriia Ukrainy/Pidruchnyk dlia inozemnykh studentiv vyshchykh navchalnykh zakladiv*. [History of Ukraine: A textbook for foreign University Students]. Kyiv, VPTs Kyivskyi universytet, 2008.

Iachim, Ion. *Istoria Rusiei*. [The history of Russia]. Chişinău, Pontos, 2006.

Inglehart, Ronald, and Christian Welzel. *Modernization, Cultural Change, and Democracy: The Human Development Sequence*. Cambridge, Cambridge University Press, 2005.

Ion, Constantin. *Basarabia sub ocupaţie sovietică de la Stalin la Gorbaciov* [Bessarabia under Soviet Occupation from Stalin to Gorbachov], Bucureşti, Fiat Lux, 1994.

Janmaat, Jan Germen. "The ethnic 'other'in Ukrainian history textbooks: The case of Russia and the Russians." *Compare*, Vol. 37, No. 3, 2007, pp. 307–324.

Janmaat, Jan Germen, and Edward Vickers. "Education and identity formation in post-cold war Eastern Europe and Asia." *Compare*, Vol. 37, No. 3, 2007, pp. 267–275.

Jennings, M. Kent, and Richard Niemi. *The Political Character of Adolescence: the Influence of Family and Schools*. Princeton, Princeton University Press, 1974.

Jørgensen, Marianne, and Louise J. Phillips. *Discourse Analysis as Theory and Method*. Thousand Oaks, Sage Publications, 2002.

Kastsiūk, Michail P., ed. *Historyiā Belarusi, t. 6: Belarus' 1996-2009*. [History of Belarus, vol. 6: Belarus, 1996–2009]. Minsk, Sovremennaiā shkola, Ekoperspektiva, 2011.

Kastsiūk, Mikhail P., Ilaryion M. Ignatsenka, Uladzimir I. Vyshynski, eds. *Narysy historyi Belarusi, ch. 2* [Essays on the History of Belarus, vol. 2]. Minsk, Belarus', 1995.

Kennedy, Michael, D. *Cultural Formations of Postcommunism: Emancipation, Transition, Nation, and War.* Minneapolis, University of Minnesota Press, 2002.

Kirillov, Viktor V. *Istoriia Rossii* [History of Russia]. Moskva, ID Iurait, 2011.

Kislitsin, Sergei A. *Istoriia Rossii v Voprosakh i Otvetakh* [History of Russia in Questions and Answers]. Rostov-na-Donu, Feniks. 1997.

Konukov, Talgat S., ed. *Istoriia Otechestva. Chast' II (Seredina XIX – Konets XX Veka)* [History of the Fatherland. Part II (mid-19th – end of the 20th Century)]. Ufa, UfGATU, 1995.

Kordonsky, Simon. "Resursnoe gosudarstvo-ot repressiy k depressiyam" [Resource State – from Repressions to Depressions] *Resursnoye gosudarstvo*, Moscow, Regnum 2007, pp. 3–46.

Koshelev, Vladimir, editor. *Vsemirnaya Istoriia, XIX – nachalo XXI 6.* [World History, XIX-beg. of XXI cent.]. Minsk, BSU, 2009.

Kosmach, Gennadiĭ A., Vladimir S. Koshelev, Marina A. Krasnova, eds. *Vsemirnaiā istoriiā Noveĭshego vremeni 1945-2005* [World History of Modernity 1945-2005]. Minsk, BSU, 2006.

Koval, Mikhail, Stanislav Kulchytskyi, Yuri Kurnosov, Vitali Sarbei. *Istoriia Ukrainy. Probnoe uchebnoe posobye dlia 10-11 klassov srednei shkoly* [History of Ukraine. Trial textbook for 10th-11th forms of secondary schools]. Kyiv, Osvita, 1991.

Kovkel, Ivan, and Edmund Yarmusik. *Istoriya Belarusi s drevneishih vremen do nashego vremeni* [History of Belarus from Ancient Times to Our Own]. Minsk, Aversev, 2010.

Kozlov, Valerii, i Aleksandr Kondakov, eds. *Fundamental'noe iadro soderzhaniia obshchego obrazovaniia* [Fundamental Core of the Substance of Public Education]. Moskva, Prosveshchenie, 2011.

Kozlovskaia, Galina. *Rossiiskoe obrazovanie v postsovetstkii period, 1991-1999* [Russian Education in the Post-Soviet Period, 1991-1999]. 2003. Moskovskii Pedagogicheskii gosudarstvennyi Universitet, Doktorskaia dissertatsiia.

Kramer, Mark "The Collapse of East European Communism and the Repercussions within the Soviet Union." *Journal of Cold War Studies*, Vol. 5, No. 4, 2003, pp. 178-256.

Kudriachenko, Andrii, Halyna Kalinicheva, Anatolii Kostyria. *Politychna istoriia Ukrainy XX stolittia: pidruchnyk dlia stud. vyshch. navch. Zakl* [Political History of Ukraine in XX century: A textbook for the University Students]. Kyiv, MAUP, 2006.

Kulchytskyi, Stanislav, and Iulia Lebedieva. *Istoriia Ukrainy. 11 klas.* [History of Ukraine. A Textbook for 11th form]. Kyiv, Heneza, 2011.

Kulchytskyi, Stanislav, and Yurii Shapoval. *Novitnia Istoriia Ukrainy (1939-2001). Pidr. Dlia 11 Klasu Zahalonosv. Navch. Zakl.* [History of Ukraine (1939-2001). A Textbook for 11th Form at Secondary Schools]. Kyiv, Heneza, 2005.

Kulchytskyi, Stanislav, and Borys Tyshchyk. *Istoriia derzhavy i prava Ukrainy. Akademichnyi kurs.* [History of the state and law in Ukraine.) Academic course Kyiv, InIure, 2008.

Kupatadze, Alexander. "Organized crime before and after the Tulip Revolution: The Changing Dynamics of Upperworld-Underworld Networks." *Central Asian Survey*, Vol. 27, No. 3-4, 2008, pp. 279-299.

Kustarev, Aleksandr. *Nervnye liudi* [Nervous People]. Moskva, KMK, 2006.

Kuz'minov, Iaroslav. "Obrazovanie v Rossii. Chto my mozhem sdelat'?" ["Education in Russia: What Can We Do?"]. *Voprosy obrazovaniia* [Issues of Education], Vol. 1, No. 1, 2004, pp. 5-30.

Lallemand, Jean-Charles. "Businessmen in Politics, in Russian Provinces: Outbreak, Consolidation, and Decline of a Type of Actor." *Politix*, Vol. 21, No. 84, 2008, pp. 61-90.

Lanovyk, Bohdan, and Mykola Lazarovych. *Istoriia Ukrainy: Navch. Posib. 3-te Vyd., Vypr. i Dop.* [History of Ukraine. A textbook. 3rd edition, improved]. Kyiv, Znannia-Pres, 2006.

Lapteva, Elena V. *Istoriia Rossii* [History of Russia]. Moskva, Akademicheskii proekt, 2009.

Laruelle, Marlene. *Russian Eurasianism: An Ideology of Empire*. Baltimore, Johns Hopkins University Press, 2008.

Lastoŭski, Vatslaŭ. *Karotkaiā historyiā Belarusi* [Brief History of Belarus]. Vil'niā, Drukarniā Martsīna Kukhty, 1918, p. 6.

Lazarovych, Mykola. *Istoriia Ukrainy: Navch. Posib.* [History of Ukraine. A textbook]. Kyiv, Znannia, 2008.

Leshchenko, Natalia. "A Fine Instrument: Two Nation-building Strategies in Post-Soviet Belarus." *Nations and Nationalism*, Vol. 10, No. 3, 2004, pp. 333-352.

Levandovskii, Andrei A., i Iurii A. Shchetinov. *Rossiia v XX Veke* [Russia in the 20th Century]. Moskva, Prosveshchenie, 1997.

Levandovskii, Andrei A., Iurii A. Shchetinov, and Sergei V. Mironenko. *Istoriia Rossii. XX – Nachalo XXI Veka* [History of Russia. The 20th – Beginning of the 21st Century]. Moskva, Prosveshchenie, 2011.

Lieven, Anatol. *The Baltic Revolution: Estonia, Latvia, Lithuania, and the Path to Independence.* New Haven, Yale University Press, 1993.

Lockhart, Charles. "Political Culture and Political Change." *Culture Matters: Essays in Honor of Aaron Wildawsky*, eds. Richard J. Ellis and Michael Thompson, Boulder, Westview Press, 1999.

Lyantsevich, Volha. *Historiya Belarusi* [History of Belarus]. Minsk, MIK Edition, 2012.

Lytvyn, Volodymyr. *Istoriia Ukrainy: Pidruchnyk – 4-e Doopratsovane ta Dopovnene Vydannia* [History of Ukraine. A Textbook – 4th Edition, Improved]. Kyiv, Naukova dumka, 2010.

Lytvyn, Volodymyr, Viktor Kolesnyk, Anatolii Sliusarenko. *Istoriia Ukrainy: Navchalno- metodychnyi Posibnyk dlia Seminarskykh Zaniat.* [History of Ukraine. A Textbook and a Guidebook for Seminars] – Ed. Volodymyr Lytvyn, Kyiv, Znannia-Pres, 2006.

"Maidan-2013." A press release from the Ilko Kucheriv Democratic Initiatives Foundation and the Kyiv International Institute of Sociology. December 2013. kiis.com.ua/? lang=ukr&cat=reports&id =216&page=1. Accessed 02 March, 2018.

Malešević, Sinisa. "Ethnicity in Time and Space: A Conceptual Analysis." *Critical Sociology*, Vol. 37, No. 1, 2011, pp. 67–82.

Malici, Akan. *When Leaders Learn and When They Don't: Mikhail Gorbachev and Kim Il Sung at the End of the Cold War.* New York, State University of New York Press, 2009.

Martirossian, Jasmine. "Russia and Her Ghosts of the Past." *The Struggle Against Corruption: A Comparative Study*, ed. Johnson, Roberta Ann, Palgrave Macmillan, 2004, pp. 81–108.

Mannheim, Karl. *Essays on the Sociology of Knowledge.* London, Routledge & Kegan Paul, 1952.

Matlock, Jack, F. *Reagan and Gorbachev: How the Cold War Ended.* NYC, Random House Trade, 2005.

Meadwell, Hudson. "Republics, Nations and Transitions to Modernity." *Nations and Nationalism*, Vol. 5, No. 1, 1999, pp. 19–51.

Merelman, Richard, M. *Partial Visions: Culture and Politics in Britain, Canada, and the United States.* Wisconsin, University of Wisconsin Press, 1991.

Mishler, William, and Richard Rose. "Trust, Distrust and Skepticism: Popular Evaluations of Civil and Political Institutions in Post-Communist Societies." *The Journal of Politics*, Vol. 59, No. 2, 1997, pp. 418–451.

Moraru, Anton. *Istoria romanilor (Basarabia si Transnistria, 1812–1993). Manual pentru clasa 12.* [The History of Romanians (Bessarabia and Transnistria, 1812-1993). Textbook for 12th class]. Chisinau, Civitas, 1995.

Nazaria, Sergiu. *Istoria universală contemporană (1914–2001). Manual pentru clasa 12.* [Contemporary World History 1914-2001. Textbook for 12th class]. Chişinău, Civitas, 2001.

Novik, Evgeniĭ K., ed. *Istoriiā Belarusi XIX-nachalo XXI β.* [History of Belarus, XIX-beg. of XXI cent.]. Minsk, BSU, 2009.

Novik, Yaŭhen K., Ihar L. Kachalau, Natalya Ya. Novik, *Historyiā Belarusi: ad starazhytnykh chasoŭ – pa 2008 g.* [History of Belarus: From Ancient Times to 2008]. Ed. Yaŭhen Novik, Minsk, Vyshĕĭshaiā shkola, 2009.

Novik, IAŭhen K., and Henadz' S. Martsul', eds. *Historyiā Belarusi* [History of Belarus, vol. 2. February 1917-1997]. Minsk, Universitetskae, 1998.

Nora, Pierre. *Les lieux de mémoire, vol 3*. Paris, Éditions Gallimard, 1997.

Nye, Joseph S. (Jr), *Soft Power: The Means to Success in World Politics*. New York, Public Affairs, 2004.

Obermann, Anja. *Die Beziehungen der Europäischen Union zu nichtdemokratischen Staaten: Europäische Außenpolitik gegenüber Algerien, Indonesien und Belarus.* Saarbrücken, AV Akademikerverlag, 2012.

O'Brien, Thomas. "Problems of Political Transition in Ukraine: Leadership Failure and Democratic Consolidation." *Contemporary Politics*, Vol. 16, No. 4, 2010, pp. 355–367.

Oppenhiem, Ian Davis. *Gorbachev: The Rise and Fall of a Hero*. Charleston, Self-published via CreateSpace, 2012 (1991).

Orlov, Aleksandr S., Vladimir A. Georgiev, Nataliia G. Georgieva, Tat'iana A. Sivokhina, *Istoriia Rossii* [History of Russia]. Moskva, Prospekt, 1997.

Orwell, George. *1984*. PlanetEBook EBook Collection, www.planetebook.com/ebooks/1984.pdf.

Ortmann, Stefanie, and John Heathershaw. "Conspiracy Theories in the Post-Soviet Space." *The Russian Review*, Vol. 71, No. 4, 2012, pp. 551–564.

Ostrovskyi, Valerii, Vitalii Startsev, Borys Starkov, Hennadii Smirnov. *Istoriia SRSR: Pidruchnyk dlia 11 klasu serednoi shkoly* [History of the USSR. A textbook for 11th form]. Kyiv, Radianska shkola, 1991.

Ostrovskyi, Valerii. *Istoriia SRSR: materialy dlia pidruchnyka do 11 klasu.* [History of the USSR. Materials for the textbook for 11th form]. Kyiv, Radianska shkola, 1991.

Parker, Stewart. *The Last Soviet Republic: Alexander Lukashenko's Belarus.* Bloomington, Trafford Publishing, 2007.

Perrault, Charles. "Sleeping Beauty." *The Fairy Tales of Charles Perrault.* The Project Gutenberg eBook Web, http://www.gutenberg.org/files/29021/29021-h/29021-h.htm

Pershái, Aliaksandr. "Minor Nation: The Alternative Modes of Belarusian Nationalism." *Eastern European Politics and Societies*, Vol. 24, No. 3, 2010, pp. 379–398.

Petrencu, Anatol. *Istoria universală: Epoca contemporană*, [World History. The Contemporary Epoch], Chisinau, Stiinta, 1995.

Petrencu, Anatol. *Istoria universala contemporana (1914–1998).* Manual pentru clasa 9 [Contemporary World History 1914-1998]. Chisinau, Prometeu, 1998.

Petrencu, Anatol. *Istoria universala contemporana*, Manual pentru clasa 9, [Contemporary World History, Manual for the 9th class]. Chisinau, Prometeu, 2000.

Petrencu, Anatol, Dobzeu, Maia. *Istoria universala. Epoca contemporana.* Material didactic pentru clasa 9. [World History. Contemporary Epoch]. Chisinau, Stiinta, 2004.

Petrencu, Anatol, *Istoria universala contemporana.* [World History. Contemporary Epoch]. Chisinau, Asociația istoricilor din Republica Moldova, 2007.

Petrencu, Anatol, Dobzeu, Maia. *Istoria universala: Epoca contemporana.* [World History. Contemporary Epoch]. Chisinau, Stiinta, 2011

Petrencu, Anatol, Chiper, Ioan. *Istoria universala.* [World History]. Chisinau, Asociatia istoricilor din Republica Moldova, 2007.

Pingel, Falk. *UNESCO Guidebook on Textbook Research and Textbook Revision.* Paris, Braunschweig, 2010.

Ploss, Sidney. *The Roots of Perestroika: The Soviet Breakdown in Historical Context.* Jefferson, McFarland & Inc. Company, 2010.

Pometun, Olena, and Nestor Hupan. *Istoriia Ukrainy. 11 klas.* [History of Ukraine. 11th form]. Kyiv, Osvita, 2011.

Propp, Vladimir. *Morfologia volshebnoi skazki* [Morphology of a Fairytale]. Moscow, Labirint, 1998.

Popper, Karl. *The Poverty of Historicism*. London, Routledge, 1957.

Puglisi, Rosaria. "The Rise of the Ukrainian Oligarchs." *Democratization*, Vol. 10, No. 3, 2003, pp. 99–123.

Purysheva, Natalia, and Michail Starovoytov. *Istoriya Belarusi: Shkolnyi kurs v kratkom izlozhenii*. [History of Belarus: School Course in Brief]. Minsk, Tetra- Systems, 2012.

Puzatich, Aleksandr. *Otsenka za rubezhom transformatsii rossiiskogo obrazovaniia v postsovetskii* [Foreign Assessment of the Transformation of Russian Education in Post-Soviet Period]. 2011. Eletskii gosudarstvennyi Universitet. Doktorskaia dissertatsiia.

Renan, Ernest, *Qu'est-ce qu'une nation?*, Paris, Presses-Pocket, 1992.

Repoussi, Maria, and Nicole Tutiaux-Guillon. "New Trends in History Textbook Research: Issues and Methodologies toward a School Historiography." *Journal of Educational Media, Memory, and Society*, Vol. 2, No. 1, 2010. pp. 154–170.

Reznik, Oleksandr. "From the Orange Revolution to the Revolution of Dignity: Dynamics of the Protest Actions in Ukraine." *East European Politics and Societies*, Vol. 30, No. 4, 2016, pp. 750–765.

Riabov, Andrei. "The Post-Soviet States: A Shortage of Development in a Context of Political and Economic Diversity." *Russian Politics and Law*, Vol. 52, No. 2, 2014, pp. 30–43.

Richardson, Tania. "Disciplining the Past in Post-Soviet Ukraine: Memory and History in Schools and Families." *Memory, Politics and Religion. The Past meets the Present in Europe*, eds. Frances Pine, Deema Kaneff, Idis Haukanes, Munster, Lit Verlag, 2004, pp. 109- 132.

Ries, Nancy. *Russian Talk: Culture and Conversation during Perestroika*. Ithaca, Cornell University Press, 1997.

Rodgers, Peter W. "Division, Difference and Diversity: Regionalism in Ukraine." *Ukraina Moderna*, 2007: pp. 210–236.

—. "(Re)inventing the Past: The Politics of 'National' History in the Ukrainian Classroom." *Studies in Ethnicity and Nationalism*, Vol. 6, No. 2, 2006, pp. 40-55.

Rontogianni, Clelia. "Belarus and East." *Postcommunist Belarus*, eds. Stephen White, Elena Korosteleva, John Lowenhardt, Lanham, Rowman & Littlefield Publishers, 2004, pp. 123–156.

Rudling, Per Anders. "Belarus in the Lukashenka Era: National Identity and Relations with Russia." *Europe's Last Frontier? Belarus, Moldova, and Ukraine between Russia and the European Union*, eds. Oliver Schmidtke and Serhy Yekelchyk, London, Palgrave Macmillan, 2007, pp. 55–78.

Sabirova, Daniia K., Iakub Sh. Sharapov. *Istoriia Tatarstana s Drevneyshikh Vremen do Nashikh Dnei* [History of Tatarstan from Ancient Times to Present]. Moskva, KnoRus, 2009.

Savchenko, Andrew. *Belarus: A Perpetual Borderland*. Leiden, Brill Academic Publishers, 2009, pp. 1–15.

Scurtu, Ioan Siscanu, Ion. *Istoria romanilor, epoca contemporana. Manual pentru clasa 12*, [Romanian History. The Contemporary Epoch. Textbook for 12th class] Chisinau, Prut international, 2007.

Sedaitis, Judith, and Jim Butterfield. *Perestroika from Below: Social Movements in the Soviet Union*. Boulder, Westview Press, 1991.

Semin, Vladimir P. *Otechestvennaia Istoriia* [History of the Fatherland]. Moskva, Akademicheskii proekt, Gaudeamus, 2008.

Shakibi, Zhand. *Khatami and Gorbachev: Politics of Change in the Islamic Republic of Iran and the Soviet Union*. London and New York, Tauris Academic Studies, 2010.

Sharova, Natalia. *Istoriya Belarusi: Opornyye konspekty dlya podgotovki k centralizovannomu testirovaniyu*, [History of Belarus: Synopsis for Preparation of Testing]. Minsk, Aversev, 2010.

Sherlock, Thomas. *Historical Narratives in the Soviet Union and Post-Soviet Russia: Destroying the Settled Past, Creating an Uncertain Future*. London, Palgrave Macmillan, 2007.

Sheveliov, Iurii. *Z istorii nezakinchenoi viiny* [On the history of unfinished war].—Collected by O. Zabuzhko and L. Masenko. Kyiv, VD KMA 20

Shevelov, George Y. "The Language Question in Ukraine in the Twentieth Century (1900–1941)." *Harvard Ukrainian Studies*, Vol. 11, No.1–2, 1987, pp. 118–224.

Shlapentokh, Vladimir. *Soviet Intellectuals and Political Power: The Post-Stalin Era*. Princeton, Princeton University Press, 1990.

Slezkine, Yuri. "The USSR as a Communal Apartment, or How a Socialist State Promoted Ethnic Particularism." *Slavic Review*, Vol. 53, No. 2, 1994, pp. 414–452.

Slyvka, Iurii. *Istoriia Ukrainy. Pidruchnyk dlia stud. vyshchykh navch. zakl. 4-te vyd.* [History of Ukraine. A textbook for University Students. - 4th edition]. Lviv, Svit, 2003.

Smith, Anthony D. *Nationalism: Theory, Ideology, History*. Malden, Polity Press, 2010.

Smolin, Oleg N. "Novaya Situatsiya v Obrazovatel'nom Zakonodatel'stve: Federal'naya i Regional'naya Kompetentsii" ["New Situation in Educational Legislation: Federal and Regional Competences"]. *Voprosy obrazovaniya* [Issues of Education], Vol. 2, No. 2, 2005, pp. 10-22.

Swedish Government; *Foreign Affairs Archives*, 1989-1991, Diplomat Reports Concerning the Situation in the Baltic States, https://issuu.com/utrikesdepartementet, Accessed 19th April, 2019.

Söderbaum, Hanna. *From Oligarch to Benefactor? Legitimation Strategies among the Wealthy Elite in Post-Soviet Ukraine*, 2018, Uppsala University, PhD dissertation.

Soulet, Jean-Francois. *Istoria comparată a statelor comuniste din 1945 pînă în zilele noastre*. [The comparative history of the Communist states from 1945 to the present]. Chișinău, Ed. Polirom, 1998.

Stashkevich, Nikolaĭ S., Georgiĭ IA. Golenchenko, Ivan I. Bogdanovich *Istoriiā Belarusi. Posobie dliā podgotovki k tsentralizovannomu testirovaniiū* [History of Belarus: Workbook for the Preparation of Centralized Testing]. Minsk, Aversev, 2012.

Sultanbekov, Bulat F., ed. *Istoriia Tatarstana* [History of Tatarstan]. Kazan, TaRikh, 2001.

Sun, Yan. *The Chinese Reassessment of Socialism, 1976–1992*. Princeton, Princeton University Press, 1995.

Suny, Ronald Grigor. *The Revenge of the Past: Nationalism, Revolution, and the Collapse of the Soviet Union*. Stanford, Stanford University Press, 1993.

Svitlychna, Valentyna. *Istoriia Ukrainy: navchalnyi posibnyk. 3-є vidannia*. [History of Ukraine. A textbook. 3rd edition]. Kyiv, Karavela, 2005.

Stefanowska, Liidia. "Back to the Golden Age: The Discourse of Nostalgia in the 1990s (Some Preliminary Remarks)." *Harvard Ukrainian Studies*, Vol. 27, No. 1/4, 2004–2005, pp. 181– 193.

Szporluk, Roman. *Russia, Ukraine, and the Breakup of the Soviet Union*. Stanford, Hoover Institution Press, 2000.

Sztompka, Piotr. "Cultural Trauma: The Other Face of Social Change." *European Journal of Social Change*, Vol. 3, No. 4, 2000, pp. 449–466.

Temko, Hryhorii, and Leonid Tupchiienko. *Istoriia Ukrainy: Posibnyk*. [History of Ukraine. A handbook]. Kyiv, Vydavnychyi tsentr Akademiia, 2001.

Tolstoy, Leo. *Anna Karenina*. 1875–1877. Moscow, Ecsmo, 2011.

Treshchenok, Yakov. *Istoriya Bielarusi, vol. 2*, [History of Belarus, vol. 2]. Mogiliov, Mogiliov State University, 2005.

Turchenko, Fedir, Petro Panchenko, Serhii Tymchenko. *Novitnia Istoriia Ukrainy (1930-2001). 11 klas.* [Contemporary History of Ukraine (1930-2001). 11th form]. Kyiv, Heneza, 2001.

Turchenko, Fedir. *Istoriia Ukrainy. 11 klas.* [History of Ukraine. 11th form]. Kyiv, Heneza, 2011.

Tiurina, Iulia A. *Transformatsiia Obrazovaniia v Sovetskoi i Postsovetstkoi Rossii: Sravnitel'nyi Analiz* [Transformation of Education in Soviet and Post-Soviet Russia: Comparative Analysis]. 2010. Sankt Peterburg, SPbGU, doktorskaia dissertatsiia.

Ukrainian Institute of National Remembrance. *Law of Ukraine on Access to Archives of Repressive Agencies of Totalitarian Communist Regime of 1917–1991.* www.memory.gov.ua/laws/law-ukraine-access-archives-repressive-agencies-totalitarian-communist-regime-1917–1991. Accessed 28 March 2018.

—. *Law of Ukraine on the Condemnation of the Communist and National Socialist (Nazi) Regimes, and Prohibition of Propaganda of Their Symbols.* www.memory.gov.ua/laws/law-ukraine-condemnation-communist-and-national-socialist-nazi-regimes-and-prohibition-propagan. Accessed 28 March. 2018.

—. *Law of Ukraine On the Legal Status and Honoring the Memory of Fighters for Ukraine's Independence in the Twentieth Century.* www.memory.gov.ua/laws/law-ukraine-legal-status-and-honoring-memory-fighters-ukraines-independence-twentieth-century. Accessed 28 March 2018.

—. *Law of Ukraine On Perpetuation of the Victory over Nazism in World War II of 1939–1945.* www.memory.gov.ua/laws/law-ukraine-perpetuation-victory-over-nazism-world-war-ii-1939–1945. Accessed 28 March. 2018.

Urban, Michael E. *An Algebra of Soviet Power: Elite Circulation in the Belorussian Republic 1966–86.* Cambridge, Cambridge University Press, 1989.

Valiullin, Kadim B., Rezeda K. Zaripova. *Istoriia Rossii. XX Vek* [History of Russia. The 20th Century]. Ufa, RIO BashGU, 2002.

Verstiuk, Vladyslav, Olexiy Haran, Olexandr Gurzhii. *Istoriia Ukrainy.* [History of Ukraine] Ed.Valeriy Smoliy, Kyiv, Vydavnychyi dim "Alternatyvy," 1997.

Voronianskyi, Oleksandr. *Istoriia Ukrainy: navchalnyi posibnyk dlia studentiv vyshchykh navchalnykh zakladiv* [History of Ukraine: a textbook for University Students]. Kharkiv, Parus, 2005.

Voslensky, Michael. *Nomenklatura: The Soviet Ruling Class.* London, The Bodley Head, 1984.

Werth, Nicolas. *Istoria Uniunii Sovietice: de la Hruşciov la Gorbaciov (1953-1985)* [The History of the Soviet Union: From Khrushchev to Gorbachev (1953-1985)]. Bucureşti, Ed. Corint, 2000.

Wesseling, Henk. "History: Science or Art?" *European Review*, Vol. 6, No 3, 1998, pp. 265-267.

Westholm, Anders. *The Political Heritage: Testing Theories of Family Socialization and Generational Change*. 1991. Uppsala University, PhD dissertation.

White, Hayden. "The Value of Narrativity in the Representation of Reality." *Critical Inquiry*, Vol. 7, No. 1, 1980, pp. 5-27.

Wilson, Andrew. *Belarus: The Last European Dictatorship*. New Haven, Yale University Press, 2012.

Wodak, Ruth, R. de Cillia, and M. Reisigi, "The discursive construction of national identities." *Discourse and Society*, Vol. 10, No. 2, 1999, pp. 149-173.

Ianguzin, Rim Z., redaktor. *Istoriia Bashkortostana (1917-1990)* [History of Bashkortostan (1917-1990)]. Ufa, BasshGU, 1997.

Ieltsin, Boris "Berite stol'ko sivereniteta, skol'ko mozhete vziat'" ["Take as much sovereignty as you can!"]. Presidential Center of Boris Yeltsin, https://yeltsin.ru/news/boris-elcin-berite-stolko-suverineteta-skolko-smozhete-proglotit/. Accessed 05 May 2019.

Zagladin, Nikita V., Sergey T. Minakov, Sergey L. Kozlenko, and Yuriy A. Petrov. *Istoriia Rossii. XX – Nachalo XXI Veka* [History of Russia: The 20th Century]. Moscow, Russkoe slovo, 2007.

Zaitsev, Iurii, editor. *Istoriia Ukrainy*. [History of Ukraine]. Lviv, Svit, 1998.

Zajda, Joseph. "Nation-building and history education in a global culture." *Nation- Building and History Education in a Global Culture*, ed. Joseph Zajda, Springer, Netherlands, 2015, pp. 185-191.

Zaruba, Viktor. *Istoriia derzhavy i prava Ukrainy: navch. posib*. [History of state and law of Ukraine]. Kyiv, Istyna, 2006.

Zinovskiĭ, Vladimir, Alekseĭ I︠A︡rkovet︠s︡, Irina Kogstevich, Elena Kukharevich, Elena Palkovskai︠a︡, Irina SHestakova, Alekseĭ Tarasenko, Inna Inna Konoshonok. "Nat︠s︡ional'nyĭ sostav naselenii︠a︡ Respubliki Belarus'" ["National Composition of the Population of the Republic of Belarus]. *Perepis' naselenii︠a︡ 2009. T. 3. Nat︠s︡ional'nyĭ sostav naselenii︠a︡ Respubliki Belarus'"* [National Composition of the Population of the Republic of Belarus]. *Perepis' naselenii︠a︡ 2009. T. 3. Nat︠s︡ional'nyĭ sostav naselenii︠a︡ Respubliki Belarus'* [*Population Census 2009. Vol. 3: National Composition of the Population of the Republic of the Respublic of Belarus*]. Minsk, National Statistic Committee of the Republic of Belarus, 2010, pp. 7-131.

Åberg, Martin. "Paradox of Change: Soviet Modernization and Ethno-Linguistic Differentiation in Lviv, 1945-1989." *Harvard Ukrainian Studies*, Vol. 24, 2000, pp. 285-301.

Index

A

Abkhazia 23
Alternative center 36, 37, 55
Armenia 22, 23, 147, 166
Assman, Jan 18, 175
Azerbaijan 23, 25, 26, 147, 167

B

Baltic States 13, 22, 23, 25, 26, 139, 140, 157, 166, 189
Barsenkov, Alexander 32, 40, 41, 43, 45, 57, 176
Bashkortostan 36, 37, 39, 58, 191
Bauman, Zygmunt 23, 176
Bellah, Robert 17, 18, 176
Bessarabia 12, 138, 139, 140, 141, 142, 144, 147, 155, 158, 159, 171, 181, 185
Bukovina 12, 171

C

Central Asia 26, 183
Chechnya 19, 29, 36, 37, 39, 48, 49, 54, 55, 56, 57, 159, 160, 164, 172, 175
Chernobyl 10, 38, 43, 49, 52, 64, 65, 78, 83, 118, 119, 120, 121, 122, 123, 124, 129, 131, 132, 133, 135, 179
Citizenship 29, 33, 72, 142
Cold War 23, 70, 96, 109, 132, 151, 177, 180, 182, 184
Collective memory 15, 17, 18, 19, 123, 158, 175, 179
community of memory 18
Crimea 9, 12, 16, 20, 23, 61, 75, 82, 147
Cultural trauma 15, 123
Czechoslovakia 12, 153, 171, 177

D

Diaspora 132
 Belarusian Diaspora 131
 Ukrainian diaspora 14, 81
Domino principle 29, 39, 41, 43, 45, 46, 47, 48, 49, 50, 51, 53, 55, 68, 115, 116
Donbas 23, 75, 76

E

Eastern Europe 10, 91, 105, 152, 169, 176, 177, 179, 180, 181, 186
Eastern Partnership 10
Eastern Ukraine 9, 12, 20, 73, 76, 82
Ethnos 29, 32, 33, 35
Europe 9, 22, 23, 63, 92, 150, 152, 176, 178, 179, 180, 187
 Central Europe 62, 73, 117, 176, 180
 common European home 146, 148, 150
 Eastern Europe 10, 91, 105, 152, 169, 176, 177, 179, 180, 181, 186
European civilization 73
European countries 63
European democracies 130
European institutions 144
European nations 150
European realities 150
Europeanization 152
 Western Europe 152
European Union 10, 20, 187

F

Feudal Machiavellianism 39, 48, 49, 53, 54
Freeland, Chrystia 24
Fukuyama, Francis 23, 180

G

Galicia 12, 73, 80, 139, 165, 171
Georgia 22, 23, 25, 26, 166
Glasnost 40, 44, 51, 65, 68, 70, 71, 72, 78, 98, 106, 108, 115, 128, 129, 130, 157, 173, 177

H

Habsburg Empire 12
Halbwachs, Maurice 17, 18, 181
Holodomor 12, 66, 167

I

Ianukovych, Viktor 16, 74, 81
Irkutskaya Oblast 36, 37

K

Kohl, Helmut 22
Komsomol 24

L

Latvia 16, 22, 73, 166, 168, 184
Le Mémoire collective 18
Ligachev, Yegor 25
Lithuania 21, 22, 53, 122, 160, 166, 168, 177, 180, 184
Lukashenko, Alexander 20, 186

M

Mannheim, Karl 14, 184
Memory Politics 15, 19
Ministry of Education and Science 31, 36, 86, 87
Molotov-Ribbentrop Pact 12, 65, 139, 140

N

Nagorno-Karabakh 23, 147
National Identity 13, 17, 25, 29, 33, 34, 35, 59, 80, 81, 91, 106, 126, 140, 159, 169, 175, 187
Nationality 26, 34, 100, 106, 158, 163, 178
Nation-building 9, 17, 53, 55, 56, 61, 67, 83, 102, 125, 159, 164, 167, 168, 183, 191
Nazi Germany 12, 139
Nomenklatura 24, 47, 117, 190
North Ossetia 32, 48

O

Orange Revolution 20, 74, 166, 173, 174, 187
Orwell, George 20, 185

P

Periphery 31, 45, 49, 55, 96, 110, 160, 169
Pingel, Falk 16, 186
Poland 12, 53, 139, 171, 177

R

Reagan, Ronald 22, 180, 184
Regional 29, 31, 35, 36, 37, 39, 45, 47, 49, 52, 53, 54, 55, 72, 82, 84, 119, 144, 162, 163, 165
regional centers 36, 37
regional composition 72
Regional differences 31
regional diversity 31, 53, 55, 72, 163
regional divisions 31, 163
regional heroes 49
regional histories 37, 72
regional history 29, 31, 144
regional languages 37, 82
regional level 31, 47, 49, 52, 119
regional perspective 39
regional political elites 48, 54
regional separatism 45
regional textbooks 36, 37
regional variety 35
religious identity 165
Revolution of Dignity 16, 79, 82, 174, 187
Romania 12, 13, 51, 137, 138, 139, 140, 141, 142, 143, 144, 146, 147, 150, 151, 152, 154, 155, 158, 159,

171, 172, 177, 178, 179, 185, 188
Russian Academy of Education 32
Russian Federation 21, 22, 29, 31, 32, 36, 41, 55, 56, 82, 103, 162, 163, 164
Russian Ministry of Foreign Affairs 16
Russian-ness 29, 35, 165

S

Secondary school 9, 16, 30, 31, 35, 60, 86, 92, 93, 114, 137, 162, 182
Shevchuk, Yuri 15
Socialization 13, 17, 191
South Ossetia 23
Statehood 9, 15, 27, 72, 83, 84, 87, 125, 157, 168, 170, 176, 178
Subtelny, Orest 15
Sweden 7, 10
Swedish Embassy 21, 26
Sztompka, Piotr 15, 189

T

Tabachnyk, Dmytro 20
Tatarstan 19, 29, 32, 36, 37, 39, 48, 50, 51, 52, 53, 54, 56, 58, 78, 159, 160, 164, 165, 172, 173, 188, 189
Thatcher, Margaret 22, 63
Tolstoy, Leo 15, 189
Transnistria 12, 23, 140, 141, 143, 152, 155, 171, 185
Trauma 15, 85, 102, 112, 123, 127, 189

Tsarist Russia 12, 23, 62, 115, 159, 164, 165, 171

U

United Kingdom 22
United States 22, 40, 63, 184

V

Vdovin, Alexander 32, 40, 41, 43, 45, 57, 176
Volhynia 12, 171

W

West 22, 72, 74, 96, 105, 106, 111, 148, 157, 161, 165, 170, 175
West Germany 22
Western 10, 12, 13, 22, 44, 68, 73, 75, 78, 79, 80, 81, 94, 98, 100, 105, 119, 152, 169, 170
Western Ukraine 12, 13, 73, 78, 79, 80
World History 41, 92, 113, 128, 129, 137, 139, 143, 144, 145, 146, 152, 154, 155, 179, 182, 185, 186
World War I 12, 16, 59, 106, 165, 190
World War II 12, 16, 59, 106, 165, 190

Y

Yeltsin, Boris 191

SOVIET AND POST-SOVIET POLITICS AND SOCIETY
Edited by Dr. Andreas Umland | ISSN 1614-3515

1. *Андреас Умланд (ред.)* | Воплощение Европейской конвенции по правам человека в России. Философские, юридические и эмпирические исследования | ISBN 3-89821-387-0
2. *Christian Wipperfürth* | Russland – ein vertrauenswürdiger Partner? Grundlagen, Hintergründe und Praxis gegenwärtiger russischer Außenpolitik | Mit einem Vorwort von Heinz Timmermann | ISBN 3-89821-401-X
3. *Manja Hussner* | Die Übernahme internationalen Rechts in die russische und deutsche Rechtsordnung. Eine vergleichende Analyse zur Völkerrechtsfreundlichkeit der Verfassungen der Russländischen Föderation und der Bundesrepublik Deutschland | Mit einem Vorwort von Rainer Arnold | ISBN 3-89821-438-9
4. *Matthew Tejada* | Bulgaria's Democratic Consolidation and the Kozloduy Nuclear Power Plant (KNPP). The Unattainability of Closure | With a foreword by Richard J. Crampton | ISBN 3-89821-439-7
5. *Марк Григорьевич Меерович* | Квадратные метры, определяющие сознание. Государственная жилищная политика в СССР. 1921 – 1941 гг | ISBN 3-89821-474-5
6. *Andrei P. Tsygankov, Pavel A.Tsygankov (Eds.)* | New Directions in Russian International Studies | ISBN 3-89821-422-2
7. *Марк Григорьевич Меерович* | Как власть народ к труду приучала. Жилище в СССР – средство управления людьми. 1917 – 1941 гг. | С предисловием Елены Осокиной | ISBN 3-89821-495-8
8. *David J. Galbreath* | Nation-Building and Minority Politics in Post-Socialist States. Interests, Influence and Identities in Estonia and Latvia | With a foreword by David J. Smith | ISBN 3-89821-467-2
9. *Алексей Юрьевич Безугольный* | Народы Кавказа в Вооруженных силах СССР в годы Великой Отечественной войны 1941-1945 гг. | С предисловием Николая Бугая | ISBN 3-89821-475-3
10. *Вячеслав Лихачев и Владимир Прибыловский (ред.)* | Русское Национальное Единство, 1990-2000. В 2-х томах | ISBN 3-89821-523-7
11. *Николай Бугай (ред.)* | Народы стран Балтии в условиях сталинизма (1940-е – 1950-е годы). Документированная история | ISBN 3-89821-525-3
12. *Ingmar Bredies (Hrsg.)* | Zur Anatomie der Orange Revolution in der Ukraine. Wechsel des Eliteregimes oder Triumph des Parlamentarismus?| ISBN 3-89821-524-5
13. *Anastasia V. Mitrofanova* | The Politicization of Russian Orthodoxy. Actors and Ideas | With a foreword by William C. Gay | ISBN 3-89821-481-8
14. *Nathan D. Larson* | Alexander Solzhenitsyn and the Russo-Jewish Question | ISBN 3-89821-483-4
15. *Guido Houben* | Kulturpolitik und Ethnizität. Staatliche Kunstförderung im Russland der neunziger Jahre | Mit einem Vorwort von Gert Weisskirchen | ISBN 3-89821-542-3
16. *Leonid Luks* | Der russische „Sonderweg"? Aufsätze zur neuesten Geschichte Russlands im europäischen Kontext | ISBN 3-89821-496-6
17. *Евгений Мороз* | История «Мёртвой воды» – от страшной сказки к большой политике. Политическое неоязычество в постсоветской России | ISBN 3-89821-551-2
18. *Александр Верховский и Галина Кожевникова (ред.)* | Этническая и религиозная интолерантность в российских СМИ. Результаты мониторинга 2001-2004 гг. | ISBN 3-89821-569-5
19. *Christian Ganzer* | Sowjetisches Erbe und ukrainische Nation. Das Museum der Geschichte des Zaporoger Kosakentums auf der Insel Chortycja | Mit einem Vorwort von Frank Golczewski | ISBN 3-89821-504-0
20. *Эльза-Баир Гучинова* | Помнить нельзя забыть. Антропология депортационной травмы калмыков | С предисловием Кэролайн Хамфри | ISBN 3-89821-506-7
21. *Юлия Лидерман* | Мотивы «проверки» и «испытания» в постсоветской культуре. Советское прошлое в российском кинематографе 1990-х годов | С предисловием Евгения Марголита | ISBN 3-89821-511-3
22. *Tanya Lokshina, Ray Thomas, Mary Mayer (Eds.)* | The Imposition of a Fake Political Settlement in the Northern Caucasus. The 2003 Chechen Presidential Election | ISBN 3-89821-436-2
23. *Timothy McCajor Hall, Rosie Read (Eds.)* | Changes in the Heart of Europe. Recent Ethnographies of Czechs, Slovaks, Roma, and Sorbs | With an afterword by Zdeněk Salzmann | ISBN 3-89821-606-3

24 *Christian Autengruber* | Die politischen Parteien in Bulgarien und Rumänien. Eine vergleichende Analyse seit Beginn der 90er Jahre | Mit einem Vorwort von Dorothée de Nève | ISBN 3-89821-476-1

25 *Annette Freyberg-Inan with Radu Cristescu* | The Ghosts in Our Classrooms, or: John Dewey Meets Ceauşescu. The Promise and the Failures of Civic Education in Romania | ISBN 3-89821-416-8

26 *John B. Dunlop* | The 2002 Dubrovka and 2004 Beslan Hostage Crises. A Critique of Russian Counter-Terrorism | With a foreword by Donald N. Jensen | ISBN 3-89821-608-X

27 *Peter Koller* | Das touristische Potenzial von Kam"janec'–Podil's'kyj. Eine fremdenverkehrsgeographische Untersuchung der Zukunftsperspektiven und Maßnahmenplanung zur Destinationsentwicklung des „ukrainischen Rothenburg" | Mit einem Vorwort von Kristiane Klemm | ISBN 3-89821-640-3

28 *Françoise Daucé, Elisabeth Sieca-Kozlowski (Eds.)* | Dedovshchina in the Post-Soviet Military. Hazing of Russian Army Conscripts in a Comparative Perspective | With a foreword by Dale Herspring | ISBN 3-89821-616-0

29 *Florian Strasser* | Zivilgesellschaftliche Einflüsse auf die Orange Revolution. Die gewaltlose Massenbewegung und die ukrainische Wahlkrise 2004 | Mit einem Vorwort von Egbert Jahn | ISBN 3-89821-648-9

30 *Rebecca S. Katz* | The Georgian Regime Crisis of 2003-2004. A Case Study in Post-Soviet Media Representation of Politics, Crime and Corruption | ISBN 3-89821-413-3

31 *Vladimir Kantor* | Willkür oder Freiheit. Beiträge zur russischen Geschichtsphilosophie | Ediert von Dagmar Herrmann sowie mit einem Vorwort versehen von Leonid Luks | ISBN 3-89821-589-X

32 *Laura A. Victoir* | The Russian Land Estate Today. A Case Study of Cultural Politics in Post-Soviet Russia | With a foreword by Priscilla Roosevelt | ISBN 3-89821-426-5

33 *Ivan Katchanovski* | Cleft Countries. Regional Political Divisions and Cultures in Post-Soviet Ukraine and Moldova| With a foreword by Francis Fukuyama | ISBN 3-89821-558-X

34 *Florian Mühlfried* | Postsowjetische Feiern. Das Georgische Bankett im Wandel | Mit einem Vorwort von Kevin Tuite | ISBN 3-89821-601-2

35 *Roger Griffin, Werner Loh, Andreas Umland (Eds.)* | Fascism Past and Present, West and East. An International Debate on Concepts and Cases in the Comparative Study of the Extreme Right | With an afterword by Walter Laqueur | ISBN 3-89821-674-8

36 *Sebastian Schlegel* | Der „Weiße Archipel". Sowjetische Atomstädte 1945-1991 | Mit einem Geleitwort von Thomas Bohn | ISBN 3-89821-679-9

37 *Vyacheslav Likhachev* | Political Anti-Semitism in Post-Soviet Russia. Actors and Ideas in 1991-2003 | Edited and translated from Russian by Eugene Veklerov | ISBN 3-89821-529-6

38 *Josette Baer (Ed.)* | Preparing Liberty in Central Europe. Political Texts from the Spring of Nations 1848 to the Spring of Prague 1968 | With a foreword by Zdeněk V. David | ISBN 3-89821-546-6

39 *Михаил Лукьянов* | Российский консерватизм и реформа, 1907-1914 | С предисловием Марка Д. Стейнберга | ISBN 3-89821-503-2

40 *Nicola Melloni* | Market Without Economy. The 1998 Russian Financial Crisis | With a foreword by Eiji Furukawa | ISBN 3-89821-407-9

41 *Dmitrij Chmelnizki* | Die Architektur Stalins | Bd. 1: Studien zu Ideologie und Stil | Bd. 2: Bilddokumentation | Mit einem Vorwort von Bruno Flierl | ISBN 3-89821-515-6

42 *Katja Yafimava* | Post-Soviet Russian-Belarussian Relationships. The Role of Gas Transit Pipelines | With a foreword by Jonathan P. Stern | ISBN 3-89821-655-1

43 *Boris Chavkin* | Verflechtungen der deutschen und russischen Zeitgeschichte. Aufsätze und Archivfunde zu den Beziehungen Deutschlands und der Sowjetunion von 1917 bis 1991 | Ediert von Markus Edlinger sowie mit einem Vorwort versehen von Leonid Luks | ISBN 3-89821-756-6

44 *Anastasija Grynenko in Zusammenarbeit mit Claudia Dathe* | Die Terminologie des Gerichtswesens der Ukraine und Deutschlands im Vergleich. Eine übersetzungswissenschaftliche Analyse juristischer Fachbegriffe im Deutschen, Ukrainischen und Russischen | Mit einem Vorwort von Ulrich Hartmann | ISBN 3-89821-691-8

45 *Anton Burkov* | The Impact of the European Convention on Human Rights on Russian Law. Legislation and Application in 1996-2006 | With a foreword by Françoise Hampson | ISBN 978-3-89821-639-5

46 *Stina Torjesen, Indra Overland (Eds.)* | International Election Observers in Post-Soviet Azerbaijan. Geopolitical Pawns or Agents of Change? | ISBN 978-3-89821-743-9

47 *Taras Kuzio* | Ukraine – Crimea – Russia. Triangle of Conflict | ISBN 978-3-89821-761-3

48 *Claudia Šabić* | "Ich erinnere mich nicht, aber L'viv!" Zur Funktion kultureller Faktoren für die Institutionalisierung und Entwicklung einer ukrainischen Region | Mit einem Vorwort von Melanie Tatur | ISBN 978-3-89821-752-1

49 *Marlies Bilz* | Tatarstan in der Transformation. Nationaler Diskurs und Politische Praxis 1988-1994 | Mit einem Vorwort von Frank Golczewski | ISBN 978-3-89821-722-4

50 *Марлен Ларюэль (ред.)* | Современные интерпретации русского национализма | ISBN 978-3-89821-795-8

51 *Sonja Schüler* | Die ethnische Dimension der Armut. Roma im postsozialistischen Rumänien | Mit einem Vorwort von Anton Sterbling | ISBN 978-3-89821-776-7

52 *Галина Кожевникова* | Радикальный национализм в России и противодействие ему. Сборник докладов Центра «Сова» за 2004-2007 гг. | С предисловием Александра Верховского | ISBN 978-3-89821-721-7

53 *Галина Кожевникова и Владимир Прибыловский* | Российская власть в биографиях I. Высшие должностные лица РФ в 2004 г. | ISBN 978-3-89821-796-5

54 *Галина Кожевникова и Владимир Прибыловский* | Российская власть в биографиях II. Члены Правительства РФ в 2004 г. | ISBN 978-3-89821-797-2

55 *Галина Кожевникова и Владимир Прибыловский* | Российская власть в биографиях III. Руководители федеральных служб и агентств РФ в 2004 г.| ISBN 978-3-89821-798-9

56 *Ileana Petroniu* | Privatisierung in Transformationsökonomien. Determinanten der Restrukturierungs-Bereitschaft am Beispiel Polens, Rumäniens und der Ukraine | Mit einem Vorwort von Rainer W. Schäfer | ISBN 978-3-89821-790-3

57 *Christian Wipperfürth* | Russland und seine GUS-Nachbarn. Hintergründe, aktuelle Entwicklungen und Konflikte in einer ressourcenreichen Region| ISBN 978-3-89821-801-6

58 *Togzhan Kassenova* | From Antagonism to Partnership. The Uneasy Path of the U.S.-Russian Cooperative Threat Reduction | With a foreword by Christoph Bluth | ISBN 978-3-89821-707-1

59 *Alexander Höllwerth* | Das sakrale eurasische Imperium des Aleksandr Dugin. Eine Diskursanalyse zum postsowjetischen russischen Rechtsextremismus | Mit einem Vorwort von Dirk Uffelmann | ISBN 978-3-89821-813-9

60 *Олег Рябов* | «Россия-Матушка». Национализм, гендер и война в России XX века | С предисловием Елены Гощило | ISBN 978-3-89821-487-2

61 *Ivan Maistrenko* | Borot'bism. A Chapter in the History of the Ukrainian Revolution | With a new Introduction by Chris Ford | Translated by George S. N. Luckyj with the assistance of Ivan L. Rudnytsky | Second, Revised and Expanded Edition ISBN 978-3-8382-1107-7

62 *Maryna Romanets* | Anamorphosic Texts and Reconfigured Visions. Improvised Traditions in Contemporary Ukrainian and Irish Literature | ISBN 978-3-89821-576-3

63 *Paul D'Anieri and Taras Kuzio (Eds.)* | Aspects of the Orange Revolution I. Democratization and Elections in Post-Communist Ukraine | ISBN 978-3-89821-698-2

64 *Bohdan Harasymiw in collaboration with Oleh S. Ilnytzkyj (Eds.)* | Aspects of the Orange Revolution II. Information and Manipulation Strategies in the 2004 Ukrainian Presidential Elections | ISBN 978-3-89821-699-9

65 *Ingmar Bredies, Andreas Umland and Valentin Yakushik (Eds.)* | Aspects of the Orange Revolution III. The Context and Dynamics of the 2004 Ukrainian Presidential Elections | ISBN 978-3-89821-803-0

66 *Ingmar Bredies, Andreas Umland and Valentin Yakushik (Eds.)* | Aspects of the Orange Revolution IV. Foreign Assistance and Civic Action in the 2004 Ukrainian Presidential Elections | ISBN 978-3-89821-808-5

67 *Ingmar Bredies, Andreas Umland and Valentin Yakushik (Eds.)* | Aspects of the Orange Revolution V. Institutional Observation Reports on the 2004 Ukrainian Presidential Elections | ISBN 978-3-89821-809-2

68 *Taras Kuzio (Ed.)* | Aspects of the Orange Revolution VI. Post-Communist Democratic Revolutions in Comparative Perspective | ISBN 978-3-89821-820-7

69 *Tim Bohse* | Autoritarismus statt Selbstverwaltung. Die Transformation der kommunalen Politik in der Stadt Kaliningrad 1990-2005 | Mit einem Geleitwort von Stefan Troebst | ISBN 978-3-89821-782-8

70 *David Rupp* | Die Rußländische Föderation und die russischsprachige Minderheit in Lettland. Eine Fallstudie zur Anwaltspolitik Moskaus gegenüber den russophonen Minderheiten im „Nahen Ausland" von 1991 bis 2002 | Mit einem Vorwort von Helmut Wagner | ISBN 978-3-89821-778-1

71 *Taras Kuzio* | Theoretical and Comparative Perspectives on Nationalism. New Directions in Cross-Cultural and Post-Communist Studies | With a foreword by Paul Robert Magocsi | ISBN 978-3-89821-815-3

72 *Christine Teichmann* | Die Hochschultransformation im heutigen Osteuropa. Kontinuität und Wandel bei der Entwicklung des postkommunistischen Universitätswesens | Mit einem Vorwort von Oskar Anweiler | ISBN 978-3-89821-842-9

73 *Julia Kusznir* | Der politische Einfluss von Wirtschaftseliten in russischen Regionen. Eine Analyse am Beispiel der Erdöl- und Erdgasindustrie, 1992-2005 | Mit einem Vorwort von Wolfgang Eichwede | ISBN 978-3-89821-821-4

74 *Alena Vysotskaya* | Russland, Belarus und die EU-Osterweiterung. Zur Minderheitenfrage und zum Problem der Freizügigkeit des Personenverkehrs | Mit einem Vorwort von Katlijn Malfliet | ISBN 978-3-89821-822-1

75 *Heiko Pleines (Hrsg.)* | Corporate Governance in post-sozialistischen Volkswirtschaften | ISBN 978-3-89821-766-8

76 *Stefan Ihrig* | Wer sind die Moldawier? Rumänismus versus Moldowanismus in Historiographie und Schulbüchern der Republik Moldova, 1991-2006 | Mit einem Vorwort von Holm Sundhaussen | ISBN 978-3-89821-466-7

77 *Galina Kozhevnikova in collaboration with Alexander Verkhovsky and Eugene Veklerov* | Ultra-Nationalism and Hate Crimes in Contemporary Russia. The 2004-2006 Annual Reports of Moscow's SOVA Center | With a foreword by Stephen D. Shenfield | ISBN 978-3-89821-868-9

78 *Florian Küchler* | The Role of the European Union in Moldova's Transnistria Conflict | With a foreword by Christopher Hill | ISBN 978-3-89821-850-4

79 *Bernd Rechel* | The Long Way Back to Europe. Minority Protection in Bulgaria | With a foreword by Richard Crampton | ISBN 978-3-89821-863-4

80 *Peter W. Rodgers* | Nation, Region and History in Post-Communist Transitions. Identity Politics in Ukraine, 1991-2006 | With a foreword by Vera Tolz | ISBN 978-3-89821-903-7

81 *Stephanie Solywoda* | The Life and Work of Semen L. Frank. A Study of Russian Religious Philosophy | With a foreword by Philip Walters | ISBN 978-3-89821-457-5

82 *Vera Sokolova* | Cultural Politics of Ethnicity. Discourses on Roma in Communist Czechoslovakia | ISBN 978-3-89821-864-1

83 *Natalya Shevchik Ketenci* | Kazakhstani Enterprises in Transition. The Role of Historical Regional Development in Kazakhstan's Post-Soviet Economic Transformation | ISBN 978-3-89821-831-3

84 *Martin Malek, Anna Schor-Tschudnowskaja (Hgg.)* | Europa im Tschetschenienkrieg. Zwischen politischer Ohnmacht und Gleichgültigkeit | Mit einem Vorwort von Lipchan Basajewa | ISBN 978-3-89821-676-0

85 *Stefan Meister* | Das postsowjetische Universitätswesen zwischen nationalem und internationalem Wandel. Die Entwicklung der regionalen Hochschule in Russland als Gradmesser der Systemtransformation | Mit einem Vorwort von Joan DeBardeleben | ISBN 978-3-89821-891-7

86 *Konstantin Sheiko in collaboration with Stephen Brown* | Nationalist Imaginings of the Russian Past. Anatolii Fomenko and the Rise of Alternative History in Post-Communist Russia | With a foreword by Donald Ostrowski | ISBN 978-3-89821-915-0

87 *Sabine Jenni* | Wie stark ist das „Einige Russland"? Zur Parteibindung der Eliten und zum Wahlerfolg der Machtpartei im Dezember 2007 | Mit einem Vorwort von Klaus Armingeon | ISBN 978-3-89821-961-7

88 *Thomas Borén* | Meeting-Places of Transformation. Urban Identity, Spatial Representations and Local Politics in Post-Soviet St Petersburg | ISBN 978-3-89821-739-2

89 *Aygul Ashirova* | Stalinismus und Stalin-Kult in Zentralasien. Turkmenistan 1924-1953 | Mit einem Vorwort von Leonid Luks | ISBN 978-3-89821-987-7

90 *Leonid Luks* | Freiheit oder imperiale Größe? Essays zu einem russischen Dilemma | ISBN 978-3-8382-0011-8

91 *Christopher Gilley* | The 'Change of Signposts' in the Ukrainian Emigration. A Contribution to the History of Sovietophilism in the 1920s | With a foreword by Frank Golczewski | ISBN 978-3-89821-965-5

92 *Philipp Casula, Jeronim Perovic (Eds.)* | Identities and Politics During the Putin Presidency. The Discursive Foundations of Russia's Stability | With a foreword by Heiko Haumann | ISBN 978-3-8382-0015-6

93 *Marcel Viëtor* | Europa und die Frage nach seinen Grenzen im Osten. Zur Konstruktion ‚europäischer Identität' in Geschichte und Gegenwart | Mit einem Vorwort von Albrecht Lehmann | ISBN 978-3-8382-0045-3

94 *Ben Hellman, Andrei Rogachevskii* | Filming the Unfilmable. Casper Wrede's 'One Day in the Life of Ivan Denisovich' | Second, Revised and Expanded Edition | ISBN 978-3-8382-0044-6

95 *Eva Fuchslocher* | Vaterland, Sprache, Glaube. Orthodoxie und Nationenbildung am Beispiel Georgiens | Mit einem Vorwort von Christina von Braun | ISBN 978-3-89821-884-9

96 *Vladimir Kantor* | Das Westlertum und der Weg Russlands. Zur Entwicklung der russischen Literatur und Philosophie | Ediert von Dagmar Herrmann | Mit einem Beitrag von Nikolaus Lobkowicz | ISBN 978-3-8382-0102-3

97 *Kamran Musayev* | Die postsowjetische Transformation im Baltikum und Südkaukasus. Eine vergleichende Untersuchung der politischen Entwicklung Lettlands und Aserbaidschans 1985-2009 | Mit einem Vorwort von Leonid Luks | Ediert von Sandro Henschel | ISBN 978-3-8382-0103-0

98 *Tatiana Zhurzhenko* | Borderlands into Bordered Lands. Geopolitics of Identity in Post-Soviet Ukraine | With a foreword by Dieter Segert | ISBN 978-3-8382-0042-2

99 *Кирилл Галушко, Лидия Смола (ред.)* | Пределы падения – варианты украинского будущего. Аналитико-прогностические исследования | ISBN 978-3-8382-0148-1

100 *Michael Minkenberg (Ed.)* | Historical Legacies and the Radical Right in Post-Cold War Central and Eastern Europe | With an afterword by Sabrina P. Ramet | ISBN 978-3-8382-0124-5

101 *David-Emil Wickström* | Rocking St. Petersburg. Transcultural Flows and Identity Politics in the St. Petersburg Popular Music Scene | With a foreword by Yngvar B. Steinholt | Second, Revised and Expanded Edition | ISBN 978-3-8382-0100-9

102 *Eva Zabka* | Eine neue „Zeit der Wirren"? Der spät- und postsowjetische Systemwandel 1985-2000 im Spiegel russischer gesellschaftspolitischer Diskurse | Mit einem Vorwort von Margareta Mommsen | ISBN 978-3-8382-0161-0

103 *Ulrike Ziemer* | Ethnic Belonging, Gender and Cultural Practices. Youth Identitites in Contemporary Russia | With a foreword by Anoop Nayak | ISBN 978-3-8382-0152-8

104 *Ksenia Chepikova* | ‚Einiges Russland' - eine zweite KPdSU? Aspekte der Identitätskonstruktion einer postsowjetischen „Partei der Macht" | Mit einem Vorwort von Torsten Oppelland | ISBN 978-3-8382-0311-9

105 *Леонид Люкс* | Западничество или евразийство? Демократия или идеократия? Сборник статей об исторических дилеммах России | С предисловием Владимира Кантора | ISBN 978-3-8382-0211-2

106 *Anna Dost* | Das russische Verfassungsrecht auf dem Weg zum Föderalismus und zurück. Zum Konflikt von Rechtsnormen und -wirklichkeit in der Russländischen Föderation von 1991 bis 2009 | Mit einem Vorwort von Alexander Blankenagel | ISBN 978-3-8382-0292-1

107 *Philipp Herzog* | Sozialistische Völkerfreundschaft, nationaler Widerstand oder harmloser Zeitvertreib? Zur politischen Funktion der Volkskunst im sowjetischen Estland | Mit einem Vorwort von Andreas Kappeler | ISBN 978-3-8382-0216-7

108 *Marlène Laruelle (Ed.)* | Russian Nationalism, Foreign Policy, and Identity Debates in Putin's Russia. New Ideological Patterns after the Orange Revolution | ISBN 978-3-8382-0325-6

109 *Michail Logvinov* | Russlands Kampf gegen den internationalen Terrorismus. Eine kritische Bestandsaufnahme des Bekämpfungsansatzes | Mit einem Geleitwort von Hans-Henning Schröder und einem Vorwort von Eckhard Jesse | ISBN 978-3-8382-0329-4

110 *John B. Dunlop* | The Moscow Bombings of September 1999. Examinations of Russian Terrorist Attacks at the Onset of Vladimir Putin's Rule | Second, Revised and Expanded Edition | ISBN 978-3-8382-0388-1

111 *Андрей А. Ковалёв* | Свидетельство из-за кулис российской политики I. Можно ли делать добро из зла? (Воспоминания и размышления о последних советских и первых послесоветских годах) | With a foreword by Peter Reddaway | ISBN 978-3-8382-0302-7

112 *Андрей А. Ковалёв* | Свидетельство из-за кулис российской политики II. Угроза для себя и окружающих (Наблюдения и предостережения относительно происходящего после 2000 г.) | ISBN 978-3-8382-0303-4

113 *Bernd Kappenberg* | Zeichen setzen für Europa. Der Gebrauch europäischer lateinischer Sonderzeichen in der deutschen Öffentlichkeit | Mit einem Vorwort von Peter Schlobinski | ISBN 978-3-89821-749-1

114 *Ivo Mijnssen* | The Quest for an Ideal Youth in Putin's Russia I. Back to Our Future! History, Modernity, and Patriotism according to Nashi, 2005-2013 | With a foreword by Jeronim Perović | Second, Revised and Expanded Edition | ISBN 978-3-8382-0368-3

115 *Jussi Lassila* | The Quest for an Ideal Youth in Putin's Russia II. The Search for Distinctive Conformism in the Political Communication of Nashi, 2005-2009 | With a foreword by Kirill Postoutenko | Second, Revised and Expanded Edition | ISBN 978-3-8382-0415-4

116 *Valerio Trabandt* | Neue Nachbarn, gute Nachbarschaft? Die EU als internationaler Akteur am Beispiel ihrer Demokratieförderung in Belarus und der Ukraine 2004-2009 | Mit einem Vorwort von Jutta Joachim | ISBN 978-3-8382-0437-6

117 *Fabian Pfeiffer* | Estlands Außen- und Sicherheitspolitik I. Der estnische Atlantizismus nach der wiedererlangten Unabhängigkeit 1991-2004 | Mit einem Vorwort von Helmut Hubel | ISBN 978-3-8382-0127-6

118 *Jana Podßuweit* | Estlands Außen- und Sicherheitspolitik II. Handlungsoptionen eines Kleinstaates im Rahmen seiner EU-Mitgliedschaft (2004-2008) | Mit einem Vorwort von Helmut Hubel | ISBN 978-3-8382-0440-6

119 *Karin Pointner* | Estlands Außen- und Sicherheitspolitik III. Eine gedächtnispolitische Analyse estnischer Entwicklungskooperation 2006-2010 | Mit einem Vorwort von Karin Liebhart | ISBN 978-3-8382-0435-2

120 *Ruslana Vovk* | Die Offenheit der ukrainischen Verfassung für das Völkerrecht und die europäische Integration | Mit einem Vorwort von Alexander Blankenagel | ISBN 978-3-8382-0481-9

121 *Mykhaylo Banakh* | Die Relevanz der Zivilgesellschaft bei den postkommunistischen Transformationsprozessen in mittel- und osteuropäischen Ländern. Das Beispiel der spät- und postsowjetischen Ukraine 1986-2009 | Mit einem Vorwort von Gerhard Simon | ISBN 978-3-8382-0499-4

122 *Michael Moser* | Language Policy and the Discourse on Languages in Ukraine under President Viktor Yanukovych (25 February 2010–28 October 2012) | ISBN 978-3-8382-0497-0 (Paperback edition) | ISBN 978-3-8382-0507-6 (Hardcover edition)

123 *Nicole Krome* | Russischer Netzwerkkapitalismus Restrukturierungsprozesse in der Russischen Föderation am Beispiel des Luftfahrtunternehmens "Aviastar" | Mit einem Vorwort von Petra Stykow | ISBN 978-3-8382-0534-2

124 *David R. Marples* | 'Our Glorious Past'. Lukashenka's Belarus and the Great Patriotic War | ISBN 978-3-8382-0574-8 (Paperback edition) | ISBN 978-3-8382-0675-2 (Hardcover edition)

125 *Ulf Walther* | Russlands "neuer Adel". Die Macht des Geheimdienstes von Gorbatschow bis Putin | Mit einem Vorwort von Hans-Georg Wieck | ISBN 978-3-8382-0584-7

126 *Simon Geissbühler (Hrsg.)* | Kiew – Revolution 3.0. Der Euromaidan 2013/14 und die Zukunftsperspektiven der Ukraine | ISBN 978-3-8382-0581-6 (Paperback edition) | ISBN 978-3-8382-0681-3 (Hardcover edition)

127 *Andrey Makarychev* | Russia and the EU in a Multipolar World. Discourses, Identities, Norms | With a foreword by Klaus Segbers | ISBN 978-3-8382-0629-5

128 *Roland Scharff* | Kasachstan als postsowjetischer Wohlfahrtsstaat. Die Transformation des sozialen Schutzsystems | Mit einem Vorwort von Joachim Ahrens | ISBN 978-3-8382-0622-6

129 *Katja Grupp* | Bild Lücke Deutschland. Kaliningrader Studierende sprechen über Deutschland | Mit einem Vorwort von Martin Schulz | ISBN 978-3-8382-0552-6

130 *Konstantin Sheiko, Stephen Brown* | History as Therapy. Alternative History and Nationalist Imaginings in Russia, 1991-2014 | ISBN 978-3-8382-0665-3

131 *Elisa Kriza* | Alexander Solzhenitsyn: Cold War Icon, Gulag Author, Russian Nationalist? A Study of the Western Reception of his Literary Writings, Historical Interpretations, and Political Ideas | With a foreword by Andrei Rogatchevski | ISBN 978-3-8382-0589-2 (Paperback edition) | ISBN 978-3-8382-0690-5 (Hardcover edition)

132 *Serghei Golunov* | The Elephant in the Room. Corruption and Cheating in Russian Universities | ISBN 978-3-8382-0570-0

133 *Manja Hussner, Rainer Arnold (Hgg.)* | Verfassungsgerichtsbarkeit in Zentralasien I. Sammlung von Verfassungstexten | ISBN 978-3-8382-0595-3

134 *Nikolay Mitrokhin* | Die "Russische Partei". Die Bewegung der russischen Nationalisten in der UdSSR 1953-1985 | Aus dem Russischen übertragen von einem Übersetzerteam unter der Leitung von Larisa Schippel | ISBN 978-3-8382-0024-8

135 *Manja Hussner, Rainer Arnold (Hgg.)* | Verfassungsgerichtsbarkeit in Zentralasien II. Sammlung von Verfassungstexten | ISBN 978-3-8382-0597-7

136 *Manfred Zeller* | Das sowjetische Fieber. Fußballfans im poststalinistischen Vielvölkerreich | Mit einem Vorwort von Nikolaus Katzer | ISBN 978-3-8382-0757-5

137 *Kristin Schreiter* | Stellung und Entwicklungspotential zivilgesellschaftlicher Gruppen in Russland. Menschenrechtsorganisationen im Vergleich | ISBN 978-3-8382-0673-8

138 *David R. Marples, Frederick V. Mills (Eds.)* | Ukraine's Euromaidan. Analyses of a Civil Revolution | ISBN 978-3-8382-0660-8

139 *Bernd Kappenberg* | Setting Signs for Europe. Why Diacritics Matter for European Integration | With a foreword by Peter Schlobinski | ISBN 978-3-8382-0663-9

140 *René Lenz* | Internationalisierung, Kooperation und Transfer. Externe bildungspolitische Akteure in der Russischen Föderation | Mit einem Vorwort von Frank Ettrich | ISBN 978-3-8382-0751-3

141 *Juri Plusnin, Yana Zausaeva, Natalia Zhidkevich, Artemy Pozanenko* | Wandering Workers. Mores, Behavior, Way of Life, and Political Status of Domestic Russian Labor Migrants | Translated by Julia Kazantseva | ISBN 978-3-8382-0653-0

142 *David J. Smith (Eds.)* | Latvia – A Work in Progress? 100 Years of State- and Nation-Building | ISBN 978-3-8382-0648-6

143 *Инна Чувычкина (ред.)* | Экспортные нефте- и газопроводы на постсоветском пространстве. Анализ трубопроводной политики в свете теории международных отношений | ISBN 978-3-8382-0822-0

144 *Johann Zajaczkowski* | Russland – eine pragmatische Großmacht? Eine rollentheoretische Untersuchung russischer Außenpolitik am Beispiel der Zusammenarbeit mit den USA nach 9/11 und des Georgienkrieges von 2008 | Mit einem Vorwort von Siegfried Schieder | ISBN 978-3-8382-0837-4

145 *Boris Popivanov* | Changing Images of the Left in Bulgaria. The Challenge of Post-Communism in the Early 21st Century | ISBN 978-3-8382-0667-7

146 *Lenka Krátká* | A History of the Czechoslovak Ocean Shipping Company 1948-1989. How a Small, Landlocked Country Ran Maritime Business During the Cold War | ISBN 978-3-8382-0666-0

147 *Alexander Sergunin* | Explaining Russian Foreign Policy Behavior. Theory and Practice | ISBN 978-3-8382-0752-0

148 *Darya Malyutina* | Migrant Friendships in a Super-Diverse City. Russian-Speakers and their Social Relationships in London in the 21st Century | With a foreword by Claire Dwyer | ISBN 978-3-8382-0652-3

149 *Alexander Sergunin, Valery Konyshev* | Russia in the Arctic. Hard or Soft Power? | ISBN 978-3-8382-0753-7

150 *John J. Maresca* | Helsinki Revisited. A Key U.S. Negotiator's Memoirs on the Development of the CSCE into the OSCE | With a foreword by Hafiz Pashayev | ISBN 978-3-8382-0852-7

151 *Jardar Østbø* | The New Third Rome. Readings of a Russian Nationalist Myth | With a foreword by Pål Kolstø | ISBN 978-3-8382-0870-1

152 *Simon Kordonsky* | Socio-Economic Foundations of the Russian Post-Soviet Regime. The Resource-Based Economy and Estate-Based Social Structure of Contemporary Russia | With a foreword by Svetlana Barsukova | ISBN 978-3-8382-0775-9

153 *Duncan Leitch* | Assisting Reform in Post-Communist Ukraine 2000–2012. The Illusions of Donors and the Disillusion of Beneficiaries | With a foreword by Kataryna Wolczuk | ISBN 978-3-8382-0844-2

154 *Abel Polese* | Limits of a Post-Soviet State. How Informality Replaces, Renegotiates, and Reshapes Governance in Contemporary Ukraine | With a foreword by Colin Williams | ISBN 978-3-8382-0845-9

155 *Mikhail Suslov (Ed.)* | Digital Orthodoxy in the Post-Soviet World. The Russian Orthodox Church and Web 2.0 | With a foreword by Father Cyril Hovorun | ISBN 978-3-8382-0871-8

156 *Leonid Luks* | Zwei „Sonderwege"? Russisch-deutsche Parallelen und Kontraste (1917-2014). Vergleichende Essays | ISBN 978-3-8382-0823-7

157 *Vladimir V. Karacharovskiy, Ovsey I. Shkaratan, Gordey A. Yastrebov* | Towards a New Russian Work Culture. Can Western Companies and Expatriates Change Russian Society? | With a foreword by Elena N. Danilova | Translated by Julia Kazantseva | ISBN 978-3-8382-0902-9

158 *Edmund Griffiths* | Aleksandr Prokhanov and Post-Soviet Esotericism | ISBN 978-3-8382-0903-6

159 *Timm Beichelt, Susann Worschech (Eds.)* | Transnational Ukraine? Networks and Ties that Influence(d) Contemporary Ukraine | ISBN 978-3-8382-0944-9

160 *Mieste Hotopp-Riecke* | Die Tataren der Krim zwischen Assimilation und Selbstbehauptung. Der Aufbau des krimtatarischen Bildungswesens nach Deportation und Heimkehr (1990-2005) | Mit einem Vorwort von Swetlana Czerwonnaja | ISBN 978-3-89821-940-2

161 *Olga Bertelsen (Ed.)* | Revolution and War in Contemporary Ukraine. The Challenge of Change | ISBN 978-3-8382-1016-2

162 *Natalya Ryabinska* | Ukraine's Post-Communist Mass Media. Between Capture and Commercialization | With a foreword by Marta Dyczok | ISBN 978-3-8382-1011-7

163 *Alexandra Cotofana, James M. Nyce (Eds.)* | Religion and Magic in Socialist and Post-Socialist Contexts. Historic and Ethnographic Case Studies of Orthodoxy, Heterodoxy, and Alternative Spirituality | With a foreword by Patrick L. Michelson | ISBN 978-3-8382-0989-0

164 *Nozima Akhrarkhodjaeva* | The Instrumentalisation of Mass Media in Electoral Authoritarian Regimes. Evidence from Russia's Presidential Election Campaigns of 2000 and 2008 | ISBN 978-3-8382-1013-1

165 *Yulia Krasheninnikova* | Informal Healthcare in Contemporary Russia. Sociographic Essays on the Post-Soviet Infrastructure for Alternative Healing Practices | ISBN 978-3-8382-0970-8

166 *Peter Kaiser* | Das Schachbrett der Macht. Die Handlungsspielräume eines sowjetischen Funktionärs unter Stalin am Beispiel des Generalsekretärs des Komsomol Aleksandr Kosarev (1929-1938) | Mit einem Vorwort von Dietmar Neutatz | ISBN 978-3-8382-1052-0

167 *Oksana Kim* | The Effects and Implications of Kazakhstan's Adoption of International Financial Reporting Standards. A Resource Dependence Perspective | With a foreword by Svetlana Vlady | ISBN 978-3-8382-0987-6

168 *Anna Sanina* | Patriotic Education in Contemporary Russia. Sociological Studies in the Making of the Post-Soviet Citizen | With a foreword by Anna Oldfield | ISBN 978-3-8382-0993-7

169 *Rudolf Wolters* | Spezialist in Sibirien Faksimile der 1933 erschienenen ersten Ausgabe | Mit einem Vorwort von Dmitrij Chmelnizki | ISBN 978-3-8382-0515-1

170 *Michal Vít, Magdalena M. Baran (Eds.)* | Transregional versus National Perspectives on Contemporary Central European History. Studies on the Building of Nation-States and Their Cooperation in the 20th and 21st Century | With a foreword by Petr Vágner | ISBN 978-3-8382-1015-5

171 *Philip Gamaghelyan* | Conflict Resolution Beyond the International Relations Paradigm. Evolving Designs as a Transformative Practice in Nagorno-Karabakh and Syria | With a foreword by Susan Allen | ISBN 978-3-8382-1057-5

172 *Maria Shagina* | Joining a Prestigious Club. Cooperation with Europarties and Its Impact on Party Development in Georgia, Moldova, and Ukraine 2004–2015 | With a foreword by Kataryna Wolczuk | ISBN 978-3-8382-1084-1

173 *Alexandra Cotofana, James M. Nyce (Eds.)* | Religion and Magic in Socialist and Post-Socialist Contexts II. Baltic, Eastern European, and Post-USSR Case Studies | With a foreword by Anita Stasulane | ISBN 978-3-8382-0990-6

174 *Barbara Kunz* | Kind Words, Cruise Missiles, and Everything in Between. The Use of Power Resources in U.S. Policies towards Poland, Ukraine, and Belarus 1989–2008 | With a foreword by William Hill | ISBN 978-3-8382-1065-0

175 *Eduard Klein* | Bildungskorruption in Russland und der Ukraine. Eine komparative Analyse der Performanz staatlicher Antikorruptionsmaßnahmen im Hochschulsektor am Beispiel universitärer Aufnahmeprüfungen | Mit einem Vorwort von Heiko Pleines | ISBN 978-3-8382-0995-1

176 *Markus Soldner* | Politischer Kapitalismus im postsowjetischen Russland. Die politische, wirtschaftliche und mediale Transformation in den 1990er Jahren | Mit einem Vorwort von Wolfgang Ismayr | ISBN 978-3-8382-1222-7

177 *Anton Oleinik* | Building Ukraine from Within. A Sociological, Institutional, and Economic Analysis of a Nation-State in the Making | ISBN 978-3-8382-1150-3

178 *Peter Rollberg, Marlene Laruelle (Eds.)* | Mass Media in the Post-Soviet World. Market Forces, State Actors, and Political Manipulation in the Informational Environment after Communism | ISBN 978-3-8382-1116-9

179 *Mikhail Minakov* | Development and Dystopia Studies in Post-Soviet Ukraine and Eastern Europe | With a foreword by Alexander Etkind | ISBN 978-3-8382-1112-1

180 *Aijan Sharshenova* | The European Union's Democracy Promotion in Central Asia A Study of Political Interests, Influence, and Development in Kazakhstan and Kyrgyzstan in 2007–2013 | With a foreword by Gordon Crawford | ISBN 978-3-8382-1151-0

181 *Andrey Makarychev, Alexandra Yatsyk (Eds.)* | Boris Nemtsov and Russian Politics. Power and Resistance | With a foreword by Zhanna Nemtsova | ISBN 978-3-8382-1122-0

182 *Sophie Falsini* | The Euromaidan's Effect on Civil Society. Why and How Ukrainian Social Capital Increased after the Revolution of Dignity | With a foreword by Susann Worschech | ISBN 978-3-8382-1131-2

183 *Andreas Umland (Ed.)* | Ukraine's Decentralization. Challenges and Implications of the Local Governance Reform after the Euromaidan Revolution | ISBN 978-3-8382-1162-6

184 *Leonid Luks* | A Fateful Triangle. Essays on Contemporary Russian, German and Polish History | ISBN 978-3-8382-1143-5

185 *John B. Dunlop* | The February 2015 Assassination of Boris Nemtsov and the Flawed Trial of his Alleged Killers. An Exploration of Russia's "Crime of the 21st Century" | ISBN 978-3-8382-1188-6

186 *Vasile Rotaru* | Russia, the EU, and the Eastern Partnership. Building Bridges or Digging Trenches? | ISBN 978-3-8382-1134-3

187 *Marina Lebedeva* | Russian Studies of International Relations. From the Soviet Past to the Post-Cold-War Present | With a foreword by Andrei P. Tsygankov | ISBN 978-3-8382-0851-0

188 *Tomasz Stępniewski, George Soroka (Eds.)* | Ukraine after Maidan. Revisiting Domestic and Regional Security | ISBN 978-3-8382-1075-9

189 *Petar Cholakov* | Ethnic Entrepreneurs Unmasked. Political Institutions and Ethnic Conflicts in Contemporary Bulgaria | ISBN 978-3-8382-1189-3

190 *A. Salem, G. Hazeldine, D. Morgan (Eds.)* | Higher Education in Post-Communist States. Comparative and Sociological Perspectives | ISBN 978-3-8382-1183-5

191 *Igor Torbakov* | After Empire. Nationalist Imagination and Symbolic Politics in Russia and Eurasia in the Twentieth and Twenty-First Century | With a foreword by Serhii Plokhy | ISBN 978-3-8382-1217-3

192 *Aleksandr Burakovskiy* | Jewish-Ukrainian Relations in Late and Post-Soviet Ukraine. Articles, Lectures and Essays from 1986 to 2016 | ISBN 978-3-8382-1210-4

193 *Natalia Shapovalova, Olga Burlyuk (Eds.)* | Civil Society in Post-Euromaidan Ukraine. From Revolution to Consolidation | With a foreword by Richard Youngs | ISBN 978-3-8382-1216-6

194 *Franz Preissler* | Positionsverteidigung, Imperialismus oder Irredentismus? Russland und die „Russischsprachigen", 1991–2015 | ISBN 978-3-8382-1262-3

195 *Marian Madeła* | Der Reformprozess in der Ukraine 2014-2017. Eine Fallstudie zur Reform der öffentlichen Verwaltung | Mit einem Vorwort von Martin Malek | ISBN 978-3-8382-1266-1

196 *Anke Giesen* | „Wie kann denn der Sieger ein Verbrecher sein?" Eine diskursanalytische Untersuchung der russlandweiten Debatte über Konzept und Verstaatlichungsprozess der Lagergedenkstätte „Perm'-36" im Ural | ISBN 978-3-8382-1284-5

197 *Alla Leukavets* | The Integration Policies of Belarus and Ukraine vis-à-vis the EU and Russia. A Comparative Case Study Through the Prism of a Two-Level Game Approach | ISBN 978-3-8382-1247-0

198 *Oksana Kim* | The Development and Challenges of Russian Corporate Governance I. The Roles and Functions of Boards of Directors | With a foreword by Sheila M. Puffer | ISBN 978-3-8382-1287-6

199 *Thomas D. Grant* | International Law and the Post-Soviet Space I. Essays on Chechnya and the Baltic States | With a foreword by Stephen M. Schwebel | ISBN 978-3-8382-1279-1

200 *Thomas D. Grant* | International Law and the Post-Soviet Space II. Essays on Ukraine, Intervention, and Non-Proliferation | ISBN 978-3-8382-1280-7

201 *Slavomír Michálek, Michal Štefansky* | The Age of Fear. The Cold War and Its Influence on Czechoslovakia 1945–1968 | ISBN 978-3-8382-1285-2

202 *Iulia-Sabina Joja* | Romania's Strategic Culture 1990–2014. Continuity and Change in a Post-Communist Country's Evolution of National Interests and Security Policies | With a foreword by Heiko Biehl | ISBN 978-3-8382-1286-9

203 *Andrei Rogatchevski, Yngvar B. Steinholt, Arve Hansen, David-Emil Wickström* | War of Songs. Popular Music and Recent Russia-Ukraine Relations | With a foreword by Artemy Troitsky | ISBN 978-3-8382-1173-2

204 *Maria Lipman (Ed.)* | Russian Voices on Post-Crimea Russia. An Almanac of Counterpoint Essays from 2015–2018 | ISBN 978-3-8382-1251-7

205 *Ksenia Maksimovtsova* | Language Conflicts in Contemporary Estonia, Latvia, and Ukraine. A Comparative Exploration of Discourses in Post-Soviet Russian-Language Digital Media | With a foreword by Ammon Cheskin | ISBN 978-3-8382-1282-1

206 *Michal Vít* | The EU's Impact on Identity Formation in East-Central Europe between 2004 and 2013. Perceptions of the Nation and Europe in Political Parties of the Czech Republic, Poland, and Slovakia | With a foreword by Andrea Pető | ISBN 978-3-8382-1275-3

207 *Per A. Rudling* | Tarnished Heroes. The Organization of Ukrainian Nationalists in the Memory Politics of Post-Soviet Ukraine | ISBN 978-3-8382-0999-9

208 *Kaja Gadowska, Peter Solomon (Eds.)* | Legal Change in Post-Communist States. Progress, Reversions, Explanations | ISBN 978-3-8382-1312-5

209 *Paweł Kowal, Georges Mink, Iwona Reichardt (Eds.)* | Three Revolutions: Mobilization and Change in Contemporary Ukraine I. Theoretical Aspects and Analyses on Religion, Memory, and Identity | ISBN 978-3-8382-1321-7

210 *Paweł Kowal, Georges Mink, Adam Reichardt, Iwona Reichardt (Eds.)* | Three Revolutions: Mobilization and Change in Contemporary Ukraine II. An Oral History of the Revolution on Granite, Orange Revolution, and Revolution of Dignity | ISBN 978-3-8382-1323-1

211 *Li Bennich-Björkman, Sergiy Kurbatov (Eds.)* | When the Future Came: The Collapse of the USSR and the Emergence of National Memory in Post-Soviet History Textbooks | ISBN 978-3-8382-1335-4

212 *Olga R. Gulina* | Migration as a (Geo-)Political Challenge in the Post-Soviet Space. Border Regimes, Policy Choices, Visa Agendas | With a foreword by Nils Muižnieks | ISBN 978-3-8382-1338-5

213 *Sanna Turoma; Kaarina Aitamurto; Slobodanka Vladiv-Glover (Eds.)* | Religion, Expression, and Patriotism in Russia | Essays on Post-Soviet Society and the State | ISBN 978-3-8382-1346-0

ibidem.eu